COURTIERS

KT-229-877

By the same author

Non-fiction

On Next to Nothing (with Susan Hinde)
The Great Donkey Walk (with Susan Chitty)
The Cottage Book
A Field Guide to the English Country Parson
Stately Gardens of Britain
Forests of Britain
Capability Brown

Autobiography

Sir Henry and Sons

Fiction

Mr Nicholas
Happy as Larry
For the Good of the Company
A Place like Home
The Cage
Ninety Double Martinis
The Day the Call Came
Games of Chance
The Village
High
Bird
Generally a Virgin
Agent
Our Father
Daymare

Portrait of a young man, possibly Sir Philip Sidney,
by Isaac Oliver

Thomas Hinde

COURTIERS

900 Years of Court Life

LONDON
VICTOR GOLLANCZ LTD
1986

First published in Great Britain 1986
by Victor Gollancz Ltd,
14 Henrietta Street, London WC2E 8QJ

© Thomas Hinde 1986

British Library Cataloguing in Publication Data
Hinde, Thomas
  Courtiers: 900 years of court life.
  1. Great Britain—Courts and courtiers—Biography
  Rn: Sir Thomas Willes Chitty I. Title
  941   DA111

  ISBN 0-575-03767-9

BEXLEY LIBRARY SERVICE			
CARD	CL No.		
CL	942.00992 HN		
PRICE	16 NOV 1989	BK	AS
12.95			
MSTAT	MAT. TYPE		
2	AD Book		
KEYER	TRACE	LANG	CH	PRV
90			NL	KY

Typeset in Great Britain by Centracet
and printed by St Edmundsbury Press,
Bury St Edmunds, Suffolk
Illustrations originated and printed by Acolortone Ltd, Ipswich

0903192

For Miranda and Jessica

NOTE

Except where noted I give quotations with their original spelling and punctuation. In *prose* quotation, however, I have adopted modern practice for capital letters, and expanded abbreviations where we would today.

Contents

The Courts of the Houses of Saxe-Coburg and Gotha, and Windsor

Illustrations

Introduction

Every tribal leader gathers around him a group of men and women to help and advise him. In one sense these form his court and could all be called his courtiers. But among them are those whose duties are military or administrative, concerned with the tribe as a whole, and those who mainly attend to his personal needs, forming his 'household'. It is these last who can best be called courtiers. Unfortunately in practice they are not so easy to distinguish. Many of those who surround the early English kings had both functions, changing at times from one to the other. To add to the difficulty they would delegate their household appointments to deputies or servants. It follows that among the hundred courtiers gathered here from nine hundred years of English (later British) history some could also be called politicians, seamen or soldiers.

There is a further complication: over the centuries our kings and queens gradually lost political power, and the ministers they appointed became in practice increasingly responsible to parliament. Often these ministers began their careers by holding household positions.

Even when ministers nominally managed the affairs of the nation, courtiers, just because they were intimate with the king or queen, kept some political power. As late as 1910 Francis Knollys, George V's Private Secretary, played a significant part in the constitutional crisis over the Parliament Bill. In the eighteenth century the career of Lord Hervey, now remembered for his memoirs, shows how a courtier, who was nominally concerned with such trivial matters as ceremonial at the King's birthday celebrations, had political influence. For years, Walpole kept him as Vice-chamberlain because he was Queen Caroline's confidant (and probably her lover), so enabling Walpole to control his king, George II, via the queen.

All this is greatly to the advantage of a biographer. Power is a fascinating subject, no less so when it is exercised deviously in the royal closet than publicly in an assembly of the people. But inevitably there have always been courtiers who had little interest in power. Because their motives are more obscure they are equally interesting.

What can have made Fanny Burney, the best known lady novelist of her time, an intimate friend of Dr Johnson and his circle, endure five years as a bullied and virtually imprisoned royal serving maid? Why did Lady Antrim for months on end abandon her husband with his Irish castle to suffer piles from endless standing in attendance on Queen Victoria and Queen Alexandra? Kings and queens, it seems, even when reduced to symbols, still possess a remarkable magnetism, as well as the power to inspire much love and loyalty.

Courtiers have been my subject, but I have interpreted the word generously. You will find here three queens, promoted from Ladies-in-Waiting, a prince, a royal duke, a clutch of royal physicians and others who attended court but held no official position there. My problem has been less to know who to include than who must sadly be left out.

Certainly I have sought for the curious, but they have not been hard to find. Perhaps it is logical, not ironic, that courtiers, condemned by tradition and in practice to formality and ceremonial, should so commonly become private eccentrics.

The Courts of the Houses of Normandy, Plantagenet, York and Lancaster

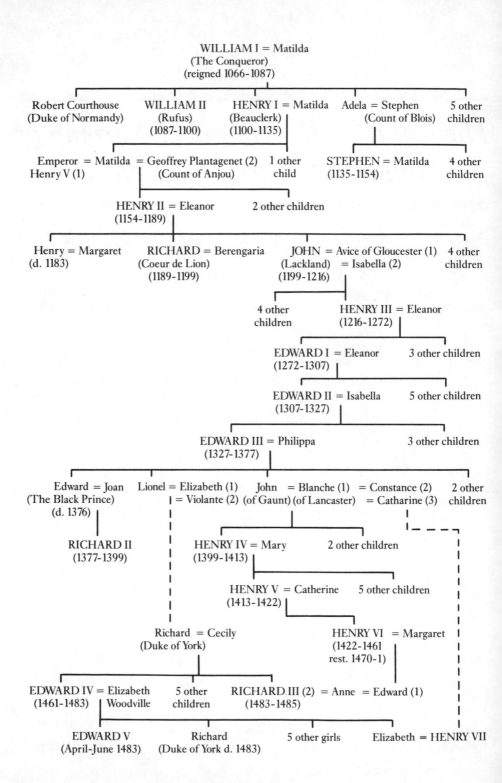

William the Conqueror to Edward V

Except for his three great courts – held at Easter, Whitsun and Christmas, either at Westminster, Winchester or Gloucester – William the Conqueror's court was perpetually on the move. Like a herd of grazing cattle, it fed on one pasture then moved to the next. In Saxon times royal manors had paid their dues to the king in the form of a night's 'farm' (keep) for the King's court, and even at the end of William's reign, when the Domesday Book was compiled, some were still doing so. Ninety years later, during the one year 1177, Henry II and his court used at least forty-four stopping places, sixteen of them in France.

So the court of these times, impressive as it must have been when at rest, can also be pictured as a huge straggle of men, wagons, beasts and hounds, shifting from place to place across the countryside, a fine procession in high summer but a chaotic one in muddy winter. It was followed by a rabble of parasites who had no official positions but were useful, from merchants, actors, singers and gamblers to prostitutes. A member of King John's household had the duty of managing these last.

All who were officially part of this procession were in a sense courtiers, from the great officers of state to the keepers of hounds, falconers and royal fools. Looking back we try to distinguish between the administrators, whose duty it was to manage the country, and the king's personal servants whose duties were, for example, to prepare his food or keep his private money. But this distinction was less clear at the time. Many who held positions which later became 'court' positions – the King's Chamberlain, for example – were regularly sent about the country to fight the King's battles or administer distant provinces, leaving behind them servants or deputies whom we barely know by name, let alone their characters.

If William I's court was sternly military and businesslike, accompanying the King here and there as he suppressed his rebellious new subjects, the court of his son, the red-headed and dislikeable William Rufus, has the reputation of being immoral – though it may have got this from monkish chroniclers who hated him for his hostility to the

Church. The court of his younger brother, Henry I, was another contrast. Once he had grabbed the throne – after Rufus's accidental death or murder while hunting in the New Forest – he married a nun and gathered around him men of civilization and learning. Next came nineteen years of civil war between Henry I's daughter, Matilda, and his nephew, Stephen, before Matilda's son, Henry II, took control.

Henry II's court is the first we know about in detail. After his Chancellor, its most important administrative officer, came the Treasurer (antecedent of the Keeper of the King's Privy Purse), the Master Butler with his 'sewers' or stewards (antecedent of the Lord Steward, in charge of the 'below stairs' department of later courts), the Master Chamberlain (antecedent of the Lord Chamberlain, responsible for the King's chamber and ceremonial), and a marshal and constable to keep order, the second of these the antecedent of that other great officer of later courts: the Master of the Horse, responsible for horses and transport.

Below these came many lesser servants, from laundresses and bakers to cellarers and the King's personal ewer, the man who was paid four pence to prepare his bath every time he took one. Since hunting was so important to the King, there were also numerous keepers of hounds and falconers, and there were keepers of his tents, watchmen and hornblowers, suggesting what a rugged but at the same time ostentatious progress the King must have made about the country. Apart from being forced continually to move and camp, the court's food and drink was disgusting. The bread, made with the sediment of beer for yeast, was like lead and full of uncooked bran. The wine had to be drunk through the teeth, to filter out the dregs.

Two hundred years later, the court of Richard II – who, on the death of his father, the Black Prince, came to the throne as a boy of fifteen in 1377 – was the most luxurious yet. He rebuilt the Palace of Westminster, where the court had now settled, and to Westminster he brought high fashion: fantastic head-dresses for the ladies which made their faces seem halfway down their bodies, and, for the men, fantastic shoes with elongated toes which had to be supported by chains to the knees. Thousands of hangers-on gathered around this court which served as many as ten thousand meals a day.

For court entertainment there were musicians playing trumpets, pipes, fiddles, kettle-drums and quainter instruments like the citole and tambour. And there were variety artists who would 'distort their bodies by lewd dance and gesture or strip themselves and put on horrible masks'. This final, splendid but degenerate Plantagenet court invited the revenge of exiled Bolingbroke, who deposed Richard in 1399 and had him starved to death at Pontefract Castle. (Richard's skeleton, examined in 1871, showed no evidence of violence to support Shakespeare's version of his murder).

By comparison the courts of Henry IV (Bolingbroke) and his son Henry V were frugal, but Henry VI allowed his to grow extravagant again, even if he disapproved of lewdness. At Christmas one year when 'a certain great lord brought before him a dance or show of young ladies with bare bosoms the King turned his back and left the room saying "Fy, fy, for shame".'

To cut his costs his successor, Edward IV, issued an elaborate description of his courtiers and their duties. Ironically, 'The Black Book of the Household', as this is called, demonstrated what a costly and complicated organization the court had become as well as how ritualized.

The King's life was as circumscribed as everyone else's. He was to sleep surrounded by courtiers to protect him, including a Squire of the Body. At night this person was in charge of the palace. At dawn he woke the King and with other Squires of the Body dressed him.

When the King emerged for breakfast twenty Squires of the Household supervised the server who went to fetch the King's food from the kitchen. During the meal thirteen minstrels played in the gallery and a doctor of physic stood beside the King to advise him on the best diet. Afterwards the squires supervised the ewer who brought him basin and water to wash his hands.

Meanwhile in the Bedchamber two squires and two grooms made the royal bed, helped by a yeoman to bring new bedding and an usher to hold back the bed curtains. The yeoman was to beat the pillows, and throw them to the squires who put them in position then turned down the ermine counterpane to the exact distance of an ell. . . . So the royal day proceeded. Hunting and making war must have been welcome reliefs from so much formality.

The young heir to the throne (the future Edward V, who was murdered in the Tower) for light relief had only the reading of 'such noble stories as behoveth a prince to understand'. As for the King's mother, Princess Cecily, her life consisted almost exclusively of praying, attending masses and being lectured on holy subjects – though she was allowed a cup of wine twice a day and a little free time with her ladies after supper.

Eudo, Dapifer (d. 1120)

Eudo, Dapifer (or steward), fourth son of Hubert de Rie, is one of the few Norman barons whose function at William the Conqueror's court is clear. He was a predecessor of the many Lord Stewards who, in succeeding centuries, had charge of the 'below stairs' section of the royal household, in particular of the King's kitchens. There is even a legend to suggest precisely what a steward's duties might then have included. In 1070 Eudo's predecessor, William FitzOsbern, Earl of Hereford, guardian of the Welsh Marches and William I's closest friend and most loyal supporter during the Conquest, is said to have served William an undercooked crane. When King William tried to strike Earl William, Eudo protected him from the blow. At this Earl William offered Eudo his stewardship, which Eudo accepted.

Eudo was William I's Steward from this date till the end of his reign. Like later Lord Stewards, however, he was probably seldom so directly concerned with the King's roasts, since he was also a great landholder with a total of about sixty-four holdings in six counties. He was related by marriage to two of the other great baronial families, among whom William had shared his new country. His wife's father was Richard Fitz Gilbert of Claire (Richard of Tonbridge), and her mother, Rohesia, was daughter of Walter Giffard, first Earl of Buckingham. Eudo's daughter married Richard de Mandeville and their child became the first Earl of Essex.

When William I died in Normandy, Eudo was largely responsible for William Rufus succeeding him. He came with Rufus to England and hurried to Winchester, then to the channel ports, securing support. As a result Rufus was proclaimed king before William's other barons, left behind in Normandy, had decided on their candidate.

Eudo remained in favour with Rufus, but was less so with Henry I, who suspected him of supporting his brother, Count Robert. Nevertheless, Henry visited him at his castle of Préaux in Normandy when he was dying. At Eudo's request his body was brought to England and buried at the Abbey of St Peter's which he had founded at Colchester. He left to the abbey £100, a gold ring set with a topaz, a cup and cover decorated with gold plate and his horse and mule.

Alan de Neville (d. c. 1191), Geoffrey de Neville (d. 1225), Hugh de Neville (d. 1222)

These three de Nevilles – all of them important servants of Henry II, Richard, John or Henry III – were only some of many de Nevilles of the time, so it is not certain exactly how they were related to each other, but they may have been uncle and nephews. Certainly the dates of their deaths suggest that Alan was of one generation, Geoffrey and Hugh of the next. Alan is the most easily pictured; a contemporary description by Battle Abbey's chronicler gives his own and Henry II's opinions of him.

> This Alan so long as he lived enriched the royal treasury, and to please an earthly king did not fear to offend the king of Heaven. But how much gratitude he earned from the King, whom he strove to please, the sequel showed. For when he was brought to his last, the bretheren of a certain monastery hoping, it seems, to secure something of his substance for their house, besought the King to allow them to carry away his body to their burial place. Whereupon, the King revealed his true sentiments towards him in these terms: 'I', he said, 'will have his wealth, you shall have the corpse, and the demons of hell his soul'.

Alan, as Henry II's Chief Forester, gave peasants and landowners equal reason to dislike him. He turned into royal forest large parts of the country which had either been lost to the king during the nineteen-year civil war of Stephen's reign, or, as many claimed, had never been forest before. Fifty years later when juries carried out their perambulations for the Great Forest Charter of 1217, they still remembered Alan's afforestations with bitterness.

The best known descendant of Alan's side of the family was Richard Neville, known as 'Warwick the Kingmaker', supporter of the Lancastrians in the Wars of the Roses.

Though Alan was an important royal servant, whether or not he was a courtier depends on how the word is interpreted. Geoffrey, however, was clearly one. Early in John's reign he is described as Seneschal, then for many years he was John's and Henry III's Chamberlain. But he must have often been away from court because he also became Seneschal of Poitou and Gascony, and during the civil war at the end of John's reign was at one time roaming the countryside between Oxford and Lincoln with an armed band, and at another acting as

John's agent in Yorkshire, crushing the rebellion there. Henry III confirmed Geoffrey's appointment as Chamberlain, but he, too, used him chiefly to protect his more remote possessions, either in the north of England or in France. In France Geoffrey considered himself so poorly supported by Henry that he threatened to abandon his post and go on a crusade.

Hugh – probably Alan's nephew and possibly Geoffrey's cousin – was at one time described as John's Treasurer, the official who managed the king's personal monies, but is better known because, like Alan, he was the king's Chief Forester. In the previous reign he had been a close companion of Richard I's, going with him on his crusade to Palestine but, unlike Richard, avoiding capture. His seal shows a man killing a lion, and according to legend he did this during the crusade. He was probably John's most powerful administrator, and also an intimate gambling companion at court.

Hugh's connection with John was even more personal, if more ambiguous. In 1204 when John visited Marlborough Castle, where Hugh had his forest headquarters, Hugh's wife Joan undertook to give John two hundred chickens for permission to spend one night with her husband. Mediaeval historians have worried for decades over this tantalizing fragment of information. Did John normally hold Joan a hostage for Hugh's good behaviour. Or was she his regular mistress, from whom she was buying a night off to spend with her husband. Sadly the Exchequer records do not show if the chickens were ever paid.

Piers Gaveston, Earl of Cornwall (d. 1312)

No royal favourite had a greater – if brief – influence on the history of his time than Piers Gaveston, boyfriend of the almost certainly homosexual Edward II. Gaveston, whose family came from Gascony, was brought to England in about 1298 to be one of ten youths who were official companions for Edward as a young prince. 'And when the king's son saw him', a contemporary chronicler wrote – perhaps with hindsight – 'he fell so much in love that he entered upon an enduring compact with him'.

Prince Edward was then about fourteen, and his father – Edward I, the Hammer of the Scots – did not at once show disapproval of his son's friendship with Gaveston. He took both of them with him to campaign in Scotland in 1301. But four years later he banished the

Prince from court for six months, in theory for poaching some of the Bishop of Coventry and Lichfield's deer, but perhaps because Gaveston had encouraged this adventure. And in February 1307 he banished Gaveston from the country.

The cause was a violent quarrel between the King and the Prince, either because the Prince had asked for Gaveston to be made Earl of Cornwall, or because the King more generally accused Edward of 'having an inordinate affection' for Gaveston. One account says that the King seized his son by the hair and pulled out as much as he could; another that he knocked him down and kicked him. Gaveston obeyed the banishment order, but the Prince went with him to Dover and gave him expensive tunics, tapestries and quilts, as well as money before he embarked.

As soon as Prince Edward succeeded his father (July 1307) he recalled Gaveston and made him Earl of Cornwall. The real conflict now began, between the new King and his favourite on one side and the old baronial families on the other. They regularly accused Edward of 'excessive love and tenderness' towards Gaveston. When his coronation had to be postponed for a week, it was probably because they refused to attend if Gaveston was there. And they disliked his cheeky French manners. But the real reason for their hostility was that he had taken from them the power they thought should be theirs. As a foreigner with no aristocratic background he should never have been allowed to marry the King's niece.

Unfortunately for them, Gaveston was no limp queer but a brave soldier and talented jouster. At the tournament at Wallingford which followed his wedding he and his young knights humiliated the Earls of Hereford, Arundel and Surrey.

Within six months Edward gave way, agreeing to Gaveston's second exile and to depriving him of all his titles. In compensation he gave Gaveston lands in England and France, and made him his lieutenant in Ireland, where he now went.

A year later Edward made concessions to the barons who as a result allowed him to bring Gaveston back, but Gaveston soon gave new offence by inventing a series of nicknames for them; these can be loosely translated 'Big-Belly', 'Son of a Whore', 'Fiddler', 'Busker', and (for the Earl of Warwick) 'Black Hound of Arden'. 'One day the hound will bite him,' Warwick said. And in November 1311 the King was forced to agree to Gaveston's third banishment.

By Christmas that year, however, Gaveston had secretly returned and in January Edward, who had retreated with him to York, officially announced his return and gave him back his titles. At once the Archbishop of Canterbury excommunicated Gaveston, and the Earls raised troops and marched north, where the Earl of Pembroke eventually captured him at Scarborough Castle.

Pembroke set out for the south, taking Gaveston with him to be tried, but when he reached Deddington he left his prisoner there to spend a night at Bampton with his wife. While Pembroke was away Warwick took his chance, captured Gaveston and brought him to Warwick Castle. Here three more earls, Lancaster, Hereford and Arundel, soon arrived and supervised Gaveston's murder on a nearby hill. One Welsh soldier ran his sword through him while another cut off his head. Since he had been excommunicated he was not buried in holy ground.

Geoffrey Chaucer (1340–1400)

At the age of about seventeen Geoffrey Chaucer became a page to the wife of Lionel, Duke of Clarence and second son of Edward III (it was the descendents of Lionel who were to become the Yorkists in the Wars of the Roses, and ultimately include Edward IV.) Chaucer remained a page for some years, though this did not prevent his going to France with the King's military expedition of 1359, where he was captured, and the King had to contribute £16 towards his ransom.

Presently he transferred to the King's Court. By 1368 he was one of the King's esquires and he was presently getting other favours, like a daily pitcher of wine, to be served him in the port of London by the King's butler. In 1374 he also became a customs officer for wool, skins and hides in the port of London.

He remained in favour when Edward III died and the boy king Richard succeeded him. On the whole his poetry makes few references to political events of his time but he mentions and may perhaps have watched the slaughter of the Flemings in London in 1381 during the Peasants' Revolt. Five years later he suddenly lost his positions, but he was not totally disgraced because he went on drawing a pension. And in 1389 when Richard regained control of the country from his barons he made Chaucer Clerk of the Works for Westminster Palace, the Tower of London, the Castle of Berkhamsted and several royal manors and forest lodges; also for the mews at Charing Cross where Richard kept his falcons.

While Chaucer was carrying out these duties he was robbed twice in one day, first at Westminster, then at Hatcham, on his way to the manor of Eltham. He lost £10 the first time and £9 3s 6d the second, as well as his horse. Though he was excused repayment, he was relieved of his job after two years. But again he continued to receive a small pension, and in the last year of Richard's reign was granted more wine – this time a tun. He seems to have been an inefficient manager of his own finances and during these years regularly asked for advances, or for letters of protection from his creditors.

Henry IV at once granted him an additional pension of 40 marks, but he only survived about a year to enjoy it. As a courtier and a recognized poet – the first great poet to write in English, author of *The Canterbury Tales* – he was buried in Westminster Abbey, in what is now known as Poets' Corner.

Sir John Bushy (d. 1399), Sir William Bagot, (d. c 1420) and Sir Henry Green (d. 1399)

> I would unfold some causes of your deaths,
> You have misled a prince, a royal king,

says Bolingbroke, the future king Henry IV, to Bushy and Green at Bristol in Shakespeare's *Richard II*, explaining to them why they are to be executed.

> You have in manner with your sinful hours
> Made a divorce betwixt his queen and him,
> Broke the possession of a royal bed,
> And stain'd the beauty of a fair queen's cheek.

Bushy and Green together with Bagot (who had escaped to Cheshire) were, in Bolingbroke's opinion,

> The caterpillars of the commonwealth
> Which I have sworn to weed and pluck away.

Shakespeare does nothing to modify Bolingbroke's words, showing Bushy, Bagot and Green as foppish, perverted courtiers, who had misled a potentially virtuous king. He got his information from the chronicler, Holinshed, who wrote that Richard was 'of good nature enough, if the wickedness and naughty demeanour of such as were about him, had not altered it'. As a result Richard had become 'much given to the pleasures of the body. . . . Furthermore, there reigned abundantly the filthy sin of lechery and fornication, with abominable adultery, specially in the king.'

About Bushy, Holinshed wrote that he was 'an exceeding cruel man, ambitious and covetous beyond measure'. When speaking to the King he would invent 'such strange names as were rather agreeable to the divine majesty of God, than to any earthly potentate'. But Richard 'seemed to like well his speech and gave good ear to his talk'. Against the three of them 'the commons bore great and privie hatred'.

Certainly by 1398, the year before Bolingbroke drove Richard from the throne, they were unpopular, as a song of the time shows:

> There is a Bush that is overgrown
> Crop it well and keep it low
>   Or else it will grow wild
> The long grass that is Green
> It must be mown and raked clean.
>   For it hath overgrown the field
> The great Bag that is so mickle
> It shall be cut and made little
>   Its bottom is nearly out. . . .

But it was the great landlords, friends of Bolingbroke, not the common people, who really disliked Sir John Bushy, Sir William Bagot and Sir Henry Green, who had been Richard's chief assistants in ruling without Parliament and in depriving them of their lands and power. And, whatever their sexual practices may have been, it was for their political activities that they were blamed.

Bagot was generally considered their leader. Like the other two, he was a shire knight and a Member of Parliament. He was a particular friend of Richard, and Richard was staying in his castle of Baginton at the time of the famous Coventry assize which ended in the banishment of Mowbray and Bolingbroke.

Bushy, on the other hand, played a more dramatic part in the story. By 1397 he had been three times Sheriff of his county, Lincolnshire, and was Speaker of Parliament, where he had sat for most of eleven years. He was known as a persuasive orator, and also acted as the King's Secretary. Now he helped Richard have his revenge on the first three of the five so-called 'Appellant Lords', Warwick, Gloucester and Arundel, who were exiled, murdered and executed respectively, and when the other two, Mowbray and Bolingbroke, met at Coventry to settle their quarrel in combat, it was Bushy who, reading from a scroll a full fathom in length, gave the King's judgement: that Mowbray should be exiled for life and Bolingbroke for ten years.

The eight months of Richard's tyranny followed, during which Bushy, Bagot and Green continued to be his close advisers, and in which he committed his greatest blunder – the seizing of the exiled Bolingbroke's Lancastrian lands.

Richard then set off on his last Irish expedition, leaving Bushy, Bagot and Green as his most important administrative officials while he was gone. He was still away when Bolingbroke landed in Yorkshire and by the time he returned, landing at Milford Haven, Bushy and Green, who had taken refuge in Bristol Castle, had been captured by Bolingbroke and executed.

Bagot, who had been sent to fetch Richard back from Ireland, took refuge in his castle in Cheshire. In due course he was captured, but Bolingbroke, now king, had had sufficient revenge, and after The Bag had given some useful evidence against another of Richard's supporters, Aumerle, he was released and allowed to die in peace.

Sir John Oldcastle, Lord Cobham (c. 1378–1417)

When Shakespeare invented the character of Sir John Falstaff, the fat and cowardly older companion of Prince Hal in the days before Hal became King Henry and abandoned the pranks of his youth, he was almost certainly thinking of Sir John Oldcastle. In the first draft of *Henry IV*, Falstaff is called Oldcastle, and at times the part was played under that name. But Shakespeare's character had little resemblance to the real man. There is nothing to suggest that Sir John Oldcastle was fat or cowardly. He probably wasn't even elderly. His name seems to have misled the Elizabethans, and the best guess at his date of birth is 1378, making him in his twenties or early thirties while Henry was a prince.

Oldcastle and Prince Henry did probably know each other. When Henry was sent by his father (Henry IV) to the Welsh marches they may have cooperated there in suppressing the rebellious Welsh. Oldcastle had been born in this part of the country, at the family manor of Almeley in western Herefordshire. And they knew each other better after Oldcastle took Joan, Lady Cobham, to be his third wife. Joan was a Kentish heiress, and brought him Cobham Manor and Cooling Castle near Rochester. Oldcastle no doubt used these as his base when in 1409 he came to London, was made Lord Cobham and was given a position in the Prince's household. Four years later he kept this position when Henry became King. Judging by Henry's reluctance to have him condemned after his arrest, the two were on friendly terms.

Oldcastle's crime was to have joined the Lollards, the sect founded by Wycliffe in the previous century which attacked the celibacy of the clergy, belief in transubstantiation, the selling of indulgences and pilgrimages. The case against Oldcastle rested on a book of subversive tracts which was found in the shop of an illuminator, who said it was Oldcastle's. Oldcastle admitted it was his but said he had barely read two pages. In June 1413 he was cross-questioned in the King's presence, in August proceedings were issued against him and in September he was arrested and sent to the Tower. Throughout, Henry tried to protect him and even now he was given forty days to recant. Instead he escaped.

Hidden in London, at one time with a parchment maker at Smithfield, Oldcastle helped organize the Lollard rising of January 10th 1414 which was such a disastrous failure. But he escaped again and spent the next four years as a hunted fugitive on the Welsh border. Eventually he was betrayed and captured after a fierce skirmish in which he was seriously wounded. This did not save him from being carried to London on a 'whirlicote' (horse-litter), condemned as a heretic and on the same day taken to St Giles's Field on a hurdle where he was 'burnt hanging', probably alive.

John Scoggin (lived 1470s and 1480s)

All we know of John Scoggin, fool at the court of Edward IV, comes originally from *Scoggin's Jests*, first published about 1565, supposed to be by the physician, Dr Andrew Boorde. This was almost certainly the source used by Elizabethan dramatists like Jonson and Shakespeare who mention him, and by the chronicler, Holinshed. Boorde credits Scoggin with jests which were sometimes credited to others but when *Scoggin's Jests* was published people were alive who could have remembered Scoggin and he was probably a real person, not merely a composite figure.

The book (of which the earliest surviving copy is dated 1626) claims that Scoggin went to Oriel College, Oxford, where he took a degree (though he also remarked that 'A Master of Art is not worth a fart').

When the plague reached Oxford in 1471 Scoggin left, and became the fool of Sir William Neville, who brought him to court. Here Edward IV and his queen, Elizabeth, so fancied him that Neville presented Scoggin to them.

Many of Scoggin's jests involved making money in such a flagrantly dishonest way that they seemed merry pranks rather than crimes. At Oxford he accepted a horse as a bribe for getting a man made a priest. When the King gave him a house in Cheapside he filled it with straw and blackmailed his neighbours by threatening to set it alight.

Less dishonestly, he won a £20 bet by standing for a long time under a spout of running cold water. The story of how he escaped from a debt of £500 to the King is clearly more apocryphal; he is said to have shammed dead and arranged for the King to meet his funeral procession. The King was moved to pity and remarked that he forgave Scoggin his debt – at which Scoggin sat up and called for witnesses.

In Normandy, where he went after he had offended the King, he conspired with a priest to share the proceeds of a complicated plot, using a skull he had found in the churchyard. The skull had spoken to him, Scoggin told the congregation, and asked them to give money and valuables for a new church to be built above it. But, Scoggin added, women who had been faithless to their husbands were to stay seated and give nothing. 'Thus received he the offerings both of the good and the bad, and by this practice got a great sum of money.'

He was buried on the east side of Westminster Abbey, where Henry VII's chapel now stands, his grave sited at his own request below a water spout, 'For I have ever loved good drink, all the days of my life.'

Anthony Woodville, Baron Scales, 2nd Earl Rivers (c. 1442–1483)

Anthony Woodville, brother of King Edward IV's queen, Elizabeth Woodville, epitomized the knightly virtues so admired in the late middle ages, first as a jousting champion, later as a pilgrim and pious man of learning.

He and his father abandoned the Lancastrians and joined the Yorkists in 1461 when Henry VI's cause seemed hopeless, but it was only after Anthony's sister married the King that he became a figure at court and was made a Knight of the Garter and Lord of the Isle of Wight.

Soon afterwards, when on his knees before the Queen one day, he was presented by her ladies with a roll of parchment tied with a golden thread, which told him that he was to prove his valour by challenging the Bastard of Burgundy (Anthony, natural son of the Duke of Burgundy) to single combat. The result was the most celebrated tournament of the century. In late May 1467 the Bastard sailed up the Thames in a fleet of four ships with pennants and banners flying, to be lodged by the Bishop of Salisbury in Fleet Street and lent his house at Chelsea for secret training.

The combat began at Smithfield thirteen days later, among the audience the King dressed in purple surrounded by twenty to twenty-five white-haired councillors.

At the first charge with lances neither scored. At the second with swords, the Bastard's horse struck a piece of iron in Scales's saddle and fell on top of him. He refused a remount and the tournament was adjourned till next day.

They then fought on foot with axes, Scales battering with the axe's head, the Bastard using 'the small end of the blade', until the King decided that they were becoming too violent and 'cast his staff and with a high voice, cried "Whoo". Notwithstanding, in the departing there were given two or three great strokes.' The English claimed that Scales had been winning, the French noted the large gashes which the Bastard had made in Scales's armour.

In 1470 when Warwick the Kingmaker temporarily drove Edward out of England to the Low Countries, Scales went with him; when Edward returned next year he helped him defeat the rebels. Now he was made the young Prince Edward's councillor, then his Governor, and as a result of his adventures determined to live a life devoted to philosophical reflection and literature. In the summer of 1473 he went on a pilgrimage to Santiago de Compostella, and in 1476 to Rome. He became a friend of Caxton's, who printed three of his translations of devotional works.

But when Edward IV died and named his brother, the Duke of Gloucester (the future Richard III), as Edward V's protector, Scales marched from Ludlow with two thousand men in an attempt to reach the young king first. Gloucester intercepted him, imprisoned him and in due course had him executed at Pontefract. He was found to be wearing a hair shirt next to his skin.

*Elizabeth Lambert, 'Jane' Shore (c. 1450–c. 1526), and William
Hastings, Baron Hastings (c. 1430–1483)*

For over three hundred years Jane Shore was remembered as the
notorious mistress of Edward IV. Her story was told in many popular
ballads, Shakespeare referred to her in *Richard III* during the dramatic
council meeting at the Tower which led to the beheading of Hastings,
Blake drew 'The Penance of Jane Shore'. Brothels were named after
her, and to call a woman a Jane Shore was to call her a whore. The
King's mistress she certainly was, but not an avaricious or malicious
one, and her fate was the result of the bad luck that her royal lover
died at the early age of forty-two. 'The King would say,' Thomas
More wrote, 'that he had three concubines which in three divers
properties diversely excelled, one the merriest, another the wiliest, the
third the holiest harlot in his realm . . . the merriest was this Shore's
wife.'

Most (but not all) we know about Jane comes from More's *History of
Richard III*, and since More wrote between 1513 and 1518 when Jane
herself and many of those who had known her at the time of her
notoriety were still alive, it is to be trusted. One fact which More did
not seem to know was that she was born Elizabeth Lambert, the
daughter of John Lambert, a city merchant. 'Jane' was a later invention,
first used in 1599. Till then More and others had merely called her
'Mistress Shore', or 'Shore's wife'.

She had married William Shore, also a prosperous city merchant,
'somewhat too soon', and 'before she was well ripe' with the result that
she never longed for her husband and did not 'very fervently love him'.
It was this which 'more easily made her incline unto the King's appetite
when he required her'. But she may have had other marriage problems.
In 1476 three bishops were appointed to judge her petition for the
annulment of her marriage on the grounds that her husband was frigid
and impotent.

From this date all records of William Shore's merchant dealings
disappear, until he returned to England from Antwerp after Edward
IV's death so he may have stayed abroad while Jane was the King's
merriest harlot. As More describes her, there was nothing about her
you would have wanted to change except that you might have 'wished
her somewhat higher'. But she 'delighted men not so much in her
beauty as in her pleasant behaviour. For a proper wit had she, and
could both read well and write.' She was 'merry in company, ready and
quick of answer, neither mute nor full of babble'. Of the King's

concubines she was the one in whom he 'took special pleasure. For many he had, but her he loved.' What was more she 'never abused to any man's hurt, but to many a man's comfort and relief; where the King took displeasure, she would mitigate and appease his mind.'

Her misfortunes began soon after Edward's death in 1483. For a few months Lord Hastings, the Lord Chamberlain, protected and lived with her, but soon Richard of Gloucester accused her of plotting with Edward IV's queen, Elizabeth, to bewitch him and cause his arm to wither. This is the scene, vividly described by More, which Shakespeare used unaltered. The accusations were transparently improbable since Jane Shore was the woman whom the Queen most disliked as the mistress the King had loved best, and since everyone knew that Richard's arm had been withered from birth.

> *Richard* See how I am bewitch'd; behold, mine arm
> Is, like a blasted sapling, wither'd up:
> And this is Edward's wife, that monstrous witch,
> Consorted with that harlot strumpet Shore,
> That by their witchcraft thus have marked me.
> *Hastings* If they have done this thing, my gracious lord,-
> *Richard* If! thou protector of this damned strumpet,
> Tellest thou me of 'ifs'? Thou art a traitor:
> Off with his head! Now, by Saint Paul I swear,
> I will not dine until I see the same.

Hastings was beheaded and Jane imprisoned, then forced to do public penance, walking through the streets of London in procession before the cross with a taper in her hand. Since by then she had no clothes except her 'kyrtle' and blushed in such a comely way and was in general 'so fair and lovely . . . her great shame won her much praise, among those that were more amorous of her body than curious of her soul'.

After this she was sent back to prison, and although briefly at liberty in the autumn when she was living in adultery with Thomas Grey, Marquess of Dorset, she was soon in Ludgate again, where Thomas Lynom, Richard's solicitor, fell in love with her. Richard disapproved, and wrote to his Lord Chancellor to tell him to dissuade Lynom, but the Lord Chancellor failed, Jane was released and made a second marriage, bearing a child named Julian.

By the time More wrote, however, her luck had changed once more. She was 'now in the most beggerly condition, unfriended and worn out of acquaintance . . .', begging from people who would themselves have been begging, but for the help she had once given them. There is nothing to show whether her new husband had died or whether her second marriage had failed like her first.

Lord Hastings, Jane's temporary protector, came of a family of courtiers (an ancestor had been Henry II's Steward). He had been Edward IV's Grand Chamberlain for twenty-two years. He held other royal appointments, including Master of the Mint, where he invented the gold Noble, worth 100 pence. But like many Chamberlains, he spent less time at court than fighting the King's wars or negotiating marriages for his relatives. While in France on one of these missions he met Louis XI who gave him a service of plate worth 10,000 marks and described him as a loyal servant to Edward IV and a person of wisdom and virtue.

His loyalty did not extend to Edward IV's queen, Elizabeth, who disliked him because he, instead of her brother, Lord Scales, had been made Governor of Calais. Perhaps she also knew of his liking for her rival, Jane Shore, the royal mistress.

The Court of the House of Tudor

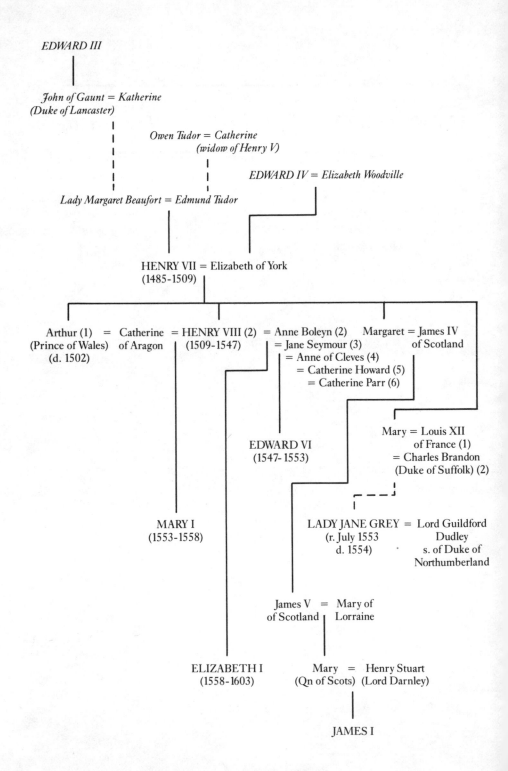

2

Henry VII and Henry VIII

Stability was Henry VII's aim. Five months after he had defeated Richard III at the battle of Bosworth Field he improved his position by marrying Elizabeth, eldest daughter of Edward IV, so uniting the houses of Lancaster and York which had spent much of the century fighting each other. But the result was a well-ordered rather than an exciting court, with few of the picturesque incidents or personalities of those of his wife's late father, Edward, or his son, Henry VIII.

True, he gave lavish entertainments on proper occasions, as when he entertained Philip, Archduke of Austria, husband of the Queen of Castile, for twelve days at Windsor. And he founded the Yeomen of the Guard, nominally for ceremonial purposes, though they were then no band of doddering ancients but a troop of fifty archers, 'hardy, strong and of agility'. He also extended the Palace of Greenwich, and built himself the important new Palace of Richmond (part of its grounds now form half the Royal Botanic Gardens at Kew). But he did not waste money, and left accumulated savings of £1,250,000.

It was a court where scholars like Thomas More and Erasmus felt welcome. And to which John Skelton was appointed as the first Poet Laureate – even if this position was not then a prize for a senior respectable poet but one which required loyal propaganda in verse. For the future of the monarchy and the court, however, the most significant event of the reign was the early death in 1501 of King Henry's eldest son, Prince Arthur.

It was his second son, Henry (soon married to his brother's widow, Catherine of Aragon) who formed around himself a court of a very different kind, and from 1509 when he came to the throne produced twenty-eight years of palace drama.

As a young man Henry VIII was entirely unlike the gross person he became in his fifties, with constantly suppurating sores on both his thighs, who had to be moved about his palaces by derricks, ropes and pulleys. He was slim, athletic and sporting, enjoying tennis and jousting and spending ferociously long days hunting, during which he would sometimes exhaust ten horses. Around him he gathered young men who enjoyed similar sports. But he also sang, wrote music and played the recorder, flute and virginals. And among his courtiers were the poets Francis Bryan, Thomas Wyatt and Henry Howard, Earl of Surrey, all three of whom became involved in intrigues and one of whom (Surrey) was executed only just before Henry's death might have saved him.

Another of the amusements of Henry and his courtiers was dressing in fancy costumes, for instance as Robin Hood and his merry men. For general court entertainment Henry had built extravagant 'conceits': for one occasion a jewel-covered mountain with space inside it for a lady of the mountain and her children of honour; for another a forest which contained a castle of gold and was pulled by a lion and an antelope.

But the greatest of all Henry's ostentatious displays was the Field of the Cloth of Gold, staged in 1520 in France at the castle of Guines, to impress the King of France. Here a thousand workmen built for him a crystal palace four hundred and thirty-seven yards long to house his own and the Queen's households, numbering in total five thousand two hundred. The French king brought a similar retinue to the town of Andres, and for a fortnight the rival courtiers feasted, jousted and showed off to each other.

More solidly, and in some cases more lastingly, Henry built or improved many royal palaces. He had inherited Windsor, Richmond, Greenwich and Eltham, where he had lived as a child. Hampton Court he was given by Wolsey, and York Place he took from him, adding to it until it grew into the great shambling palace of Whitehall which for nearly two hundred years was the most important English royal palace. He also started to build St James's Palace, taking over a leper hospital there, and built for himself the new palace of Nonsuch in Surrey which he planned to connect to Windsor Forest by a new stretch of hunting reserve.

As at many courts there was much petty pilfering and backstairs licence at Henry VIII's. Wolsey in 1526 drew up the Eltham Statutes, which vividly suggest the sort of characters who were taking shelter or practising as whores under palace roofs. The Knight Harbinger was to punish or banish them. The statutes described in detail the sort of meals to which every grade of courtier was entitled (the Lord Chamberlain's midday dinner was to consist of sixteen dishes, his supper of eleven), their precise accommodation (the senior courtiers invariably had too few beds for their servants) and their precise duties (Equerries of the Body were to put on the king's undergarments, Gentlemen of the Privy Chamber were to be ready at seven a.m. with his outer ones.)

At few courts in few periods can courtiers have felt less sure of their lives, let alone their jobs. The poet Surrey was only one of a remarkable number of men and women who were executed for religious offences, for political plotting or for adultery with one of the King's queens. Life was often merry under Henry VIII but it could be short.

Henry VIII's sores are sometimes said to have been symptoms of syphilis, but there is no evidence that he took the remedies for venereal disease usually taken at this time, and they were more probably ulcerated varicose veins or symptoms of osteomyelitis of the thigh bone, this perhaps the result of a jousting injury.

John Skelton (c. 1460–1529)

John Skelton, the first Poet Laureate, had previously been made a laureate of Oxford (an honour given for a degree in rhetoric) before he came to court as Henry VII's laureate in November 1488. Though he was of humble background, he had also studied at Cambridge and by this time was considered a man of learning. His face was described as frowning and frost-bitten. At court he was no mere composer of birthday odes, but had serious duties: to write verse propaganda for Henry VII, a king whose claim to the throne was not the best, and who had seized it only three years previously by defeating Richard III at Bosworth. Skelton's earliest loyal poem was his 'Northumberland Elegy', celebrating the defeat of the north country rebels who had murdered the 4th Duke of Northumberland.

Ten years later Skelton was given the additional post of Tutor to the king's second son, Prince Henry – later Henry VIII. During the summer of that year, to qualify him for this new job, he had been ordained subdeacon, deacon and priest all within four months. Prince Henry's residence was at Eltham, near Greenwich, and Skelton lived there with him, but was entitled to 'bowge' at court – free board and lodging at Westminster when he went there. 'The Bowge of Court' was the title of the poem he wrote during his first year at Eltham, a vigorous attack on the sorts of vice he had met at court and now felt free to comment on because of his priesthood and his detached position at Eltham.

Skelton claimed that he taught Prince Henry how to spell. He also wrote for the young prince 'Speculum Principis', a guide to proper princely behaviour, which ended, ironically, with the advice, 'choose yourself a wife who you will always and only love'.

When Henry's elder brother, Prince Arthur, died and Henry became the heir to the throne Skelton lost his position at court and retired to a country parsonage at Diss on the Norfolk–Suffolk border. Here, judging by his verses, he made enemies. One was a neighbouring cleric. Arriving at his own church door one day, Skelton found it barred. This cleric was inside together with his hawk which had pursued and caught a pigeon and was now tearing it to pieces on the altar.

More picturesque details of Skelton's life at Diss are given in *Merry Tales of Skelton*, and though this was first published thirty-eight years after Skelton's death, its author seems to have been a contemporary of Skelton's and it is probably reliable. Skelton, it says, kept a mistress there, by whom he had a child. Called before the Bishop of Norwich to defend himself, he took two capons as a gift. When the Bishop was not satisfied Skelton told him that they were called Alpha and Omega respectively, since one was the first capon he had ever given the Bishop and the other would be the last.

Back at Diss, Skelton defended himself in the pulpit, calling his mistress to bring him his child. 'And he, showing his child naked to all the parish, said, How say you neighbours all? is not this child as fair as is the best of all yours? It hath nose, eyes, hands, and feet, as well as any of yours: it is not like a pig, nor a calf, nor like no fowl nor no monstrous beast. If I had, said Skelton, brought forth this child without arms or legs, or that it were deformed, being a monstrous thing, I would never have blamed you to have complained to the bishop'. (Spelling modernized.)

Skelton's early biographer, Braynewode, concluded the story of his mistress by telling how, on his death bed, Skelton admitted that she had always been his wife. Certainly for a priest to have married was a more serious offence than to take a mistress, but a secret marriage would not have been in keeping with Skelton's orthodox religious views.

Skelton probably left Diss in about 1512 and spent the last seventeen years of his life at Westminster, where he was again closely connected with the court, this time that of Henry VIII, his old pupil. Once more he wrote loyal propaganda and was given the new honour of King's Orator. He also wrote light verse for performance at court theatricals, including (but sadly lost) 'The Ballad of the Mustard Tart'. Another, 'Mannerly Margaret Milk and Ale', was set to music by the King's musician, Cornish, and survives.

In the early 1520s Skelton acquired a new patron, Elizabeth Stafford,

Countess of Surrey, and it may have been she and her husband who encouraged him to write his most dangerous satires. In these he attacked Cardinal Wolsey with increasing openness. 'Bo-ho [the King] doth bark well, but Hough-ho [Wolsey] he ruleth the ring', he wrote, in, 'Speak, Parrot', one of the earliest.

Eventually in about 1522 or 1523, Skelton took refuge with his old friend, Abott John Islip, at Westminster Abbey. Presently a compromise was reached. Wolsey would forgive him for his early poems and allow him his freedom provided in future he agreed to perform his proper court duties as Poet Laureate and King's Orator, and write only poems in the national interest. His real opinions no doubt remained well known to all who remembered his earlier 'hot choler kindled against the cankered Cardinal, Wolsey'.

Sir Thomas Wyatt (c. 1503–1542)

Though Thomas Wyatt's portrait shows a man with a long bald forehead and long black beard, he died comparatively young – and naturally, unlike his son, also Thomas, who in the next reign led 'Wyatt's Rebellion', and unlike many of his contemporaries at Henry VIII's court. As well as becoming a courtier, diplomat and soldier, he was a poet. He, rather than Surrey (who was fifteen years younger), probably introduced the sonnet from Italy to England.

As a young man at court – where in 1516 he became a 'Sewer Extraordinary', then an Esquire of the Body – he was equally admired for his physique and sporting qualities. At Christmas 1524, by which time he was also Clerk of the King's Jewels, he took part in one of those remarkable events – part tournament, part dramatic performance, part genuine battle – with which the court amused itself, as one of sixteen gentlemen who were to defend a structure known as The Castle of Loyalty, occupied by four ladies. When the castle was set up at Greenwich some who saw it said that it was so strong 'it could not be won by sport but by earnest'. On the first day of the performance two ancient knights appeared to challenge six of the defenders and when given permission threw off their disguises to reveal themselves as the King and the Duke of Suffolk. About the day's play, in which the king broke seven spears, Hall reported: 'I think that there was never battle of pleasure, better fought than this one.'

Wyatt probably first met his cousin, Anne Boleyn, when she returned from the French court in 1522. Although married he soon became her lover, a dangerous condition once Henry also grew interested in her. Henry warned Wyatt during a bowls match, at which Wyatt measured the distance between the bowls with a locket and Henry pointed with a finger wearing a ring, each of these trophies taken from Anne. Wyatt later told Henry precisely what his connection with Anne had been and warned him against making a queen of such a woman.

In January 1526 Wyatt went for a while to live in Italy. He is said to have hitched a lift there with the Ambassador to the Papal Court, John Russell, whose ship he met as it was passing down the Thames. It was now that he studied Italian literature, in particular the sonnets of Petrarch.

Back in England he became involved in 'a great affray' with 'the sergeants of London, in which one of the sergeants was slain', and was sent briefly to the Fleet prison. But within the month he was released and given command of 'all the men able for war' in parts of Kent, including Tenterden, Goudhurst, Staplehurst and the Isle of Oxney, with licence to dress twenty of them in livery.

He was in more serious trouble in the summer of 1536, when Queen Anne (Boleyn) was arrested and accused of incest and adultery. Wyatt, along with her brother and her four lovers, was sent to the Tower, and here, if a poem he wrote soon afterwards tells the literal truth, he watched his friends being executed through a grating. He expected to die too, but Thomas Cromwell, always his friend, saved him. He was never brought to trial and within a month of the executions had been released.

He was in equally serious danger in 1540, after the execution of Thomas Cromwell, when old rivals claimed that while an ambassador in France he had tried to make contact with the King's enemies, and that at Barcelona he had said 'that he feared the King would be cast out of a cart's arse and that, by God's blood, if he were so, he were well served, and he would he were so.' In January 1541 he was sent to the Tower. In his defence he claimed that the first accusation was true but had been a stratagem to gain information and that the second was a lie.

After three months he was released at the request of Queen Catherine Howard, on condition that he confessed his guilt and 'resumed conjugal relations with his wife' from whom he had been living apart for fifteen years because of her adultery. There is no knowing whether or not Wyatt kept these conditions, but he was certainly soon back in royal favour, making exchanges of land with the king and receiving royal appointments. In October 1542 he was sent by the king to meet the

Spanish envoy at Falmouth, but he never got there. He rode so hard, using relays of horses, that he developed a severe fever at Sherborne and died three days later.

Anne Boleyn, Queen (1507–1536)

If Anne Boleyn, Henry VIII's second queen, had been less virtuous (or less ambitious) English history might have been very different. By persistently refusing to become the King's mistress she so excited him that he determined to marry her. True, he was already bored with his queen, Catherine of Aragon, who was four years older than himself and had disappointed him by producing only one daughter (the future Queen Mary) among many miscarriages, still births and infants who had died within a few weeks. But Anne's obstinacy was an important, perhaps the most important, reason for Henry's decision that he must divorce Catherine.

As a girl of twelve Anne had gone to France to the household of Queen Claude, but had returned to the English court, to become part of Wolsey's household, in 1522 when England and France went to war. Later she was Maid of Honour to Queen Catherine. Apart from her long dark hair she was not beautiful. But she soon had suitors, including her cousin Thomas Wyatt. And from this time (if not before) Henry – who was already having an affair with her older sister, Mary – took an interest in Anne. At first he and Wolsey tried to marry her to an Irish chieftain, Sir James Butler. When this failed and she began to be pursued by Henry Percy, heir to the Duke of Northumberland, the King employed Wolsey to warn Percy off. Perhaps Anne was genuinely in love with Percy, and this episode explains her later dislike of Wolsey.

To obtain his divorce from Catherine, Henry convinced himself that his marriage to her was illegitimate because she was the widow of his brother, Prince Arthur. There was, however, a problem with this argument: though Leviticus forbade marriage to a brother's widow, Deuteronomy specifically ordered it. There was also a difficulty about Henry's plan to marry Anne. If he argued that he should not have married Catherine because of her previous marriage to his brother, so Anne should not marry Henry because of *his* previous relationship to *her* sister, who was well known to have been his mistress. For six years Henry tried to get the Pope's permission to do what he wanted. Finally, on January 25th 1533, still without permission, he secretly married Anne; it was only later the same year that Archbishop Cranmer pronounced Henry's first marriage invalid. Meanwhile Anne had lived more and more openly with the King, and in increasing splendour. She and her supporters, the Dukes of Norfolk and Suffolk, had succeeded in having Wolsey dismissed. And she had become pregnant.

This may have happened when it did, in December 1532, because until then she had still been refusing to sleep with Henry, and had only agreed when she was made Marquis of Pembroke. Whatever the reason, it was her pregnancy which forced Henry to act and ended his appeals to the Pope.

Anne began to describe herself as Queen soon after her marriage to Henry. She was not popular. At one London church most of the congregation left when asked to pray for the new queen. Nevertheless on May 23rd, six days after Cranmer had declared Henry's first marriage null and void, she arrived by river at the Tower of London accompanied by a fleet of three hundred decorated ships, with music playing and banners flying. Two days later she was carried in procession through the streets of Westminster on a litter canopied with cloth of gold, and next day she was crowned Queen.

From this moment Anne's luck changed. A great bed was prepared at Greenwich for the delivery of her child and astrologers forecast a son, but, alas, it was a girl (the future Queen Elizabeth). Henry was so disappointed that he did not attend the christening.

Next year Anne miscarried, and in January 1536, gave premature birth to a dead child. These accidents were the underlying cause of the charges of adultery and incest which Henry soon afterwards began to bring against her. He stage-managed their climax at a May Day tournament that year, which he left abruptly, claiming to have seen her drop a handkerchief for one of her lovers to pick up and use to mop his brow. Next afternoon Anne was arrested and taken to the Tower. Within three weeks she was dead, her head cut off with a sword by the executioner of Calais.

Her supposed lovers, Francis Weston, Henry Norris, William Brereton, and Mark Smeaton, had been tried first and found guilty by peers who included her own father. She and her brother were then accused of incest and unanimously found guilty by twenty-six peers who included her uncle, the Duke of Norfolk.

Neither Anne nor any of her supposed lovers admitted their guilt except Smeaton, a musician, and he only when threatened with torture. The truth is that, quite apart from Anne's failure to provide him with a male heir, Henry had long fallen out of love with her. Within eleven days of Anne's execution he had married one of *her* Ladies-in-Waiting.

Jane Seymour, Queen (1509–1537)

As soon as Henry VIII heard the news that Anne Boleyn had been executed, he went by barge to visit Jane Seymour, where she was staying in Chelsea. Next day they became engaged and ten days later they were married.

Jane had first been a Lady-in-Waiting to Queen Catherine of Aragon, then when Catherine died, to Anne Boleyn. Henry no doubt saw her during this time, but he seems to have taken no special notice of her till the late summer of 1535 when her family, who had been wardens of Savernake Forest in Wiltshire since the Norman Conquest, entertained him at their house of Wolf Hall, in the forest. Early the next year he began to send her 'dishonourable proposals', one of them accompanied by a purse of sovereigns. But Jane, like Anne Boleyn in similar circumstances, knew that virtue would pay better in the end and sent back the purse and letter unopened. And though, when she came to stay in Thomas Cromwell's apartments, she lived in 'almost regal splendour', she only allowed Henry to visit her if others were present.

Such evidences of scheming to succeed Anne Boleyn qualify the character of quiet decency which historians often give Jane, and which, fortunately for these suggestions, is not spoiled by any of the sort of memorable or bitchy remarks made by Anne Boleyn when *she* became queen. Catholic historians favour Jane because she reconciled Henry with Princess Mary (ignoring the possibility that this was part of Jane's campaign against Anne and her rival daughter, Princess Elizabeth). Protestant historians favour her because she was the mother of the future Edward VI.

Her brief period as Queen included one picturesque event and one important one. In January 1537 she accompanied the King and his court when they rode across the frozen Thames. In October the same year she at last produced for Henry the legitimate son who, in due course, became king. Twelve days later she died, according to contemporaries because of the combined effects of a cold, of 'eating things that her fantasy called for', and of over-excitement at her son's christening, but more probably of puerperal fever. When Henry died in 1547 he was buried, at his own request, by Jane's side in St George's Chapel, Windsor.

Catherine Howard, Queen (c. 1520–1542)

Catherine Howard was at least the fifth young woman at court to be seduced by Henry VIII, and the third to become one of his queens. In 1539 she had been appointed a Maid of Honour to Anne of Cleves who was due shortly to become his fourth queen. He was marrying Anne for political reasons – the story that he was misled by Holbein's portrait of Anne is a picturesque invention – but he was also anxious about her looks, and soon after she landed in England he went in disguise to Rochester to get an early view of her. He was so disappointed that he was only with difficulty persuaded by Thomas Cromwell to marry her.

And although, after they were married on January 6th, 1540, he spent nights with Anne, he called her his 'Flanders Mare' and found her so repulsive that he never consummated the marriage. Within a few months it was Catherine Howard, Anne's Maid of Honour, who was receiving lavish gifts from the King. Catherine was nineteen, short and plump, but high-spirited. Henry was forty-nine.

Now there was a power struggle between Thomas Cromwell, Henry's principal minister since Wolsey's fall, and Catherine's supporters, the Duke of Norfolk and Henry Gardiner, Bishop of Winchester. These encouraged Henry to abandon Anne of Cleves and substitute Catherine, in order (as the Council put it) to provide 'some more store of fruit of succession'. Henry seemed willing to co-operate with them, crossing the Thames by day and night to meet Catherine at one or other of their residences on the south bank. On July 10th, still a mere six months after his marriage to Anne of Cleves, this was declared null and void. Eighteen days later the climax came when, on the same day, Thomas Cromwell was executed and Henry married Catherine.

A honeymoon period followed, Henry apparently revivified by his young bride and more in love with her than with any previous wife. Catherine was less satisfied. She was able to make comparisons, since she had had earlier affectionate relationships with at least two men. One, Henry Manox, had taught her to play the virginals and claimed that she had promised to be his mistress; the other, Francis Dereham, she had given shirt sleeves and a shirt band as tokens of love, and he had given her 'a silk heart's-ease' and had brought her wine, strawberries and apples after the Duchess of Norfolk, in whose house they were living, had gone to bed. As a result of such experiences, or because Catherine was bored with Henry and oversure of her position, by 1541 she was not only flirting with such courtiers as Thomas

Culpeper junior, her cousin, but had even obtained a position at court for her old love, Dereham.

That summer Henry and Catherine set out on a splendid royal journey to York. Throughout this trip he was cuckolded by Thomas Culpeper, who was regularly let into Catherine's apartments by Lady Rochford, Matron of the Queen's Suite, widow of Anne Boleyn's executed brother, George. Catherine may well have been having a parallel affair with Dereham, and to conceal this have appointed him her secretary, as she did at Pontefract.

Back in London, Henry was told about Catherine's previous relationship with Dereham. At first he refused to believe it, but after Dereham had confessed and Henry had been presented with the full evidence at an all-night meeting of the Council, he was convinced. In turn he wept, raged, called for a sword to kill Catherine, blamed the Council for misadvising him, then spent several long days hunting.

Catherine eventually confessed that she had been no virgin when she had married Henry, but refused to admit that she and Dereham had promised to marry each other. If they had done so, this would have been considered at the time to have invalidated her later marriage to Henry, and he might have agreed merely to part from her. Certainly he announced that he intended to show her mercy.

Soon, however, Dereham and Culpeper were arrested and enough evidence of their more recent intimacies with Catherine extracted from them and others by torture to have them found quilty. Both were executed.

Catherine meanwhile was imprisoned at Syon House. Here she was described as 'very cheerful and more plump and pretty than ever; as careful about her dress and as imperious and wilful as at the time she was with the King'. But in January 1542 an Act of Attainder was passed by Parliament against her to which commissioners gave royal assent early in February. This procedure was used so that Henry could seem only reluctantly to break his promise of mercy. Two days later she was beheaded on Tower Green. So was Lady Rochford, who should have been tried with Culpeper and Dereham but after her arrest had for three days 'gone completely out of her mind with the horror of the situation', and had had to be carefully nursed to make her fit for execution with Catherine.

Sir Nicholas Carew (c. 1495–1539)

Nicholas Carew was one of Henry VIII's companions in the early years of his reign, enjoying with the young king his life of hunting, jousting, dicing, tennis-playing and music-making. At court Carew was a Squire of the King's Body, and one of the King's 'Cypherers' (Cupbearers); his wife, Elizabeth, was a daughter of Queen Catherine of Aragon's Vice-Chamberlain. Soon he was knighted.

But he twice fell out of favour and was temporarily banished from court. When forgiven the first time Wolsey wrote: 'Mr Carew and his wife to be returned to the King's grace – too soon in my opinion.' In compensation for his second banishment (when he and other young courtiers were accused of imitating French court behaviour, although he had not himself yet been at the French court) he was given a well-paid position at Calais, but found this exile 'sore to his displeasement'.

By the following year he was back in favour, attending the King at the Field of the Cloth of Gold, and defeating all comers in the lists; two years later he was at court again as Master of the Horse. During the next seventeen years he was sent on a number of foreign missions by Henry, some of them concerned with getting his divorce from Catherine, and at this time made such a good impression that the King of France pressed Henry to make Carew a Knight of the Garter. This he became in 1536.

Disaster followed quickly. According to Thomas Fuller it occurred because Carew was over-familiar with the king during a game of bowls but, even if the incident was real, it was probably only another example of Henry staging a public fall from favour, as he did when he supposedly saw Anne Boleyn drop a handkerchief for her lover at a May Day tournament. High treason was the charge on which Carew was arrested. During the trial of the Marquis of Exeter, in which Carew had acted as interrogator, he had apparently said that he thought Exeter innocent.

In the Tower he was examined about treasonable correspondences he had had with Princess Mary, and with Exeter. Though he and Exeter had both burned their letters this did not save Carew, and he was beheaded on Tower Green. Before he died he apparently confessed his error in supporting the old and superstitious faith, and thanked God for having him imprisoned in the Tower, where for the first time he had 'savoured the life and sweetness of God's most holy word' in the form of the Bible translated into English.

Henry Howard, Earl of Surrey (c. 1517–1547)

Henry Howard, the poet, generally known simply as Surrey, was unlucky to lose his head only nine days before Henry VIII died, but he had been arrested and condemned partly as a cumulative result of his own quarrelsomeness and conceit. He was the eldest son of the third Duke of Norfolk, one of the most important political figures throughout Henry's reign, and his maternal grandfather was the Duke of Buckingham. To further improve his opinion of himself, he was brought up at Windsor as the companion of Henry Fitzroy, Duke of Richmond, Henry VIII's illegitimate son by Elizabeth Blount (whom his sister married), and in 1530, when he was still about thirteen, he was considered as a possible husband for Princess Mary (the future Queen Mary).

Though he was probably less responsible than Thomas Wyatt for importing the sonnet to England, he was a better poet; when a child his tutor praised his translations from Spanish, Italian and Latin, and his poetry, which he circulated in manuscript though it was not published till ten years after his death, was admired by contemporaries. One poem, 'A Description and Praise of his Love Geraldine', referred to Lady Elizabeth Fitzgerald, and produced an elaborate legend about his love for this nine-year-old girl (as she must have been when he first admired her). The legend claimed that in Florence Surrey issued a challenge to 'all who disputed her supreme beauty'. In fact he never went to Italy.

His quarrelsomeness led to two periods of confinement, the first at Windsor after he had struck a courtier who had accused him of secretly sympathizing with the Catholic rising known as the Pilgrimage of Grace, the second in the Fleet prison, after a dispute with John à Leigh, which he admitted and blamed on 'the fury and recklessness of youth'. A year later he was in the Fleet again, accused of eating flesh in Lent, and of breaking the windows of London houses by shooting at them with a 'stone bow'. In a poem about this third offence he claimed to have done it to prepare the citizens for divine retribution which they would soon receive for their irreligious life.

His conceit was noted by one of Thomas Cromwell's spies, who described him as 'the most foolish and proud boy that is in England', and by the landlady of a house he rented in the city for private amusement, who said that he made his friends treat him as if he were a prince. His long-standing dislike of Cromwell was in part because of Cromwell's common background.

But he was a brave and sometimes successful soldier. When he returned to court at the end of 1543 Henry made him his Cupbearer as a reward for his part in the year's campaign. Next year, now a Marshal, he fought again in France, under his father who reported with enthusiasm on his son's bravery; he had almost died of his wounds when attempting to storm the town of Montreuil.

In 1545 he was given command of the English troops defending Boulogne. Henry VIII had personally led the capture of this town and was determined to keep it. Surrey encouraged him, but was defeated in a nearby battle at St Etienne, and further irritated the king by asking afterwards to have his wife with him in France. There would soon be 'trouble and unquietness unmeet for woman's imbecilities', Henry wrote, and Surrey was presently replaced.

When he (and his father, the Duke of Norfolk) were arrested and sent to the Tower in December that year (1546) it was, however, for political reasons, not for military incompetence, and the work of their political enemies, rather than the King. Henry was expected to die soon and the Seymours and their allies (relatives of Prince Edward's mother, Queen Jane Seymour) had the Howards put away to make sure that they would control the young Prince when he became King.

Surrey was accused of various offences, including having an Italian jester, and of suggesting to his sister (widow of the Duke of Richmond) that she make herself the King's harlot, so establishing control over him. But the underlying accusation was that he and his father had plotted not only to make his father Regent when Henry died, but to murder Prince Edward and make his father king.

The precise charge against Surrey was for an offence which symbolized this plan: that he had included the arms of Edward the Confessor in his own coat-of-arms. He was found guilty and beheaded on Tower Green on January 19th 1547. Eight days later commissioners gave royal assent to a Parliamentary Act of Attainder by which his father would also have been executed, but Henry died early the next morning and the Duke survived, though he was kept in prison for the whole six years of Edward VI's reign and only released by Queen Mary.

Sir Francis Bryan (d. 1550)

Francis Bryan was another of Henry VIII's lusty young courtiers during the early years of his reign; unlike many, he still had his head on his shoulders at its end. This was more surprising since he was closely related to others who were less lucky. Anne Boleyn was his cousin, and his sister married Nicholas Carew. It was for his callousness in taking Jane Howard (Henry's third queen) the news that his cousin Anne Boleyn (Henry's second queen) had been condemned to death, that Thomas Cromwell called him 'the vicar of hell'. He was an admired poet in his lifetime, described by another poet fifty years later as 'the most passionate among us to bewail and bemoan the complexities of love'. He had only one eye, and was later reported by the French Ambassador to be usually drunk.

Briefly he was a seaman, Captain of the *Margaret Bonaventure*, but by 1516 he was the King's Cupbearer, and two years later 'Master of the Toyles' at Greenwich Park, responsible for managing the driven deer which the Tudors shot for sport.

Next year he was one of several young courtiers, Nicholas Carew among them, who were temporarily banished from court for copying French court behaviour. When in France they were said to have joined the French king in his daily sport of riding 'in disguise through Paris, throwing eggs, stones and other foolish trifles at the people'. Back in England these young courtiers had been 'all French in eating, drinking and apparel, yea, and in French vices and brags', affecting to despise everything English. But Bryan was soon back in favour, attending Henry at the Field of the Cloth of Gold and becoming again a royal Cupbearer.

At first he did his best to forward Henry's divorce from Catherine of Aragon and his proposed marriage to Anne Boleyn (Bryan's cousin). He went with three others for Henry on a mission to Rome in 1528 (which failed); and four years later he helped to deliver the summons to Catherine to attend Cranmer's court and say why Henry should not divorce her. She refused, taking particular offence that this relative of Anne Boleyn's should have been sent to her.

However, when Bryan saw that Anne's fortunes were declining, he wisely switched sides and manufactured a quarrel with her brother, Lord Rochford, to give Henry the opportunity to break with Rochford by taking his (Bryan's) part. Just the same he was lucky to escape when Anne's lovers were executed and Cromwell, who disliked him, sent for him from the country. But he was not charged, and, once Anne had been executed, was freed within a month.

He had a second near-escape when examined about whether or not he had spread the rumour that Henry had forgiven Princess Mary. On this and other occasions he was careful to avoid becoming involved with any Catholic reactionary group, as his brother-in-law, Nicholas Carew, so fatally did, and he survived the rest of the reign, to act as 'Master of the Henchmen' at Henry VIII's funeral and be rewarded soon afterwards with much confiscated monastic land.

Early in the next reign he did Edward VI a peculiar service when, to prevent the two most powerful Irish clans becoming united by marriage, he himself married Joan, widow of the Earl of Ormonde, the lady who had been proposing such a union. Now he was rewarded by being made Lord Deputy of Ireland, and he died there three years later.

William Summers [Somers] (d. 1560), Jane the Fool and Patch

Will Summers, best known Tudor fool, was fool to Henry VIII, Edward VI and Mary; as late as October 1558 when Mary was dying he was granted seven and a half ounces of silk, a hundred and eighty buttons of various kinds, eight green and yellow silk tassels, two ells of Holland cloth, fifteen pairs of hose of various sorts and six handkerchiefs.

Numerous stories accumulated around him, some credible, some not, the most dramatic concerned with Cardinal Wolsey. Summers is said to have visited his cousin Patch, who was Wolsey's fool, and to have been taken by Patch to the Cardinal's cellars for a drink. Here they tapped a hogshead of wine and found it full of gold coin. So were forty more in the cellar, they discovered. Summers reported this to the King, the story concludes, who sent and found a total of a hundred and fifty hogsheads of gold coin.

Legend as this may be, Robert Armin, himself a stage fool, who wrote at a time when many remembered Summers, confirms that Wolsey and Summers disliked each other and tells a more credible story of how Summers tricked Wolsey into paying a debt of £10 to the poor.

Wolsey was present and snubbed on another legendary occasion when he, the King and Summers rode past a house occupied by one of the King's mistresses, and challenged each other to a game of rhyme-capping of the sort Summers often played with the King.

King   Within yon tower
There is a flower
That hath my heart

Summers   Within this hour
She pist full sower,
And let a fart

Wolsey   A rod in the school
And a whip for the fool
Are always in season

Summers   A halter and a rope
For him that would be Pope
Against right and reason.

At which 'the cardinal bit his lip', the story concludes.

Summers came from Shropshire and was lean and hollow-eyed with a stoop, but popular at court, no doubt because he dared to say things to the King which others would have liked to say. He would make comic faces and gestures and ask the King riddles. According to Armin, many people who were still living at Greenwich remembered an occasion when the King was particularly gloomy and Summers retired behind the arras to prepare three questions for him. 'At last out comes William with his wit, as the foole of the play does, with an antick look to please the beholders' and asked the King his three questions of which the last was: 'What is it that, being born without life, head, nose, lip or eye, and yet runs terribly roaring through the world till it dies.' When told the answer (a fart) 'the King laughed heartily, and was exceeding merry and bids Will ask him any reasonable thing and he would grant it', but Summers replied that at present he had all he needed and 'layes him down amongst the spaniels to sleep'.

On the whole Summers's often scatological jokes seem laboured today. Once he told a miller there was nothing he could imagine more valiant than the collar of a miller's shirt. Why was that, the miller asked. 'Marry, because every morning it hath a thief by the neck', Summers told him.

Summers was also popular for his good-heartedness.

> . . . he was a poor man's friend
> And helped the widow often to her end;
> The king would ever grant him what he crave

For well he knew Will no exacting knave
But wished the king to do good deeds great store
Which caused the court to love him more and more.

When an uncle came to court from Shropshire to protest against the enclosure of a local common, Summers dressed him in his own fool's costume. In this he was able to plead his case successfully with the King.

[Summers] loved sweet wine exceedingly, and it was as natural to him as milk from a calf; and having drunk somewhat too much, that his stomach would not bear it, and fearing to be seen lest he should be whipt at the Porters Lodge the better to conceal this oversight, runs to a closestool, and opening the top, puts in his head, because he would not be heard to vomit; and when he had eased his stomach, he could not get his head out of the seat: so at length he cried out, and no body heard him for the present, and he not able to endure the smell, strived to pull his head out, which he could not do; but often forcing himself, at length pulled the stool out, which hung about his neck like a band; which some espying brought him before the king, and told the story, which made the king laugh heartily at his folly.

For the coronation of Queen Mary, Summers was given 'a gown of blue satin, the ground yellow striping with a slight gold, a jerkin furred, with sleves of same, furred with conie'. On the whole, however, his grants of clothing, apart from handkerchiefs of which he was given an astonishing number, were less ample or luxurious than those of his counterpart, 'Jane the Fool'. Jane had been with Queen Mary's household since 1537 when Mary was a princess, and was regularly given gowns, petticoats, kirtles and above all shoes, often by the dozen. But, unlike Summers, no book was made of her riddles and mishaps, and she disappears after Mary's death in 1558.

Patch, Wolsey's fool, was much valued by the Cardinal who once said he was worth £1,000. When Wolsey was sick and in disgrace at Esher he made a present of Patch to the King, 'which Patch hearing, fell a crying, and would by no means have gone from him, till the Cardinal was forced to command six of his tallest yeomen to conduct him to the King'. When Patch arrived, however, and was shown the court by Summers, this 'pleased him very well'. While Summers was an 'artificial' fool, Patch was a 'natural' one and had his keeper. He remains a more legendary figure than Summers and no king or queen seems to have given him clothes.

Summers died in 1560 and was buried at St Leonard's, Shoreditch, but no one knows when or where Jane or Patch died or were buried.

3

Edward VI, Mary and Elizabeth I

Edward VI was nine years old when he came to the throne and sixteen when he died. He never knew his mother, Queen Jane Seymour, Henry VIII's third wife, for she died twelve days after he was born. Among those who brought him up was Sybil Penne, a warm-hearted woman who became something of a mother to him.

At the age of six Richard Cox, already his tutor, was given full charge of his education, and John Cheke employed as Cox's assistant. Henry VIII's appointment of Cox and Cheke was important. They were both Protestant sympathizers and were responsible for Edward becoming one too, so ensuring that the Reformation and the break with Rome continued after Henry's death.

A group of young aristocrats was brought to court to be educated alongside Edward, one of them, Barnaby Fitzpatrick, to be his whipping boy, who was punished in the Prince's place for the Prince's offences. Surprisingly, Edward and Fitzpatrick liked each other, corresponded when Fitzpatrick went to France and remained friends for the rest of Edward's short life.

Edward grew into a pious, humourless young man – he is said to have laughed only once – and his court was equally dull. This did not prevent it becoming corrupt. 'The court was corrupt and extremely covetous, especially towards the declining of the King's reign,' John Strype wrote, 'raking continually from the King . . . for the enrichment of themselves and making preys also of one another.'

Meanwhile politicians fought for power. First his uncle, Edward Seymour (Earl of Hertford, Duke of Somerset) made himself Lord Protector, but soon he was displaced and executed at the instigation of the Duke of Northumberland. It was Northumberland who persuaded Edward to leave the throne in his will to Lady Jane Grey, by then married to Northumberland's son, and who marched to Cambridge to meet Mary's forces, but surrendered to her when he saw that he could not defeat her.

Early in Mary's reign she herself was almost toppled by Thomas Wyatt (son of the courtier-poet of Henry VIII's reign) whose rebel force marched from Kent via Knightsbridge to Ludgate before surrendering. Many were executed. But during the rest of her reign it was heretics, rather than traitors, that Mary executed in large numbers, in an attempt to bring back the old faith, thus earning the name of Bloody Mary. At court she tried just as unsuccessfully to produce a Roman Catholic heir. In July 1554 she married Prince Philip (later Philip II of Spain) and next year it was announced that she was pregnant. But no child arrived.

For fourteen months Philip stayed in England, mainly at Hampton Court, along with numerous conceited and unpopular Spanish courtiers, before finding an excuse for leaving and never coming back. When he left, Mary, encouraged by her Ladies-in-Waiting, believed again that she was pregnant, but in fact she was dying.

Catholic biographers have written of various improbably virtuous lady courtiers who attended Mary. Magdalen Dacre is said to have used a staff to whack the hand of Philip of Spain which he playfully inserted through her bathroom window. Viscount Montague – who became Magdalen's husband, and the Queen's Master of the Horse – is said when in Spain to have refused to sleep with a whore although doctors assured him that this would cure him of 'a most perilous and molestful disease'. Even if such tales were true, the atmosphere of the court must have been more strongly influenced by the Queen's progressive illness and by her increasing paranoia which made her live like a recluse and, according to rumour, sleep in body armour.

Today the success of Queen Elizabeth in sustaining England for the next forty-five years as an independent protestant country may seem to have been inevitable. She saw it – more correctly – as by no means so, but requiring from her continuous political manoeuvring and the backing of daring yet competent seamen and soldiers. Her court was an important part of the robust, independent image she wished the country to show to foreigners. The fact that she was a queen made her especially determined that manliness and handsomeness should be the main qualifications for attending on her. Those who did not have such qualities were rejected or at best tolerated.

In appropriate contrast, the maids of the court were to be chaste. Whatever she might personally do – about which there remains some doubt – they were not to turn the Coffer Chamber, where they lived, into a brothel.

Surrounding herself with the beautiful and brave anyway suited the queen temperamentally, and the history of her court is the history of a succession of favourites. First came the Earl of Leicester, whom she almost married and probably did sleep with. Next, during Leicester's later years, came the gallant Sir Walter Raleigh, with his curly beard and broad Devonshire accent. Finally came Leicester's stepson, the young and foolish Earl of Essex. Only two years remained after she had had Essex's head cut off, and by then she was in her late sixties.

But to suggest that these three were ever continuously in favour is the opposite of the truth. Regularly they fell from grace and were banished from court or sent for punishment to the Tower or the Fleet. The offences they committed were precisely those which came naturally to the sort of 'proper men' they were: threatening to desert the queen by going to the wars and compounding the error by escaping from court without her permission; or insulting her by making love to her Maids of Honour and compounding the error by secretly marrying.

Sir Philip Sidney (1554–1586)

The famous incident in which Philip Sidney, himself fatally wounded and about to be given a drink of water, ordered it to be given to a wounded foot soldier with the words, 'Thy necessity is yet greater than mine,' occurred at Zutphen in the Netherlands where Sidney had gone to fight under his uncle, the Earl of Leicester, against the Spanish. Before the battle Sidney, in a typically chivalrous gesture, had left behind his leg armour when he saw that a friend was wearing none. He then formed one of a troop of five hundred English horsemen which charged three thousand Spanish. The English were driven back and the engagement nearly over when he was hit by a bullet in the thigh. He died twenty-six days later, still aged only thirty-one.

His funeral illustrates two other aspects of his life: his astonishing reputation for someone so young, who had done so little, and his perennial poverty. Though the States-General offered to spend half a ton of gold on having him buried in the Netherlands the English insisted that he should be brought home. Here his friends considered that he deserved nothing less than a processional public funeral, but he and his father had so many creditors that his embalmed body had to be kept for three months before they could afford it.

As soon as Sidney left Oxford, early in 1571, he began to pay regular visits to Elizabeth's court, where his uncle was the Queen's favourite. By this time he had impressed everyone who knew him with his precocious learning. At the age of eleven he had been writing letters to his father in Latin and French. For the next four years he travelled about Europe making an equally good impression – though he had to leave Paris hurriedly after the massacre of the Huguenots on the eve of St Bartholomew's day, 1572, because some of these had been his particular friends.

From the time he returned to court in 1575 until his death his standing there steadily improved. Sometimes the Queen would send him abroad on missions, sometimes use him at home to receive distinguished visitors. He would give her expensive presents which he could not afford, for example a gold-headed whip, a chain of gold and a heart of gold on New Year's Day 1581. For her benefit he wrote 'The Lady of May', a fantastic masque which was performed at Wanstead on May Day 1579.

But he was by no means always in favour with the Queen, who considered him involved in Leicester's secret marriage to Lettice Knollys, and who resented a long paper he sent to her arguing against the marriage she was considering to the French Duke of Anjou. She was also displeased with him for refusing to apologize to the Earl of Oxford when he and the Earl had quarrelled in the Whitehall Palace tennis-court. The Earl had started to take part in a game which Sidney was playing and, when Sidney objected, had called him a puppy and ordered all the players to leave. As a result Sidney had challenged Oxford to a duel which the Queen forbade. She suggested that he apologize to Oxford because of the Earl's superior rank.

Apart from such incidents, Sidney was a discontented courtier, and several times he planned to escape, once by buying an interest in Martin Frobisher's attempt on the North-West Passage, once by taking out a patent which allowed him to discover new land in America, once by riding secretly to Plymouth and trying unsuccessfully to persuade Drake to let him join his expedition to attack the Spanish mainland.

Meanwhile he had fallen in love with Penelope Devereux, daughter of the Earl of Essex, whom he first met when he was twenty and she was twelve. Two years later he became seriously interested in her; in 1581 his poems to her grew more passionate when she married Lord Rich; and in 1583 they reached a crescendo of loving despair when he himself married Frances Walsingham. By then he was probably Penelope's lover, and his marriage did not interrupt their affair.

About Sidney, John Aubrey wrote, he 'was the most accomplished cavalier of his time'. He was not only an excellent wit, but extremely beautiful. His hair was a 'dark amber colour. If I were to find a fault in it, methinks 'tis not masculine enough; yet he was a person of great courage.'

According to Aubrey, when Spenser brought Sidney his *Faerie Queene*, Sidney 'layed it by, thinking it might be such kind of stuff as he was frequently troubled with'. But when he read it he was so delighted with it that he hunted out Spenser in his lodgings and there 'mightily caressed him, and ordered his servant to give him so many pounds of gold. His servant said that that was too much. No said Sir Philip, and ordered an addition.'

Whatever his relationship may have been with Penelope Devereux, Aubrey says that he loved his wife so well that, after he had been wounded at Zutphen, despite the advice of his physicians and surgeons, he insisted on having 'carnal knowledge of her; which cost him his life; upon which occasion there were some rogueish verses made'.

Robert Dudley, Earl of Leicester (c. 1532–1588)

Robert Dudley, Earl of Leicester, Queen Elizabeth's great favourite and lover for the first half of her reign, was the fifth son of the Duke of Northumberland. Like other members of his family, he had been involved in the failed coup at the start of Queen Mary's reign, when his father had tried to put Lady Jane Grey on the throne. Robert had proclaimed Lady Jane as Queen at King's Lynn. When Mary defeated the coup, he, like his father and elder brother (who was married to Lady Jane) was sent to the Tower, but unlike them he was not executed and eventually released.

While Mary lived he fought abroad and for his services was 'restored in blood' by Parliament, but he stayed away from court. When she died, however, he quickly returned there. Already, in Edward VI's reign, when he had been a Gentleman of the King's Privy Chamber and Master of the Buckhounds, he had met Princess Elizabeth who had noticed his 'very goodly person'. Now as Queen she made him her Master of the Horse, and he soon became her lover.

Within a year it was being said that he would marry the Queen. In January 1560 the Spanish Ambassador described him as 'the King that is to be'. That year the first of a number of people was sent to the Tower for suggesting that the Queen was pregnant by Dudley. But there was a problem. He was already married to Amy Robsart. Though Amy only occasionally came to London and lived usually at Denchurch near Abingdon, Dudley regularly visited her there and they seem to have been on friendly terms.

In early 1560 Amy moved to Cumnor Place, a nearby house which was being rented by Dudley. Here, on Sunday September 8th, she was found lying at the bottom of the stairs with a broken neck.

The official story was that she had died from an accidental fall, and the coroner's jury agreed, giving a verdict of death by misadventure. Historians have argued ever since about whether or not this is the truth. One has recently suggested that she died of 'spontaneous fracture' of the spine, the result of disease. Others have suggested that she committed suicide because of her husband's affair with the Queen. Most have concluded that Dudley had her murdered, or that his servants murdered her for what they would gain if he became King. Lady Dudley was poisoned, they suggest, then had her neck broken and was placed at the foot of the stairs to suggest an accident. Two days before the event Lord Cecil had told the Spanish Ambassador that he knew of a plot to poison Lady Dudley, though she was at present quite well; and the following day the Queen herself had told the same Spaniard that Amy was dead or nearly so.

The scandal of Lady Dudley's death may have finally persuaded Elizabeth that she could not marry Dudley. Dudley, however, continued to plot with the Spanish Ambassador, da Quadra, to marry her. As a condition for his help da Quadra required Dudley to persuade the Queen to re-admit the supremacy of the Pope. Such a plan was of course violently opposed by the English puritans, and they may have influenced Elizabeth. So may the old English nobility, led by Cecil, who were deeply hostile to Dudley. Just the same he remained at court and seemed at first to be even more intimate with the Queen. And though he and the Queen sometimes quarrelled, she presently made him Earl of Leicester and gave him the castle of Kenilworth. Here, in 1575, he entertained her to one of the most spectacular pageants of her reign.

He may still have been hoping to marry her. True, he had been conducting a long affair with Lady Douglas Sheffield, and in 1573 they had had a child who later claimed to be legitimate because Dudley and his mother had married two days before he was born. But the story seems unlikely. During the 1575 festivities, however, Dudley had staying with him at Kenilworth Lettice Knollys, Countess of Essex, and three years later at seven o'clock one morning at his country house at Wanstead he secretly married her.

When the Queen heard of this marriage she was furious, and had Dudley confined at Greenwich. Dudley was equally furious with de Simier, the French Ambassador, who had told the Queen, and was rumoured to have tried to poison him, then when a shot was fired on the royal barge on the Thames, to have been using an agent to try to shoot him. But the Queen as usual forgave Dudley.

With others at court and in the country he grew increasingly unpopular, and in 1585 he was violently attacked in a pamphlet called *Leicester's Commonwealth*, which claimed that he had made himself virtual ruler of the country. Elizabeth forbade the circulation of the pamphlet.

Meanwhile Dudley, frustrated in England, was trying to have himself made Prince of the Netherlands. In 1586 the Queen at last allowed him to go there in charge of an English army. Here the States-General at once offered to make him the country's ruler. When Dudley accepted Elizabeth was again furious with him, but once again forgave him and agreed. In the Netherlands Dudley conducted two campaigns with notable inefficiency, during the first of which his nephew, Philip Sidney, was killed.

Back in England in 1588, Dudley was made Lieutenant and Captain General of the Queen's Armies and Companies when the country was threatened by the Armada. That August he set out from London to Kenilworth, and on the way died of 'a continual fever'.

There are strong suspicions that his wife poisoned him. One story is that *he* had tried to poison *her*, and she accidentally gave him the poisoned cordial. Another is that she knew he had tried to have her lover (Christopher Blount, whom she afterwards married) killed in the Netherlands and deliberately poisoned her husband.

He was buried at Warwick where his funeral cost the huge sum of £4,000.

Sir Walter Raleigh (c. 1552–1618)

Walter Raleigh was twenty-nine years old when, late in 1581, he threw down his cloak in a muddy road for the Queen to walk across. Perhaps it was this fine gesture which brought him to her notice, though perhaps she would anyway have been attracted by his 'thick dark hair', 'bright complexion', lively appearance and the broad Devonshire accent which he had learned as a child on the beaches of Budleigh Salterton and kept for the rest of his life. Surprisingly, John Aubrey says that his voice was small, but agrees that his presence was formidable. 'He had a most remarkable aspect, an exceeding high forehead, long-faced and sour eye-lidded, a kind of piggy-eye. His beard turned up naturally.

Tho: Wiatt Knight.

Sir Thomas Wyatt by Holbein

NON SINE SOLE IRIS

Queen Elizabeth I. The Rainbow Portrait
attributed to Isaac Oliver

... He had that awfulness and ascendancy in his aspect over other mortals.'

'Queen Elizabeth', Aubrey adds, 'loved to have all the servants of the court proper men'. There were reasons apart from his looks for her finding Raleigh a proper man. He already had a reputation as a brave soldier and sea captain. But men of this sort found court life tedious, and for the rest of his life Raleigh was continually asking to be allowed to take part in naval and military expeditions against the Spanish.

To keep him at court Elizabeth made him Captain of the Queen's Guard. She gave him many other positions and possessions, including Warden of the Stannaries (the body which controlled Devonshire tin mining), Lord Lieutenant of Cornwall and Vice-Admiral of both counties. In 1584 she knighted him and in 1586 gave him a forty thousand acre estate in southern Ireland.

It was in Ireland in 1588 that Raleigh perhaps planted the first potatoes to reach the British Isles, as a result of the interest he took in the colonization of Virginia. He never went to Virginia himself but his servant, Harriot, may have brought him some to plant at Youghal. Potatoes, however, had been taken to Spain by the Spanish conquistadores many years earlier and they may have reached England by this route. Raleigh's claim to have introduced tobacco to England is better. At court he and his fellow courtiers smoked it in pipes with silver bowls.

Raleigh actively helped to prepare for the land defence of England when the nation was threatened by the Armada in 1588, but there is no evidence that he took part in the action at sea. This was the year after his rival, Essex, had become the Queen's new favourite. For the rest of her reign (until Essex's execution) he and Essex conducted a smouldering quarrel, though strangely they co-operated in one of the most successful expeditions that either of them ever took part in: the great attack on Cadiz in 1596. It was Raleigh who led the English fleet into the harbour in the *Warspite*, and he might have helped in Essex's capture of the city if he had not been badly wounded.

Meanwhile at court Raleigh had found the other sure way to offend the Queen: he had begun an affair with one of her Maids of Honour, Elizabeth Throgmorton. Both were sent to the Tower. There is no telling whether or not she was the maid described by Aubrey.

He [Raleigh] loved a wench well; and one time getting up one of the Maids of Honour up against a tree in a wood ('twas his first lady) who seemed at first boarding to be something fearful of her honour, and modest, she cried, sweet Sir Walter, what do you me ask? Will you undo me? Nay, sweet Sir Walter! Sweet Sir Walter! Sir Walter! At last, as the danger and the pleasure at the same time grew higher, she cried in the ecstacy Swisser Swatter Swisser Swatter. She proved with child, and I doubt not but this hero took good care of them both, as also that the product was more than an ordinary mortal.

After a few months Raleigh was released and he married Elizabeth Throgmorton, but he remained out of favour at court and they settled in his new house at Sherborne.

During the last years of Elizabeth's reign he was back at Court. When Essex attempted his rebellion in 1601 his aim, he claimed, was to protect himself from the plots of Raleigh and friends. Raleigh's triumph was to watch Essex having his head cut off. Before Essex died he asked Raleigh to forgive him.

Raleigh's success was brief. Soon after James I succeeded to the throne he was accused of plotting, deprived of all his offices, sentenced to death and, although reprieved, kept prisoner in the Tower for the next twelve years. Here he spent his time carrying out chemistry experiments and writing his *History of the World*. He was eventually released in 1615 to lead another expedition to South America, but when this failed disastrously and he returned to England with no gold he was executed for the offence of which he had been convicted fifteen years earlier.

Robert Devereux, 2nd Earl of Essex (1566–1601)

Robert Devereux, Earl of Essex, Queen Elizabeth's favourite for twelve years towards the end of her reign (until she had him executed) was the stepson of the Earl of Leicester, who had been the Queen's favourite for most of the previous thirty years (until he died or was poisoned). Essex's mother had become Leicester's second wife when the young Essex was twelve.

The boy had already at the age of ten been brought to court, where he had declined to let the Queen kiss him. His stepfather, Leicester, brought him there again at seventeen, by which time he was considered notably handsome and courteous. But it was only in 1587 – after he had fought under his stepfather in the Netherlands for a year – that he became the Queen's closest friend and most usual companion. In the daytime she was regularly seen accompanied by him alone, and at night he was 'at cards, or one game or another with her [so] that he cometh not to his own lodgings till the birds sing in the morning'. In December that year he was given the position at court which Leicester had held for so long: Master of the Horse.

He was involved in several ways with Sir Philip Sidney. Like Sidney, he fought at Zutphen, where Sidney was fatally wounded. His sister, Penelope, was Sidney's great love, to whom Sidney wrote many verses. And in 1590 he secretly married Frances, Sidney's widow. Elizabeth was furious, as she had been with Leicester for *his* secret marriage, but after a few months forgave Essex provided he agreed that his wife should live a 'very retired' life in her mother's house.

Like Sidney, Essex was a discontented courtier and in just the same way escaped secretly from London to Plymouth to join one of Francis Drake's expeditions. He was more successful than Sidney, getting as far as Lisbon where he appeared in front of the besieged city and challenged all comers in the name of his mistress. But when angry messages arrived from Elizabeth, Drake sent him home.

Two years later, however, she let him go to France where much to her annoyance he made a similar gesture at the siege of Rouen, challenging the defending commander to single combat. And in 1596 she let him take part in the great attack on Cadiz, where he and Raleigh destroyed the Spanish fleet and he led the capture of the town.

For the next two years Essex was sometimes in, sometimes out of favour with the Queen. Though his friend, Francis Bacon, advised him to concentrate on politics rather than military glory, he went on another naval expedition – a less successful one to the Azores. And in 1598 he blundered again when he helped his friend, the Earl of Oxford, to marry secretly. He was also accused by gossip of having affairs with no fewer than four ladies of the court. But it was when in council with the Queen, discussing the appointment of a new Lord Deputy of Ireland, that his most serious quarrel with her occurred. Eventually he turned his back on her, telling her that 'her conditions were as crooked as her carcase' at which she hit him 'a violent blow on the ear' and told him to go and be hanged. Essex put his hand to his sword – but was persuaded to leave peacefully.

Next year he unwisely agreed to take charge of an Irish expedition, where he once more angered the Queen by making an unauthorized truce with an Irish chieftain, and by knighting large numbers of his followers. To explain himself he returned to England and early on the morning of September 28th forced his way into the Queen's bed-chamber. At first she seemed friendly, but her attitude changed during the day, and Essex was arrested, tried and sentenced to lose all his offices and remain in prison at the Queen's pleasure.

In the autumn he was released and spent the last five months of his life plotting the rebellion which led to his death. On February 8th he and his friends made their attempt, but the citizens of London failed to join them and Essex received a bullet through his hat before escaping to Essex House. Here, threatened with bombardment, he eventually surrendered on condition his friends were fairly tried.

Later that month he was sentenced to death, but the Queen hesitated, recalling the first death warrant she signed. Eventually his head was cut off, three strokes of the axe being needed. Afterwards Derrick, the executioner, was almost caught and killed by the London mob, which now belatedly made Essex its hero.

Henry Wriothesley, 3rd Earl of Southampton (1573–1624)

The career of the beautiful, quarrelsome courtier, politician and patron of the arts, Henry Wriothesley, third Earl of Southampton, almost came to a premature end in 1601 when he and his friend, Queen Elizabeth's favourite, the Earl of Essex, were sent to the Tower and Essex was executed. Southampton survived to become a controversial figure at court throughout James I's reign.

In total during the two reigns he was placed under restraint or sent to prison four times, but none of this is so well remembered as his patronage of William Shakespeare. Shakespeare, who was some ten years older than Southampton, dedicated his poems 'Venus and Adonis' and 'Lucrece' to Southampton, and there is strong internal evidence that Shakespeare's sonnets were also written for him. The expressions of love they include may not have meant what we would take them to mean today and may have merely been a convention of the time, but they could imply a homosexual relationship. Certainly Southampton was a beautiful young man. He had blue eyes and his long auburn hair fell below his shoulders. More portraits of him survive than of any of his contemporaries – at least fifteen.

At the age of eight, when his father died, he had become a royal ward, with Lord Burleigh, the Prime Minister, as his guardian. Burleigh first brought him to court in 1690. It was now that he became Essex's close friend.

One of his early quarrels was with an Esquire of the Body, Ambrose Willoughby, who told Southampton to stop the game of 'primero' he and Raleigh were playing in the Presence Chamber, since the Queen had gone to bed. Southampton hit Willoughby. Willoughby pulled out some of Southampton's auburn locks. The Queen took Willoughby's side and next day thanked him.

Southampton was in more serious trouble with the Queen when he secretly married Elizabeth Vernon, one of the Queen's Ladies-in-Waiting. Southampton and his wife were both sent to the Fleet prison. Though he was soon released, Elizabeth did not forgive him and he was excluded from court. Now he and Essex began to plot a palace revolution to remove their enemies from the Queen's court, which they staged in February 1601, but it was a total failure.

As soon as James I came to the throne next year he released Southampton, who had been sentenced to life imprisonment, and gave him many honours and positions. At the new court he became a particular favourite of the Queen's. Within two years, however, he was in more trouble for insulting Lord Grey, an old enemy of Essex's, and was once more sent to the Tower for infringing the peace of the palace. Although he was soon released and returned to court, for the next fifteen years he was given no important political appointment and employed himself in organizing voyages of exploration around North America, or in more court brawls, including one with the Earl of Montgomery conducted with tennis rackets.

Finally in 1619 he was made a Privy Councillor and for the next four years systematically opposed the royal favourite, Buckingham. Once this almost led to a fight in the House of Lords. It also led to Southampton's arrest on a charge of plotting with the members of the Commons, though this time he was merely confined to a friend's house.

In 1624 he was given charge of a body of six thousand volunteers which went to fight in the Netherlands, but caught a fever and died there.

The Court of the House of Stuart

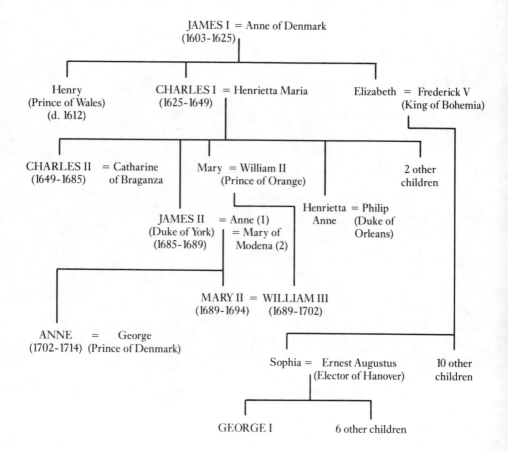

JAMES I = Anne of Denmark
(1603-1625)

Henry
(Prince of Wales)
(d. 1612)

CHARLES I = Henrietta Maria
(1625-1649)

Elizabeth = Frederick V
(King of Bohemia)

CHARLES II = Catharine
(1649-1685)   of Braganza

Mary = William II
(Prince of Orange)

2 other
children

JAMES II   = Anne (1)
(Duke of York) = Mary of
(1685-1689)   Modena (2)

Henrietta = Philip
Anne   (Duke of
Orleans)

MARY II = WILLIAM III
(1689-1694)   (1689-1702)

ANNE   =   George
(1702-1714) (Prince of Denmark)

Sophia = Ernest Augustus
(Elector of Hanover)

10 other
children

GEORGE I   6 other children

4

James I and Charles I

If Queen Elizabeth's court was dominated by a succession of male favourites, so was James I's. There may be some doubt about whether he was a practising homosexual, but there is none about his homosexual instincts. True, he managed to engender children, and to remain on surprisingly friendly terms with his queen, Anne of Denmark; he would get her agreement before committing himself to a new male favourite. But there is no suggestion of a royal mistress. 'He was the chastest prince for women that ever was', Sir John Oglander wrote. In contrast there are full accounts of how he would kiss and slobber in public over his boyfriends. About these Francis Osborne wrote that 'in w—— looks and wanton gestures they exceed any part of womankind'.

The principal three were Philip Herbert, Earl of Montgomery, later Earl of Pembroke; Robert Carr, Earl of Somerset; and George Villiers, Duke of Buckingham. Philip Herbert stepped aside gracefully for Somerset; Somerset ended in country exile, a convicted murderer. Buckingham, however, survived into the next reign, trusted as fully by Charles as he had been by James, until he was murdered by a discontented army officer.

The court was extravagant as well as immoral, and eventually Lionel Cranfield, Earl of Middlesex, was appointed to control expenses. Ironically, his appointment was made by Buckingham, whose personal extravagances were as great as the king's. They included accompanying Prince Charles to Madrid and taking part there in the most dramatic débâcle of the reign: the Prince's attempt to woo the Infanta.

When Charles I succeeded James I, 'the face of the court was much changed', Lucy Hutchinson wrote in her memoirs of her husband, the Parliamentarian soldier, Colonel Hutchinson, 'for King Charles was temperate, chaste, and serious, so that the fools and bawds, mimics and catamites of the former court grew out of fashion; and the nobility and courtiers, who did not quite abandon their debaucheries, had yet that reverence to the king to retire into corners to practise them.'

Though Buckingham remained not only the favourite at court but the most important politician in the country, and Charles still wrote to him by his nickname, Steenie, the new king's inclinations were hetero-sexual and he soon married the fifteen-year-old French princess, Henrietta Maria. One of the conditions of the marriage was that she should be allowed to bring a retinue of sixty courtiers with her. It was these (soon increased to four hundred and forty) who caused the most dramatic court event of the early years of the reign. Like their mistress, they were Roman Catholics and included a bishop and twenty-nine priests. Rumours spread that they were imposing extraordinary pen-ances on the Queen, like walking barefoot to Tyburn where so many Catholics had been martyred.

On one occasion when the King and Queen were dining in public, and the King's chaplain began to say an Anglican grace, the Queen's confessor began a Latin one. At this the Chaplain gave the confessor 'a zealous push', but he moved to the Queen's side and continued in Latin. The King stopped the competition by setting the carvers to work, but at the end of the meal chaplain and confessor began again, each trying to shout the other down.

Eventually the King decided to expel the French, first ordering them from Whitehall to Somerset House, then to leave the country. When he told the Queen she was so angry that she pulled hair from her head and ran her hands through a window, severely cutting them. And for a month the courtiers refused to leave. Eventually the King was forced to send 'the captain of the guard, attended with a competent number of his yeomen, as likewise with heralds, messengers, and trumpeters' to Somerset House with orders to turn them out 'by head and shoulders' and shut the gate after them. At this 'their courage came down and they yielded.' Nevertheless it took four days for them to leave and forty carts to transport them to Dover. And they took with them all the Queen's clothes except for a gown and two smocks. At Dover, as Madam St George, the Queen's Mistress of the Wardrobe, stepped into the boat one of the crowd threw a stone at her 'strange head-dress', at which a gentleman escort ran the man through with his sword, killing him. From France the expelled courtiers sent the Queen a bill for £19,000 in unpaid debts.

The Queen's religion continued to cause difficulties at court even when her French retinue had gone. The wet-nurse she employed for the Duke of York (the future James II) was a Catholic and refused to take the oath of allegiance. When courtiers tried to convert her she was so frightened that it 'spoilt her milk' and she had to be excused the oath. But on the whole the King and Queen lived on improved terms with each other. Puritans inevitably claimed that he had mistresses but they have left no convincing evidence.

The Queen's negroes, monkeys and dwarfs provided such levity as there was at court. They included Little Sarah and 'Sir' Jeffery Hudson. The king inherited his father's fool, Archie Armstrong, but eventually sacked him for insulting Archbishop Laud. For the most part the court was a sober place, entertained only by decorous masques which were supervised by Sir Henry Herbert, Master of the Revels. In 1633 one courtier wrote, 'I never knew a duller Christmas than we had at court this year, but one play all the time at Whitehall and no dancing at all.' The king's manner did not improve the atmosphere. All his life he suffered from a stammer which often made him speechless. Later it was said that Charles II, his son, refused favours with more grace than Charles I granted them.

As the reign progressed Parliament steadily increased its financial pressure on the King, and courtiers suffered with him. Their salaries remained unpaid for months or even years, and the lesser gentry who hung about the court, sponging on it, were ordered home to the shires.

Robert Carey, 1st Earl of Monmouth (c. 1560–1639)

As a gentleman at the court of Queen Elizabeth, Robert Carey 'kept men and horses far above [his] rank'. According to his cousin, the Earl of Suffolk, there was no one at Queen Elizabeth's court that lived in a better fashion and he was especially noted for his 'handsome and comely' dress. So it was not surprising that James VI of Scotland (the future James I of England), with his eye for male beauty, noticed Carey when he visited Scotland in 1583 and tried to persuade Elizabeth to send him back.

Elizabeth refused, but she used Carey for some years in managing the Scottish borders. He was in London, however, twenty years later, when he realized that the Queen was dying and decided that the best way to secure his future was to be the first to tell King James. As soon as he heard that the Queen had finally died he went to Richmond Palace, but here the Lords of the Council forbade him to go to Scotland and he only escaped from the palace by forcing his way through the gates behind his brother. Later that morning he sent to Whitehall where the Lords were now assembled to try again to get their permission, but was warned that if he went in person to ask them they would stop him. He therefore set off without permission.

By the evening, using horses he had had posted along the route, he had reached Doncaster – a hundred and sixty-two miles. By the next night he was at his own house at Widdrington – another hundred and thirty-five miles. By noon next day he was at Norham – another thirty-three miles – and 'might well have been with the king by supper time; but I got a great fall by the way; and my horse, with one of his heels, gave me a great blow on the head that made me shed much blood. It made me so weak, that I was forced to ride a soft pace after: so that the king was newly gone to bed by the time I knocked at the gate.'

Carey had to admit that he had brought no papers from the Council, but convinced the King that the news was genuine by showing him a ring which James had once given to Elizabeth. Carey had apparently been thrown the ring from a window after he had escaped from Richmond Palace, by his sister, Lady Scrope, who had taken it from the dead queen.

For a while Carey did not get the rewards he had hoped for. The Council persuaded James that his ride to Scotland had been a serious disobedience. But presently his wife was accepted at court and given charge of Prince Charles, and by 1605 Carey had become Governor of the Prince's Household. In 1611 he became Master of the Prince's Robes, observing that the one thing he did know about was the making of good clothes, and in 1617 his Chamberlain. Five years later he followed Prince Charles to Spain on his unfortunate expedition to woo the Infanta. The year after Charles succeeded to the throne he was made Earl of Monmouth, but was given no further honours or important positions. During the remaining thirteen years of his life he wrote his memoirs, but it was only in 1759, after Horace Walpole had admired the section dealing with Carey's great ride, that they were published in full.

William Herbert, 3rd Earl of Pembroke (1580–1630), Mary Fitton (b. c. 1572), Philip Herbert, 4th Earl of Pembroke (1584–1650)

William Herbert, third Earl of Pembroke, has been identified as the WH to whom the first edition of Shakespeare's sonnets was dedicated, and Mary Fitton as 'the dark lady' of the sonnets, but the evidence is slight. The dedication was the printer's (Thomas Thorpe), and the words 'to *the onlie begetter* of these insuing sonnets' probably refer to a friend who had brought him the manuscript for his unauthorized edition. Furthermore, by this time, 1609, Pembroke was generally known as Lord Herbert, and the other two books which Thomas Thorpe dedicated to him he did, not in this simple way, but 'in a trembling tone of subservience'.

If Pembroke was not WH, there is no reason to think that Mary Fitton was 'the dark lady'; the claim rests entirely on her connection with Pembroke. This connection, however, was genuine, and occurred in about 1600 when she was a Maid of Honour at Queen Elizabeth's court and Pembroke had newly arrived there.

There are contradictory views of Pembroke's character at this time. He had first attended on the Queen at the annual musters of the previous year, bringing with him two hundred horsemen, and been described as 'swaggering it among the men of war'. But he was also said to be 'a melancholy young man' with a want of spirit, and a 'cold and weak manner of pursuing her majesty's favour'.

On the other hand according to the historian, Clarendon, he was 'immodestly given up to women', and partook of 'pleasures of all kinds, almost all in excess'. And early in 1601 he was found to have got Mary Fitton with child. They had been having an affair for some months, and to reach him in secret she would 'put off her head-tire, and tuck up her clothes, and take a large white cloak and march as though she had been a man to meet the said earl out of the court'.

The queen sent the said Earl to the Fleet prison, and threatened to do the same with Mary, but seems to have relented. Her child died soon after he was born, and later she married twice but never again came to court.

Although Pembroke had been released after a month, he remained out of favour as long as Elizabeth reigned. But when James I succeeded her (1603) he returned to court, where the king 'regarded and esteemed him', though he never 'loved or favoured him'. In 1615 Pembroke became Lord Chamberlain and in 1626, the year after Charles I had succeeded James I, was made Lord Steward. During these years he was active in politics, usually opposing the policies of James's favourite, the Duke of Buckingham.

In later years Pembroke was described as 'rather majestic than elegant, and his presence, whether quiet or in motion . . . full of stately gravity'. He was enormously wealthy. At his seat in Wilton he kept over a hundred and ten servants to attend on a family of six or seven. Here he entertained both James I and Charles I. And his marriage to Mary, daughter of the Earl of Salisbury, brought him another fortune. But it was a 'most unhappy' marriage for his wife had a vile temper.

He was known to have a horror of frogs and on one occasion James I pushed one down his neck. The king, however, had a horror of pigs and the next time he visited Wilton Pembroke hid one under the commode in the royal bedchamber. 'His Majesty was extremely annoyed when he made the discovery.'

Though Pembroke was generally liked he managed to quarrel with Sir George Wharton, when he objected to Wharton's manners at cards and refused to continue to play with him. Next day out hunting Wharton lashed Pembroke's page across the face with his crop, and Pembroke hit Wharton in the face so violently that it 'drove him almost upon his horse's croup'. They arranged a duel, which had to be twice forbidden by the King.

Pembroke's tutor, Sandford, and 'the mad prophetess', Eleanor Lady Davies, both foretold that Pembroke would die on his fiftieth birthday. Because of this he arranged a great entertainment on the day at his London residence, Baynard's Castle. During the meal he was 'very merry' and said that he would never trust a woman's prophecy again. That night he died of an apoplexy.

In spite of his enormous wealth and his devastation of the ancient oaks of the Forest of Dean (of which he was Keeper) to make charcoal for his blast furnaces, he died with debts of £80,000.

Philip Herbert, who succeeded his brother as Earl of Pembroke in 1630, had been made Earl of Montgomery twenty-six years earlier by James I. He was a man of entirely different character from his brother: quarrelsome, foul-mouthed, interested only in dogs and horses and so illiterate that he could hardly write his own name. But, while James only respected William, he made Philip his first great English favourite. They shared a passion for hunting.

Philip had come to court at the end of Elizabeth's reign where he was described by a contemporary as 'one of the forwardest courtiers that I ever saw in my time; for he had not been here two hours, but he grew as bold as the best'. By James he was soon made a Gentleman of the Privy Chamber, then in 1605 a Gentleman of the Bedchamber.

His quarrels at court were numerous. 'There were few great persons in authority, who were not frequently offended by him by sharp and scandalous discourses, and invectives against them,' Clarendon wrote. At Croydon race-course he was horse-whipped by William Ramsay, one of the King's pages. Three years later he and the Earl of Southampton struck at each other with tennis rackets in the Whitehall Palace court. During the next reign he hit the poet Thomas May over the head with his staff of office. May accepted £50 in compensation, the way in which Pembroke calmed most of those he offended.

His first marriage, in 1604, to Lady Susan Vere, daughter of the Earl of Oxford, was celebrated with a sumptuous banquet and an elaborate masque. The couple were given lodgings for the night in the Council Chamber, where James I visited them next morning '*in his shirt and night gown* ... before they were up, *and spent a good time in or upon the bed*; choose which you will believe'.

He was succeeded in the King's favour by Robert Carr, but was content to remain at court as the King's second favourite, and when Charles I succeeded James I he followed his brother as Charles's Lord Chamberlain. By the early 1640s, however, he was openly supporting Parliament against the King, because, in Clarendon's opinion, he thought it would win, and he was dismissed from his court offices. The excuse was yet another quarrel, this time with Lord Maltravers in the House of Lords.

About the same time he became Chancellor of Oxford University, a position which showed him at his most ridiculous. 'He would make an excellent chancellor for the mews were Oxford turned into a kennel of hounds,' one pamphleteer wrote, and in Wood's opinion he was more suited by 'his eloquence in swearing to preside over Bedlam than a learned academy'.

Robert Carr, Earl of Somerset (d. 1645), Elizabeth Howard, Countess of Somerset (c. 1593–1632), Sir Thomas Overbury, (1581–1613)

In 1607, during a tilting match at the Palace of Whitehall, Robert Carr, a Scottish gentleman who had once been a royal page, was thrown from his horse in front of James I and broke his leg. James had him nursed in the palace, where he visited him for one or two hours every day and fell in love with him. As soon as Carr recovered James knighted him and made him a Gentleman of the Bedchamber.

Also at court at this time was Elizabeth Howard, daughter of the Duke of Suffolk, who four years earlier had become the child wife of the Earl of Essex (son of Queen Elizabeth's executed favourite). Elizabeth Howard had been thirteen and Essex fourteen. After the wedding Essex had been sent abroad to mature, but had now returned, keen to consummate his marriage. Elizabeth had other ideas for she, too, had fallen in love with Robert Carr.

As a young girl she had been described as the best natured and most sweetly disposed of her father's children, 'exceeding them all also in the delicacy and comeliness of her person'. Her great uncle, the Duke of Northampton, was perhaps responsible for her far from sweet behaviour during the next few years.

At court she had also attracted the attention of Prince Henry, the King's eldest son, but it was to seduce Carr and to repel her husband, Essex, that she schemed. For these purposes she went to a Mrs Anne Turner, described as 'a doctor of Physic's widow' and the keeper of a brothel; and to a doctor named Forman, also called a conjurer and a juggler. Forman made models of Elizabeth and Carr 'whom he must unite and strengthen' and models of Essex 'whom he must debilitate and weaken'. The models were later produced in court at her trial. He also devised debilitating powders and drugs to feed to Essex and aphrodisiacs to give Carr. Mrs Turner tested one aphrodisiac on a lover of her own and it affected him so violently that 'through a storm of rain and thunder he rode fifteen miles one dark night to her house, scarce knowing where he was till he was there. Such is the devilish mad rage of lust, heightened with art and fancy.'

Eventually Elizabeth's great uncle petitioned the King to have her marriage annulled because of Essex's impotence. When the commission of bishops and others heard the case they ordered a jury of midwives and matrons to check her virginity. Since she was by now Carr's mistress, this was a problem, but she protested modesty, was allowed to undergo the examination veiled and substituted a young lady whose conduct had been 'more immaculate' than her own. Her marriage to Essex was annulled in September 1613 and in December she married Carr, who had meanwhile been made Earl of Somerset, and next year became Lord Chamberlain.

Some while before this the poet and courtier, Sir Thomas Overbury, had begun to take part in these intrigues. He had been Carr's closest friend since they had met in Scotland, and Carr had brought him to the English court where he had been appointed a Sewer to the King. According to Ben Jonson, who was Overbury's friend till they quarrelled, he was a highly civilized man, responsible for bringing to the court an appreciation of literature and art.

At first Overbury encouraged Carr in his pursuit of Elizabeth, writing letters and love poems for him to send her. But he changed his mind when he realized that Carr meant to marry Elizabeth, not merely make her his mistress, describing her as a 'strumpet, and her mother and brother bawds'. It may have been to prevent Overbury interfering with Elizabeth's divorce case that Carr and the King between them had Overbury arrested on the contrived charge that he had refused to go abroad as an ambassador.

Queen Henrietta Maria by Van Dyck

George Villiers, 1st Duke of Buckingham,
attributed to William Larkin

To simplify events, three and a half months later Overbury died in the Tower, two years after that in July 1615 a witness first came forward to say that he had been poisoned, and the same autumn Carr and his wife (now Earl and Countess of Somerset) were arrested and charged with Overbury's murder.

Two facts emerge for certain from the welter of conflicting evidence that surrounds Overbury's death: that he was indeed poisoned and that Elizabeth organized it. She had had the Lieutenant of the Tower replaced by a protégé of her family, Sir Gervasse Helwys, who in turn had employed one of her creatures, Richard Weston, to be Overbury's gaoler. She had gone to Mrs Turner again, and to an apothecary named James Franklin, for poisons which included arsenic, mercury, powder of diamonds and great spiders. These were usually put into tarts which were sent to Overbury. When, after three and a half months, Overbury still would not die she bribed a doctor's assistant to give him 'a clyster of corrosive sublimate' (an injection into the rectum) which finally killed him.

Three questions remain unanswered. Why did Elizabeth do it? Was her husband her accomplice? And why, when her husband had been arrested, did the King try to persuade him to plead guilty and so prevent a trial?

The theory that Elizabeth's motive was merely anger with Overbury for the rude things he had said about her seems too simple. Equally implausible is Carr's defence that he was merely trying to make Overbury look ill, so that the King would pity him and release him.

It is possible that Elizabeth and her husband conspired to murder Overbury because he knew things which they did not want revealed. One rumour was that Carr and Overbury had been involved in a plot to murder Prince Henry (who had died in 1612). Though it is now thought that the Prince died of typhoid, this does not prove that there had been no plot. Unfortunately, anything that Overbury might have revealed about such a plot is lost. While in the Tower he wrote a full account of his relationship with Carr and gave it, sealed, to a friend, but it disappeared.

A more likely explanation of the murder is that Elizabeth and the King conspired to have it done (or at least that the King was aware of it), both of them wanting to remove Overbury permanently because of the influence he had over their husband and boyfriend respectively. If James was involved and Carr knew it, this would explain why Carr behaved throughout his imprisonment as if he had nothing to fear since the King 'durst not bring him to trial'. It would explain, too, why

James tried to persuade Carr to plead guilty and throw himself on his mercy, if he was terrified that at his trial Carr would reveal 'a thing greatly concerning my honour and service.'

Four accomplices – Mrs Turner, Franklin, Sir Gervasse Helwys and Richard Weston – were executed soon after their arrest in November 1615; Carr and Elizabeth were found guilty the following July and sentenced to death. But they made no revelations during the trial, and were reprieved. Till 1622 they were kept in the Tower, then allowed to live and die in retirement at their country seat.

The disgrace of the Somersets was not just the court sensation of the reign, but remembered long afterwards. Overbury's father, who lived for another thirty years after his son's murder, was regularly followed about the streets by a crowd which would tell itself: 'There goes Sir Thomas Overbury's father.'

George Villiers, 1st Duke of Buckingham (1592–1628)

From the age of thirteen (when his father died) George Villiers was systematically educated by his mother to be a courtier. She had him taught to dance and fence rather than to study, then sent to France to learn French. She was 'a busy, intriguing, masculine and dangerous person, not deficient in personal beauty ... but rendered odious by every possible irregularity of mind.' According to one contemporary she had been a kitchen maid in the household of George's father (whose name was also George). After his first wife had died he had given her £20 to improve her dress then married her.

George Villiers, the son, arrived at court when James's current favourite, Somerset, was beginning to bore the King with his sulks, and James soon took notice of the pretty young man. At first Somerset was able to prevent Villiers being appointed anything more than a Royal Cupbearer, but in the spring of 1615 he was made a Gentleman of the Bedchamber.

Somerset's enemies realized that this new favourite gave them their opportunity. Several of them, including the heads of the Herbert, Seymour and Russell families, returning down Fleet Street one evening, over-excited and slightly drunk, told one of their servants to throw mud at a portrait of Somerset which they saw displayed for sale by the roadside. But success only came that autumn (1615) with the dramatic arrest of Somerset and his wife on a charge of poisoning Sir Thomas

Overbury. The following January James made Villiers Master of the Horse and a year later Earl of Buckingham.

All contemporaries, even those who had little reason to like Buckingham, agree about his remarkable beauty, and many say that he had charm too. Sir Symonds D'Ewes, who saw him with some 'swarthy hard-featured' French noblemen, noticed that 'his hands and feet seemed to be specially effeminate and curious'. Bishop Goodwin said 'he was the handsomest bodied man in England; his limbs so well compacted, and his conversation so pleasing'. James was besotted with him. He nicknamed him Steenie, short for St Stephen, who is said in the Acts of the Apostles to have had the face of an angel.

He gave his new favourite honour after honour, including Master of the King's Bench, Lord High Admiral of England, and Constable of Windsor Castle. At first Buckingham had been poor, with an income of only £50 a year, and needed help from William, Earl of Pembroke, among others, but he soon became hugely rich and used his money for fantastically expensive costumes and jewels. 'It was common with him at an ordinary dancing to have his clothes trimmed with great diamond buttons, and to have diamond hat-bands, cockades, and earrings; to be yoked with great and manifold ropes and knots of pearl; in short, to be manacled, fettered, and imprisoned in jewels.' On a visit to Paris he took twenty-seven suits, one decorated with diamonds valued at £80,000, 'besides a great feather stuck all over with diamonds; as were also his sword, girdle, hat band and spurs'. When later he went with Prince Charles to Spain he was said to have purposely had his diamonds loosely set so that, as he passed groups of Spanish beauties at court, he could shake a few off and graciously tell those who picked them up to keep them.

In London he drove a coach and six – coaches had only reached England forty years before and were at first drawn by only two horses. The citizens of London applauded, but were less pleased when he was the first to use a sedan chair, considering it 'a shame that men should be brought to a servile condition as horses'. His entertainments were as fantastic as his clothes; at one banquet the king and queen, dining at separate tables, were 'served by a complete ballet at each course ...' and '... all things came down in clouds; amongst which was a representation of the French King and the two queens, with their chiefest attendants, and so to the life that the Queen's majesty could name them'.

Buckingham claimed that it was his idea that Prince Charles should marry Mary, second daughter of Philip, King of Spain. To secure himself the credit he persuaded James to let him go with Charles, both incognito, to Madrid. On February 18th, 1623, they arrived together at Dover, wearing false beards, and calling themselves Mr John Smith and Mr Thomas Smith. Though they stayed briefly in Paris and attended a court function (at which Charles saw for the first time the French princess he eventually married) they managed to reach Madrid without being discovered, where they declared themselves to the astonished English ambassador.

Throughout their stay, which lasted all summer, Buckingham shocked the Spanish by his extravagance, flamboyance and openly lecherous behaviour. He and Charles regularly sent to the King for fresh supplies of jewels to distribute. A contemporary estimated that £600,000 worth were sent to Spain from the Tower of London. The other expenses of the visit came to £50,000. Buckingham would sign his letters to the king, 'Your humble, slave and dog, STEENIE,' and began one of them, 'Dear Dad, gossip and steward.' The King in reply would address the pair as his 'sweet boys'.

Buckingham gave particular offence to Count Olivarez, the Spanish chief minister, and there were rumours that he had tried to seduce the Countess. She and Olivarez were said to have substituted a 'lady not of the most immaculate virtue, and suffering moreover under a disgraceful disease', and to have had this plot 'fully answer their expectations'. But Clarendon doubts the whole story, pointing out that the Countess was by this time 'so crooked and deformed' that she could not have tempted Buckingham.

The Spanish also considered Buckingham offensively familiar with Prince Charles, staying seated when the Prince stood and wearing his hat when the Prince was bareheaded. The marriage plan eventually failed for none of these reasons but because they realized that Prince Charles had no intention of being converted to Roman Catholicism.

When Charles succeeded James, Buckingham remained the royal favourite, and the virtual ruler of the country. Charles sent him to Paris to fetch Henrietta Maria to be his Queen. Here Buckingham attempted to seduce the French Queen, to the annoyance of the French King. At the Channel, on his way to England with Henrietta Maria, he turned back to Amiens where the French Queen had said goodbye to her daughter, forced his way into her bedchamber and knelt by her bed, kissing her sheet. He seems to have been genuinely in love with her and the Queen only after some hesitation decided that she was being insulted. From England Buckingham carried on a secret correspondence with her.

Now, however, he grew increasingly unpopular with Parliament, which tried to impeach him, and with the country generally. To regain popularity he planned to relieve the city of La Rochelle where the French Protestants were being besieged by Richelieu. Buckingham led the expedition himself and behaved with great bravery, staying ashore till all that survived of his men had re-embarked, but almost three thousand out of about seven thousand were lost.

Three years later he proposed a new expedition to La Rochelle. Deputies from the city came to Portsmouth to discuss the plan and there Buckingham arrived on August 2nd 1630. Next morning as he stepped into the hall after breakfast at Captain Mason's house where he was staying, a discontented officer named Felton stabbed him in the heart and he died at once. The Duchess and the Countess of Anglesea came out on to the gallery and 'looked into the hall, where they might behold the blood of their dearest gushing from him,' Lord Carleton wrote: '... such were their screachings, tears, and distractions, that I never in my life heard the like before'.

Jeffery Hudson (1619–1682)

Jeffery Hudson, court dwarf, was born in Rutland to parents of a normal size. At nine years old he was only eighteen inches high and – if Fuller can be trusted – was without deformity, his various parts in proportion. His father was a butcher, who as a sideline baited bulls for the First Duke of Buckingham. When the Duke entertained Charles I and Queen Henrietta Maria at his seat of Burghley on the Hill in about 1628 he had a large cold pie brought to the dinner table from which Hudson emerged. The Queen was delighted, Buckingham presented Hudson to her and she brought him to court where she had him dressed in satin and he became a favourite. At one court masque Charles's gigantic porter, William Evans, produced Hudson from his pocket.

In 1630 the Queen sent Hudson on a mission to France to bring back a midwife for her. At the French court he was equally well liked, and set out for home with £2,500 in presents as well as the midwife, but he was captured in the North Sea by pirates who landed him at Dunkirk where all his possessions were stolen.

During the Civil War Hudson stayed with the Queen, and escaped with her to Paris. By now he had acquired a sense of his own dignity and when a young man named Crofts insulted him, issued a challenge.

Crofts added a fresh insult by coming to the appointed place armed only with a 'squirt'. A new duel, with pistols on horseback, was arranged at which Hudson shot Crofts dead.

He was forced to escape from Paris, but was captured by Turkish pirates who landed him in North Africa and sold him as a slave. It was now, according to the Rutland historian Wright, who had it from Hudson himself, that his misfortunes made him suddenly grow to three feet six or nine inches.

Somehow he escaped from slavery because he was back in England after the Restoration, living in retirement in the country. But eventually he returned to court, and in 1679 was imprisoned during the Popish-Plot scare because he was a Roman Catholic. He survived, dying some three years later at the age of sixty-three. He may have earned the rank of Captain which he is sometimes given by serving as a Captain of Horse in the Civil War, but the 'Sir' with which he is also sometimes credited was probably ironic.

— 5 —

Charles II, James II, William III and Mary, and Anne

Few sovereigns have ever been so popular as Charles II during the last days of May, 1660, when he returned from abroad to become King of England. Cheering crowds lined the roads for much of his route from Dover to Canterbury then to London. At the end of the day of his arrival he wrote that he was 'disordered by my journey ... with the noise still sounding in my ears'. When he died twenty-five years later he was still much liked, although his reign had included three major disasters (the Plague of London, the Fire of London and a calamitous war with the Dutch) and a serious religious scandal (the so-called Popish-Plot), besides his own notoriously amoral life.

His good looks, easy-going character and wit had much to do with his popularity. If the second half of the epigram, 'He never said a foolish thing, never did a wise one', is unjust, the first half is fair. Life at court paralleled his own. It was informal compared to courts of continental sovereigns. The Spanish King, Charles said, would 'not piss but another must hold the chamber pot'. His male companions were rakes, like John Wilmot, Second Earl of Rochester, who added gambling and drinking to Charles's own predilection for whoring.

For the most part the King and his court occupied the great rambling palace of Whitehall, which was less like a palace as the word is normally understood, than a village, consisting of 'a heap of houses erected at diverse times and of different models ... made continuous'. It had some two thousand rooms, stretched for half a mile along the Thames and reached inland as far as today's Downing Street and New Scotland Yard.

Here the public could come and go with little restriction, watch the king pray in his chapel or eat in his banqueting hall, and meet him strolling about the lawns – trying to avoid the many royalist gentlemen who had come to London to claim rewards for their loyalty during the Civil War. Some he did reward. Above the official number of forty-eight Gentlemen of the Privy Chamber, he created four hundred and ninety Gentlemen and of the Privy Chamber in Extraordinary.

Even his Bedchamber was open to visitors, and only the King's Closet, a smaller upper room, was comparatively private. Here Keepers of the Closet like the brothers Chiffinch would bring only those who were invited – including whores who entered by back stairs from the river and who were rewarded by payments of Secret Service money.

Already during his exile Charles was said to have had seventeen mistresses, by one of whom, Lucy Waters, he had fathered the child who became the Duke of Monmouth. During his reign Barbara Villiers (Countess of Castlemaine), Frances Stuart (Duchess of Richmond), Louise Renée de Kéroualle (Duchess of Portsmouth), Hortensia Mancini (Duchess of Mazarin) and the actress Nell Gwyn were his best known, but by no means his only women. Many held official positions at court as the Queen's Maids of Honour or Ladies of her Bedchamber in addition to their unofficial occupations. His principal mistresses also had political influence, though less than Louis XIV believed, who continually tried to use them to convert Charles to Roman Catholicism, and to persuade him to join in war against the Dutch.

Across St James's Park Charles's brother, the Duke of York and future James II, held his own court at St James's Palace. Though he was a duller young man with a worrying conscience, he too had a fair number of women, even if some of them (Arabella Churchill and Catharine Sedley for example) were less lovely than Charles's. It was ironic that the earnest James married his first wife, Anne Hyde, for love, while Charles married his Queen, Catharine of Braganza, for money.

The most important event at court during James II's unhappy three-year reign was the birth of the child who was to become the Old Pretender. This led directly to the Glorious Revolution of 1688. James's open Roman Catholicism had already made him unpopular; two days after his brother Charles's death he publicly attended mass in the Queen's chapel at St James's, 'surrounded by all the insignia of royalty, and the splendid paraphernalia of the Romish Church'. At court 'the papists now swarmed', Evelyn reported. Five Gentlemen of the Privy Chamber were retired and so was the Duke of Somerset, first Lord of the Bedchamber, for refusing to co-operate in a visit of the papal nuncio. Others like Admiral Herbert, Master of the Robes, resigned. But at least until 1688, by which time James had been married for seven years to his Roman Catholic second wife, Mary of Modena, he had not produced a Catholic heir. He would therefore be succeeded by one of the two daughters of his first wife: either Mary, married to William of Orange, or Princess Anne, both Protestants. But now Queen

Mary delivered a son and there was every probability of a Roman Catholic dynasty.

As a result Protestants devised ways of suggesting that something so disastrous had not happened. To prove their case was difficult. Twenty ladies and forty-six gentlemen, including eighteen Privy Councillors, had been present at Mary's lying-in, which took place in her Bedchamber at St James's Palace. While it was in progress, however, a warming-pan was brought to the Queen's bed to comfort her, and 'it was not opened that it might be seen that there was fire and nothing else in it; so here was matter for suspicions with which all were filled'.

And if the supposed child had *not* been brought in the warming-pan in order to complete a false pregnancy, then, according to another suggestion, the real child had died and been replaced by a substitute. The Pretender was only judged genuine after a public inquiry, for which each of the sixty-six witnesses made a signed statement. Less than five months later crowds on the cliffs of Dover watched William of Orange's fleet of six hundred ships pass down the Channel on its way to land his sixteen thousand soldiers at Torbay.

William and Mary became joint King and Queen, forming what Bishop Burnet called a 'double-bottomed monarchy'. Her claim, as James II's daughter, was better than his, as Charles I's grandson – but he refused to become a gentleman usher to his wife. From the first he made an unfavourable impression. He was silent, unsmiling and, when he did speak, hoarse. This was the result of chronic chest trouble and to avoid the foul air of the city he lived mainly at Hampton Court, coming to London only on council days. As a result court life ceased to be the public spectacle it had been in the two previous reigns.

Mary attempted to be more amiable. 'She came into Whitehall, jolly as a wedding,' Evelyn wrote. Her enemy, Sarah Churchill, described her behaviour less kindly.

Queen Mary wanted bowels; of this she gave unquestionable proof the first day she came to Whitehall. She ran about it, looking into every closet and conveniency, and turning up the quilts of the beds, just as people do at an inn, with no sort of concern in her appearance. ... I thought this strange and unbecoming conduct; for whatever necessity there was of deposing King James, he was still her father, who had lately been driven from that very chamber, and from that bed.

Both Mary and William feuded with her sister, Princess Anne. On one occasion William made Anne wait among general suitors for an audience, on another ate all the peas at dinner without offering her any. Anne called him Caliban.

After Mary's death of smallpox at the end of 1694 William abandoned his mistress, Elizabeth Villiers, grew more morose and took to heavy drinking. He had from the start brought Dutchmen to his court and insulted his English courtiers. When he entertained Dutch officers 'such of the English nobility as filled offices in the royal household were compelled to stand, as menials, behind the King's chair'. Now two Dutchmen, William Bentinck (Earl of Portland) and Arnoud van Keppel (Earl of Albemarle, Lord of the Bedchamber and Keeper of the Robes) became such intimate friends that homosexuality was suspected.

In another way English court life was transformed during William's reign. In 1698 a Dutch servant accidentally set the Palace of Whitehall alight. The fire burned for seventeen hours, destroying a hundred and fifty houses including twenty which were blown up in an attempt to stop it, leaving the palace an irreparable ruin.

Two ladies influenced politics in Queen Anne's reign in a way few courtiers have influenced them since. The first was Sarah Jennings (Mrs Churchill, Duchess of Marlborough), the second was Abigail Hill (Mrs Masham). A third, Elizabeth Percy (Duchess of Somerset) was also important. All held positions in the Royal Bedchamber. When Sarah fell from favour her more important offices were divided between Mrs Masham and the Duchess of Somerset. All three influenced events by the power they had over the Queen.

This may seem strange, since Queen Anne was far from being weak or vacillating, but the sort of obstinate and opinionated person her stout figure suggested. At court she insisted on great formality. Horse-racing, deer-hunting, card-playing, gambling and food all interested her but none of them so much as court etiquette. According to the Duchess of Marlborough she spoke chiefly 'upon fashion and rules of precedence'. She had a good memory 'but chose to retain in it very little besides ceremonies and customs of courts'.

The result of this obsession was less than entertaining. At Windsor her Drawing-rooms would sometimes be attended by only twenty people, few enough to be received in her Bedchamber. Here, according to Swift, they would stand about 'while she looked at us round with her fan in her mouth, and once a minute said about three words to some that were nearest her and then she was told dinner was ready and went out'.

As she grew fatter she could no longer ride and hunted instead from a high-wheeled chariot in which she would drive up to forty miles a day. At Windsor she had to be raised and lowered from floor to floor through a trap door by ropes and pulleys. Her coffin was rumoured to have been nearly square.

Barbara Villiers, Countess of Castlemaine (1641–1709)

Barbara Villiers, daughter of the Second Viscount Grandison, first came to London during the Commonwealth, when she 'became the object of divers young gentlemen's affections'. She had a plump baby-face and dark auburn hair. In 1659 she married a Buckinghamshire gentleman, Robert Palmer. But she had begun to sleep with Charles II at the latest by May 28th 1660, the day of his return to the Palace of Whitehall, where she spent the night with him. Nine months later her first child, Anne, was born. Though the child resembled the Earl of Chesterfield, with whom Barbara had previously been sleeping, Charles eventually acknowledged her as his. At the end of the same year Roger Palmer, her husband, was given the title of Earl of Castlemaine, making Barbara the Countess.

On the day that Charles's Queen, Catharine of Braganza, reached England from Portugal, Charles spent the evening with Barbara. He sent for scales and they amused themselves by weighing each other. About the Queen he said that instead of a woman they had sent him a bat, referring to the way one of her front teeth stuck out, lifting her upper lip.

The Queen refused to meet Barbara, but a month later, on the day Barbara's second child was baptized with the King as Godfather, Charles engineered a meeting at Hampton Court. When the Queen realized to whom she had been introduced she had a violent nose-bleed, fainted and had to be carried out. To justify Barbara's presence at court Charles proposed her as a Lady of the Bedchamber to the Queen. The Queen struck out her name. But after two months of bitter controversy, during which Charles sent home most of her Portuguese Ladies-in-Waiting, she accepted Barbara, and on September 7th Pepys saw the three of them driving together in the royal carriage.

At this time the King was spending four nights a week with Barbara, going home 'through the privy gardens all alone privately, so as the very sentries take notice of it and speak of it.'

But Barbara had other lovers. Charles hurried forward the marriage of the Duke of Monmouth to keep him from her. And when her third child was born in September 1663 he refused to acknowledge it, though he later changed his mind. Later again he threatened not to acknowledge another of her children (suspecting it was Sir Harry Jermyn's) but she told him that when it was born she would bring it to court and bash out its brains. Charles pacified her with a gift of 5,600 ounces of plate from the royal jewel-house.

Meanwhile Charles was newly infatuated with the beautiful but reluctant fifteen-year-old Frances Stuart. Barbara would invite Frances to her bed, and point out to Charles that *she* could get what *he* couldn't.

By now Barbara was known at Whitehall as the mistress *en titre*, roughly translated by a fellow courtier as 'Miss of State'. She had Thomas Killigrew banished from court for calling her a wanton, and helped dismiss her enemy, Clarendon. When she heard the news of this she was seen to rush into her aviary in her smock to celebrate with her Ladies-in-Waiting. Louis XIV's Ambassador, Colbert de Croissy, believing in her power, tried to use her to obtain state secrets, but abandoned the idea, complaining that he had spent 'all that I brought from France, not excepting the skirts and frocks made up for my wife' in ineffectual bribes.

When the London apprentices sacked the whore-houses of the city (a disturbance for which eight of them were hanged) a libellous appeal was circulated, entitled 'The Poor Whores Petition to the most Splendid, Illustrious, Serene and Eminent Lady of Pleasure, the Countess of Castlemaine', and presently a fictitious answer as if from Barbara. The King pacified her with the gift of Berkshire House, St James's. Two years later she sold it, and sold all but a corner of its large garden for building sites.

Charles made her many other gifts including one of £30,000. And she received annual grants from the post office, starting in 1669 with £4,700. Next year he gave her Nonsuch Palace, which she gutted of its contents to meet her extravagances. In one night at cards she lost £20,000. At the theatre one afternoon her jewels were estimated to be worth £40,000.

In 1670 she was made Baroness Nonsuch, Countess of Southampton and Duchess of Cleveland. But during the next four years her influence declined as the King transferred his attentions to Louise Renée de Kéroualle, Duchess of Portsmouth.

Barbara now took a succession of fresh lovers, including Jacob Hall, a rope dancer she had met at Bartholomew Fair, and the young John Churchill, later Duke of Marlborough. When the King knocked at her door and Churchill escaped by jumping out of the window Barbara rewarded him with £5,000. On another occasion when Charles *did* catch them in bed together he is said to have told Churchill: 'I forgive you for you do it for your bread.'

In 1672 Barbara lost her position in the Bedchamber, under the Test Act. (She had become a Roman Catholic towards the end of 1663). This did not prevent her, in 1675, from intriguing to marry her eldest son to Elizabeth Percy, the enormously rich Northumberland heiress. The boy was thirteen, and already married for four years to a girl whom Barbara had fraudulently extracted from the protection of her guardians when she was seven. This time the wily Dowager Countess of Northumberland, Elizabeth's grandmother and guardian, outwitted Barbara and saved Elizabeth.

Barbara's husband, the Earl of Castlemaine, died in 1705. The same year Barbara, now sixty-three, married General Robert Fielding. Eight months later Fielding was committed to Newgate Prison for threatening and maltreating his wife. The marriage was dissolved when it was conveniently discovered that a previous wife of Fielding's was still alive.

Barbara died in 1709 of dropsy, which had 'swelled her gradually to a monstrous bulk'. At the height of her success she had been described as 'the fairest and lewdest of the royal concubines'.

Frances Teresa Stuart, Duchess of Richmond (1648–1702), and Charles Stuart, Duke of Richmond (1639–1672)

Among Charles II's mistresses, Frances Stuart, known as La Belle Stuart, was the most beautiful – though not the most intelligent. The Count of Grammont thought it hardly possible for a woman to have less wit and more beauty. Louis XIV had been reluctant to allow her to leave Paris, where she had been a member of the household of the Dowager Queen Henrietta Maria (Charles I's widow). Nevertheless she left, arriving at the English court early in January 1663. She was fifteen.

Here she became a Maid of Honour to Queen Catharine of Braganza. Here Charles first saw her when she was sleeping in the room of his current mistress, Barbara Villiers, Countess of Castlemaine. By July Pepys noted that he was 'besotted with Miss Stuart, getting her into corners; and will be with her half an hour together kissing her, to the observation of all the world; and she now stays by herself and expects it, as my Lady Castlemaine did use to do'. Pepys 'fancied himself sporting with her with great pleasure'. Watching the court ladies one day 'fiddling with their hats and feathers, and changing and trying one another's by one another's heads, and laughing' he reckoned that: 'Miss Stewart in this dress, with her hat cocked and a red plume, with her sweet eye, little Roman nose, and excellent *taille*, is now the greatest beauty I ever saw, I think, in my life.'

Her intelligence did not improve. 'She had a habit of laughing immoderately at the merest trifle.' Her favourite game was blind-man's buff, and her favourite amusement building card houses. 'She was surrounded on these occasions by the danglers of the court, who of course affected an interest in her folly, and supplied her with the cards.' But the King remained so infatuated that, at the time of the Queen's illness in November 1668 when she was not expected to live, he considered marrying Frances. When the Queen recovered he made inquiries about a divorce by consent, on the grounds that the queen could not bear children.

For a disappointingly long time Frances refused to oblige the King, but when a new calèche arrived from France a bargain was struck. Frances had first ride in the calèche, something the Queen had hoped for, and the King had his way.

Other gentlemen fell in love with Frances. One of them, Philip Rotier, the medallist, used her as his model for the relief of Britannia which appeared for over two hundred years on the reverse of British coins. Another was Charles Stuart, Duke of Richmond.

Charles Stuart had returned to England with Charles II at the Restoration, soon afterwards being made Duke of Lennox and Duke of Richmond and given the hereditary posts of Great Chamberlain of Scotland and Great Admiral of Scotland. In Scotland he behaved with conspicuous extravagance, before returning to the English court to see what more he could obtain from the King. Here in 1663 he was made a Gentleman of the Bedchamber with a pension of £1,000 a year.

Two years later he had a difference with Charles II and was sent to the Tower for three weeks. Meanwhile his first wife, Elizabeth Rogers, had died and his second wife, Margaret Banister, fallen ill. It was now that he offered to marry Frances Stuart as soon as his second wife died. To this the King objected so, 'on a dark and stormy night' in March 1667 Frances escaped from her lodgings, met the Duke at the 'Beare by London Bridge' and eloped with him into Kent where they were privately married.

The King was enraged but the Queen acted as mediator, and within fifteen months Frances was back at court where she became one of

Catharine's Ladies of the Bedchamber. The King was also less angry with Richmond than he might have been, possibly – as he told him one night when drunk in Norfolk – because Frances was now more willing than she had been.

Just the same, in 1671, he found a reason for sending Richmond abroad where he was to negotiate with Denmark about a joint attack on the Netherlands, and the following year he died at Elsinore. (Because he was childless his titles of Lennox and Richmond reverted to the King, enabling Charles to give them soon afterwards to his three-year-old bastard by his new mistress, Louise Renée de Kéroualle).

Back at the English court, Frances had meanwhile contracted smallpox which left her badly scarred. But Charles visited her when ill and remained fond of her. And for many years she stayed at court. In 1688 she was one of the twenty ladies present at the accouchement of James II's Queen, Mary of Modena, and she attended Queen Anne's coronation. When she died the same year she left annuities to certain of her gentlewoman friends, nominally for the keep of her cats, but in fact as a tactful form of pension.

Eleanor [Nell] Gwyn (1650–1687)

Nell Gwyn, the actress, was another of the incidental women to whom Charles II made love, in parallel with his principal mistresses, but one of whom he was particularly fond. She was a poor girl whose mother had drowned at Millbank, Chelsea, when she fell into the Thames, drunk.

Nell was beautiful, as Sir Peter Lely's portrait of her (reclining naked with cupid) shows, well built but not too plump even by today's unnatural standards. 'A mighty pretty soul she is,' Pepys wrote, when he had seen one of her performances and kissed her afterwards. She was also sharp. He called her 'pretty witty Nell' and there are many examples of her quick answers.

According to Rochester she was a herring seller:

> Her first employment was, with open throat
> To cry fresh herrings, even ten a groat.

More famously, she worked as an orange seller at the Theatre Royal, Drury Lane. At the same time or before, she was associated with the notorious Mother Ross, 'a celebrated courtesan of the period'. Charles

Hart the actor was one of her early lovers and taught her to act. Dryden wrote parts to suit her.

Presently she was seduced by two well-known rakes of the court. When Pepys was at the King's Head at Epsom he heard that, 'My Lord Buckhurst and Nelly are lodged at the next house, and Sir Charles Sedley with them; and keep a merry house. Poor girl!' He was more sorry that the theatre should lose Nell, since he admired her acting. About Dryden's *The Maiden Queen* he wrote that there was 'a comical part done by Nell . . . that I never can hope ever to see the like done again by man or woman . . . so great performance of a comical part was never, I believe, in the world before as Nell do this, both as a mad girl, then most and best of all when she comes in like a young gallant; and hath the motions and carriage of a spark, the most that ever I saw any man have'.

Charles had met her before her affair with Buckhurst. And after her return to the theatre he was reduced to convulsions of laughter by her appearance 'in a hat the size of a large coach wheel'. But he only finally fell for her after hearing her recitation of the epilogue of Dryden's 'Tyrannic Love'.

He made her a Lady of the Bedchamber to the Queen; and though at first he refused her a pension of £500 a year, according to Bishop Burnet she ultimately had from him some £60,000. With £4,520 of it she bought Prince Rupert's 'great pearl necklace'. She had one house in Chelsea – the King's Road is supposed to have got its name because Charles used it so frequently to visit her – and another near St James's Park, probably 79 Pall Mall. She was standing in the garden of this, which faced on to the park, when Evelyn 'both saw and heard a very familiar discourse between [the King] and Mrs Nelly, as they called an impudent commedian, she looking out of her garden on a terrace at the top of the wall, and [the King] standing on the green walk under it. I was heartily sorry at this scene. Thence the king walked to the Duchess of Cleveland, another lady of pleasure, and curse of our nation.' Nell was regularly impudent to the King; she called him *her* Charles III, because she had had two previous Charleses.

When Louise Kéroualle, Duchess of Portsmouth (who was French and a Roman Catholic), became Charles's principal mistress in the 1670s Nell was popular as an English Protestant rival. 'She's now the darling strumpet of the crowd', Rochester wrote. At Oxford when a mob surrounded her coach, thinking the Duchess was inside, Nell put out her head and told them, 'Pray, good people be civil; I am the Protestant whore.' At court it was reported that Nell was 'as haughty as

Charles II when Prince of Wales by Dobson

Nell Gwyn and the infant Duke of St Albans by Lely

mademoiselle [the Duchess]: she insults her, she makes grimaces at her, she attacks her, she frequently steals the king from her, and boasts whenever he gives her the preference. She is young, indiscreet, confident, wild, and of an agreeable humour: she sings, she dances, she acts her part with a good grace. She had a son by the King, and hopes to have him acknowledged.'

To this end she called him a bastard in front of the King, saying that she had no other name for him. Charles made him Earl of Burford when he was six and Duke of St Albans seven years later.

He planned to make Nell Countess of Greenwich but died before he had done so. His last words were, 'Let not poor Nelly starve'. James II did much to prevent that happening. Out of the Secret Service monies he paid her debts to her tradesmen (£729 2s 3d), for which she 'stood outlawed', gave her two sums of £500 each and settled Bestwood Park in Sherwood Forest on her and her male descendants via her natural son, the Duke of St Albans. But for a time Nell was so poor that she had to melt her plate, and she only survived Charles by two years.

John Wilmot, Earl of Rochester (1647–1680)

John Wilmot, poet and rake, son of a successful Royalist soldier, was an exceptional child. At twelve he was admitted to Wadham College, Oxford. Twenty months later he obtained his MA degree. The Restoration occurred while he was there and already some of his verses were published in the university collections which celebrated the event.

During the next few years he travelled abroad, then took part in two sea battles against the Dutch. About this time, when he was still seventeen, he first presented himself at court. Next year, on May 26th 1665, he perpetrated his wildest frolic when he employed armed men to lie in wait at Charing Cross, stop the coach of the wealthy Somerset widow, Elizabeth Mallet, with whom he was in love, and kidnap her. He was sent to the Tower. Two years later, in January 1677, he married Elizabeth, but by this time the excitements of court life had trapped him and though she had four of his children, he usually left her with them in the country.

He had already been made a Gentleman of the Bedchamber. The duties of this office were still real. The First Gentleman, or Groom of the Stole, had the 'honour to present and put on his Majesty's first garment or shirt every morning'. If he was absent the Gentleman on duty for the week would do it instead, and would anyway sleep by the King all night on a pallet bed. The salary was £1,000.

But it was Rochester's informal activities which entertained the king. He fought or nearly fought several duels, including one with the Earl of Mulgrave from which he excused himself because of 'a distemper'. He had been treated with mercury for the pox a month before. On the Newmarket road he and friends ran an inn where they systematically made gentlemen drunk in order to seduce their wives. In the King's presence he boxed the ear of Thomas Killigrew, the court's unofficial jester. The King forgave him, but Rochester went to France in self-imposed though only temporary exile.

More seriously, at Epsom in 1676 he became involved in a fight with the watch, during which he abandoned his friend Mr Downes who had his skull split with a 'spittle staff', his side run into with 'half a pike' and died. Rochester, afraid to return to court, but unable to keep away from Town, disguised himself as a quack doctor and astrologer by the name of Alexander Bendo and set up his stall on Tower Hill. Here he offered to give ladies Italian remedies, which 'without destroying your complexions (as most of your paints and daubings do) shall render them purely fair, cleaning and preserving them from all spots, freckles, heats and pimples, nay marks of the small-pox, or any other accident'.

As for his women, he was fashionably promiscuous – his friend George Etherege put him into a play as 'The Man of Mode, or, Sir Fopling Flutter'. He had an affair with Mrs Roberts, one of the King's mistresses, but his own best-known mistress and longest infatuation was with the actress, Elizabeth Barry. It was Rochester who, for a bet, taught her in six months how to act. 'In order to accomplish his intention, besides the many private instructions he gave her, he caused her to rehearse the part no less than thirty times upon the stage ... about twelve times in the dress in which she was to play.' Mrs Barry was unfaithful to him and Rochester removed their only daughter from her care, but the girl died, aged fourteen.

He became even more addicted to drink than to women. It was his misfortune to be his wittiest when drunk. 'The natural heat of his fancy,' Bishop Burnet wrote, 'being inflamed by wine, made him so extravagantly pleasant, that many, to be more diverted by that humour, studied to engage him deeper and deeper in intemperance: which at length did so entirely subdue him, that ... for five years together he was continually drunk; not all the while under the visible effect of it, but his blood so inflamed, that he was not cool ... enough to be perfectly master of himself.'

He was sent several more times to the Tower – once a year, according to the Count de Grammont – but as regularly forgiven. This is the more surprising since libellous verses attacking the King and his mistresses were often his offence. For the King he invented the name of Old Rowley, and wrote about him:

> Restless he rolls from whore to whore,
> A merry monarch, scandalous and poor.
> Nor are his high desires above his strength;
> His sceptre and his —— are of a length.

To collect material for his verses he employed a servant disguised as a sentinel who would place himself at closet doors and report observations.

About Barbara Villiers, Countess of Castlemaine, Duchess of Cleveland, he wrote,

> When she has jaded quite,
> Her almost boundless appetite . . .
> She'll still drudge on in tasteless vice,
> As if she sinn'd for exercise.

and

> [Cleveland] I say is much to be admir'd,
> Although she ne'er was satisfied or tired.
> Full forty men a day provided for this whore,
> Yet like a bitch she wags her tail for more.

And about the state of the country as a whole:

> Who can abstain from satire in this age?
> What nature wants I find supply'd by rage.
> Some do for pimping, some for treach'ry use;
> But none's made great for being good or wise.
> Deserve a dungeon, if you would be great,
> Rogues always are our ministers of state;
> Mean prostrate bitches, for a Bridewell fit,
> With England's wretched Queen must equal sit.

Despite such outspokenness the King made him Earl of Rochester before he was twenty-one, insisting on his right to sit in the House of Lords although he was a minor, and later in succession made him Keeper of the King's Game in the County of Oxfordshire, joint tenant for ever of Bestwood Park in Sherwood Forest, joint Master of the King's Hawks, and Keeper and Ranger of Woodstock Park with the right to live at its High Lodge.

Rochester died when only thirty-three, as a cumulative result of his debaucheries. Bishop Burnet visited him at High Lodge for four days during his final illness and wrote optimistically, 'I do verily believe he was then so entirely changed that, if he had recovered, he would have made good all his resolutions.'

Talbot Edwards and Colonel Blood

Talbot Edwards, Keeper of the King's Regalia, was eighty in 1671 when he was visited by an unknown man dressed as a parson (in fact the notorious Colonel Blood) and a woman described as his wife, though she wasn't. They asked to see the King's crown. When the woman saw it she 'feigned to have a qualm come upon her stomach' and had to be revived with spirits by Edwards and his wife in their private rooms.

Blood came back a few days later with a present for Mrs Edwards of four pairs of white gloves, and suggested introducing the Edwards's pretty daughter to a nephew of his who had two or three hundred pounds a year in land. To discuss this interesting proposition the Edwards invited Blood to dinner, where he said grace, adding a prayer for the King, Queen and royal family. Afterwards he persuaded Edwards to sell him his case of pistols, which he said he wanted to give to a nobleman neighbour. He arranged to return with his nephew at seven o'clock on May 9th to introduce him to Miss Edwards.

Blood arrived, not with his nephew but with two armed companions. All three had a dagger and rapier cane each and a pair of pistols. They overpowered Edwards by smothering him with a cloak, and gagged him with 'a great plug of wood with a small hole in the middle to take breath at. This they tied on with a waxed leather, which went round his neck. At the same time they fastened an iron hook to his nose, that no sound might pass from him that way.'

Sounds, he made however, so they knocked him down with a mallet and beat and stabbed him until they thought him dead. Blood then crushed the crown and put it under his parson's cloak, one of his companions put the globe in his breeches and the other began to file the sceptre in two.

At this moment Edwards's son returned home – he had been serving in Flanders. Alarmed, Blood and his companions escaped with their plunder. But Edwards senior now regained consciousness and made enough noise to alarm his daughter who ran into the street, crying: 'Treason, the crown is stolen.' Edwards junior and a friend set off in pursuit, and Blood and his companions were captured still carrying the jewels.

Blood refused to confess except to the King in person. Astonishingly, the King forgave him, perhaps because Blood claimed to have had the chance to shoot the King when he was bathing in the Thames at Battersea, but to have refrained, or perhaps because Blood said that he had 'hundreds of sworn friends who would avenge the death of any one of them'. Instead of punishment he was given £500, and for a time 'admitted into all the privacy and intimacy of court'. Talbot Edwards, whose courage and gallantry had saved the crown jewels, was given £200 and his son £100.

Louise Renée de Kéroualle, Duchess of Portsmouth (1649–1734)

Louise de Kéroualle, who succeeded Barbara Villiers, Countess of Castlemaine, as Charles II's principal mistress, was a Breton by birth. Her first court appointment was Maid of Honour to Charles II's sister, Duchess of Orleans. In 1670 she came to London with the Duchess, where Charles saw and liked her. Soon afterwards, when the Duchess returned to France and died, he sent a royal yacht to meet Louise at Calais and bring her back to Whitehall. Here he made her Maid of Honour to Queen Catharine.

She had, according to Evelyn, 'a childish simple baby face' but she was more intelligent than her predecessor, and Louis XIV tried to make use of her to influence Charles, even if he did not actually plant her in London. When she first slept with Charles (during a visit to Newmarket in 1671) the French king wrote to congratulate her, and he asked successfully for her to be made an English subject. She was a Roman Catholic and he hoped she would convert Charles. Two years later Charles created her Duchess of Portsmouth and promoted her to become one of the Queen's Ladies of the Bedchamber.

As a Catholic and a foreigner she was never popular with the English who called her Madam Carewell. This unpopularity rose to a climax during the 'Popish Plot' (in fact no plot but an invention of the clergyman, Titus Oates). It was then that an Oxford mob surrounded the royal coach, believing she was inside, but instead found Nell Gwyn (see p.94). In December 1679 Parliament demanded that Louise be removed from court, and she thought it wise to dismiss her Catholic servants, but she herself remained.

She also successfully kept her position as Charles's mistress *en titre* despite occasionally successful attempts by others, in particular the Duchess of Mazarin, to seduce him away, and his own infatuation with 'La Belle Stuart'. Floods of tears were her most usual and effective weapon.

She was even more extravagant (and better rewarded) than Barbara Villiers, receiving from 1674 onwards £10,000 a year from the wine licences, and from about 1682 £10,000 a quarter from the privy purse. Her private apartment at Whitehall was especially luxurious; she had it two or three times 'pull'd down and rebuilt to satisfy her prodigal and expensive pleasures'.

The day before the start of Charles's final illness Evelyn saw Louise and others at court:

I can never forget, the inexpressible luxury and profaneness, gaming and all dissoluteness and, as it were, total forgetfulness of God (it being Sunday evening) which . . . I was witness of; the King sitting and toying with his concubines, Portsmouth, Cleveland, Mazarin etc. A French boy singing love songs in that glorious gallery whilst about twenty great courtiers and other dissolute persons were at basset round a large table, a bank of at least £2,000 in gold before them; upon which two gentlemen who were with me made reflections with astonishment.

When the King lay dying Louise was not allowed to remain with him, but it was she who now claimed that he was a secret Catholic and obtained for him a Catholic priest.

She was never again so successful. Though James II protected her, and she continued to live in London during his reign she failed to ingratiate herself with William III by reminding him of favours she claimed to have done him. In 1698 her fine apartment was burnt down with the rest of Whitehall Palace and she spent most of her remaining life on her estate at Aubigny. Occasionally she visited the English court, and at Queen Caroline's Drawing room after George II's coronation met William III's mistress, the Countess of Orkney and James II's mistress, the Countess of Dorchester. 'God, who would have thought', the Countess of Dorchester said, 'that we three whores should have met here'. In old age Voltaire said that Louise was still beautiful. She was eighty-five when she died in 1734.

Arabella Churchill (1648–1730)

Arabella Churchill was two years older than her more famous brother John, who became the First Duke of Marlborough. Like her brother, she was given a court appointment soon after the Restoration, becoming Maid of Honour to Anne Hyde, who had married James, Duke of York, Charles II's brother. Arabella was 'tall . . . pale-faced, nothing but skin and bone', and 'one of the most indolent creatures in the world'.

James fancied her, but had begun to 'cool in his affections' when an accident changed his mind. The court was watching greyhound coursing on open downland near York, Arabella mounted on a more high-spirited horse than the Maids of Honour were generally given, which bolted. The Duke pursued but could not save her and she was thrown to the ground where she was 'so greatly stunned that her thoughts were otherwise employed than about decency'. The Duke and others who crowded round her 'could hardly believe that limbs of such exquisite beauty belonged to Miss Churchill's face'.

As a result James renewed his pursuit of Arabella and the Count de Grammont noted that she did not make him 'languish with impatience'. She had four children by him, of whom the best known became the Duke of Berwick. When James abandoned her in favour of Catharine Sedley she married Colonel Charles Godfrey, who became Clerk Controller of the Green Cloth and Master of the Jewel Office, first to William III then to Queen Anne.

Catharine Sedley, Countess of Dorchester (1657–1717)

Catharine Sedley, who succeeded Arabella Churchill as James, Duke of York's mistress, was well known at court by the time she was fifteen; in 1673 Evelyn described her as 'none of the virtuous but a wit'. She was at least as ugly as Arabella – pale and thin with a squint. By the time James favoured her he had admitted to being a Roman Catholic, and Charles II said that James's priests must send his brother his mistresses as penances. Catharine was equally surprised. 'It cannot be my beauty for he must see I have none,' she said, 'and it cannot be my wit for he has not enough to know that I have any'. In spite of James's religion she remained a Protestant, and used her sharp tongue in particular against his fellow Catholics.

As a result when James succeeded Charles in 1685 he dropped Catharine, doubling her pension and sending her to live at Arabella Churchill's previous house in St James's Square. Protestants like Rochester tried to prolong the affair, hoping to embarrass James with a Protestant mistress just as Charles had been embarrassed by his Catholic ones. Within three months they arranged a secret meeting at William Chiffinch's, which produced the results they hoped for. The following year James again increased Catharine's pension, this time to £5,000 a year, and made her Countess of Dorchester. James's queen, Mary of Modena, 'took very grievously' this honouring of a rival, and for two dinners hardly ate 'one morsel, nor spake one word to the King, or to any about her, though at other times she used to be extremely pleasant, full of discourse and good humour. The Roman Catholics were also very angry.' Even James regretted what he had done. He acquired a scourge to punish himself and told Catharine to go to Flanders.

Catharine refused – there were too many convents there, she said – and only went briefly to Dublin. When she returned she and James had at least one more secret meeting. But the affair was in practice over.

After the revolution William III gave her a modest pension; Anne raised it to £5,000 again, and Catharine continued sometimes to come to court, on one occasion meeting Louise de Kéroualle and Elizabeth Villiers there and making the comment quoted above on this gathering of ancient royal mistresses.

Elizabeth Villiers, Countess of Orkney (c. 1657–1733)

Elizabeth Villiers, mistress of William III, was as lacking in good looks as her predecessors, Arabella Churchill and Catharine Sedley, two of James II's principal mistresses. Swift wrote that she 'squinted like a dragon'.

Elizabeth was first cousin to Barbara Villiers, Charles II's principal mistress for the first ten years of his reign. But it was Elizabeth's mother, governess to James II's two daughters Mary and Anne, who arranged for her to go with Mary to Holland in 1677 after Mary's marriage to William of Orange. When William and Mary came back to England in 1688 as King and Queen, Elizabeth came too.

As William's principal mistress she made use of her opportunities, obtaining from him the income from 90,000 acres of his Irish estates. And though it was one of William's jokes to syphon off some of this to maintain James II's abandoned mistresses, Elizabeth was left with a comfortable £5,000 a year.

Politically she intrigued against the Churchills, John, Duke of Marlborough and Sarah, the close friend of Mary, despite the fact that John Churchill had played an important part in putting William and Mary on the English throne. Since Mary and her sister Anne were now enemies, Mary and Elizabeth should have been brought together by similar political interests, but in practice Mary always resented Elizabeth, and when Mary died of smallpox at the end of 1694 she left William a letter asking him to abandon Elizabeth.

This was perhaps why, the following year, William arranged for Elizabeth to marry George Hamilton, who soon afterwards became Earl of Orkney. Hamilton was a Tory and Elizabeth now became 'a high tory if not a Jacobite, and was very busy with Harley and Swift in expelling the whigs' during the political manoeuvrings of the later years of Queen Anne's reign. Swift, also a Tory, said she was the wisest woman he ever knew. She survived into George II's reign and was noticed at his coronation by Mary Wortley Montagu.

She that drew the greatest number of eyes was indisputably lady Orkney; she displayed a mixture of fat and wrinkles, and no little corpulence. Add to this the inimitable roll of her eyes, and her grey hairs, which by good fortune stood directly upright, and it is impossible to imagine a more delightful spectacle. She had embellished all this with considerable magnificence, which made her look as big again as usual.

John Churchill, Duke of Marlborough (1650–1722) and Sarah Jennings, Duchess of Marlborough (1660–1742)

John Churchill, younger brother of Arabella Churchill, spent a number of years at court before matters of state and war took over his life and led him to fame. It was probably Arabella who persuaded James, Duke of York, to appoint her brother page at the age of sixteen when his school, St Paul's, was burnt down by the fire of London. A year later James obtained for John a commission as ensign in the King's Own Regiment of Foot Guards.

After serving abroad for several years, John returned to court in the winter of 1670/71 and soon became the lover of Barbara Villiers, Countess of Castlemaine, the mistress of whom Charles II was tiring. When Barbara gave John £5,000 – as a reward, according to Bishop Burnet, for his agility in jumping out of her window when they were in bed together and Charles knocked at the door – John, who knew the importance of money, bought himself a life annuity of £500.

In 1672 he fought as a soldier on board the Duke of York's flagship in the Battle of Sole Bay against the Dutch, and then for three years in France and the Netherlands for Louis XIV, before returning to court, now promoted to be one of the Duke of York's Gentlemen of the Bedchamber. By this time Sarah Jennings, who was to become his wife, was Maid of Honour to James's second wife, Mary of Modena. John courted Sarah. At a party given by the French Ambassador, 'Colonel Churchill took special pleasure in tying and untying the garters of Mistress Jennings'.

But he did not propose to her, and was pressed by his father, Sir Winston Churchill, to abandon someone so poor, who would not be able to buy him army promotion, and to marry instead Catharine Sedley, who had a fortune and was witty even if she was ugly and squinted. It was when this plan failed that Catharine Sedley became the Duke of York's principal mistress, succeeding John's sister, Arabella. In 1678 John and Sarah Jennings were secretly married, so forming one of the great partnerships of English history.

For the next ten years John remained attached to the court of James, Duke of York. Sometimes he went on missions for him, sometimes accompanied him abroad or to Scotland, where Charles sent James for safety at the time of the Popish Plot. When James succeeded Charles, John was appointed one of the King's Gentlemen of the Bedchamber, and he remained loyal to James, despite his own Protestantism, until November 24th 1688. That night he deserted James's army and joined William of Orange's, which had advanced as far as Axminster. Three months later William reappointed him a Gentleman of the Bed-chamber.

John lost all his positions, including his court ones, in 1692, when he was suspected of plotting to bring back James II, or perhaps to replace William with Anne. Though politics, plotting and soldiering now became his main preoccupations, his wife, as Lady of the Bedchamber to Princess Anne, remained at court where, as soon as Anne became queen, she became as politically influential as her husband.

Sarah's friendship with Princess Anne had begun when they had played together as children in the nursery. It had survived Sarah's marriage to John Churchill, and when Anne herself married Prince George of Denmark in 1683 she appointed Sarah to be one of her Ladies of the Bedchamber.

For ten years they were such passionate friends that Sarah later claimed their relationship had been homosexual. She also claimed that the passion had been Anne's. Her own 'sprightliness and cheerfulness' had been 'perpetually chained as it were to a person whose other accomplishments had not cured the sullenness of her temper nor wholly freed her conversation from an insipid heaviness'. Certainly Anne might well have fallen in love with a woman so lively, witty and intelligent, who would take her mind off her own sad life. Prince George loved the Queen to excess. When he asked Charles II how he might grow no fatter, Charles advised him to: 'Walk with me, hunt with my brother and do justice to my niece.' Of the eighteen resulting pregnancies, most ended in miscarriages, and the child which lived longest died at the age of eleven. But Sarah may have been more emotionally involved with Anne than she admitted. In the letters which she and the Queen exchanged, she writing as Mrs Freeman, the Queen as Mrs Morley, the Queen claimed that Sarah 'wrote to me as I used to do to her'. Whether or not this is true it is hard to say since Sarah made Anne destroy most of her letters.

Such recriminations came later. At first Anne and Sarah were aligned against Anne's sister, Mary, who in 1688 became Queen with her husband, William of Orange. Mary believed that Anne's obstinate independence (she refused to let William manage her finances and successfully asked Parliament for a personal income) stemmed from her friendship with Sarah. To get rid of Sarah she encouraged William to sack Churchill, now Earl of Marlborough, assuming that Anne would then part with Sarah. Instead Anne infuriated her sister by bringing Sarah to one of the Queen's receptions at Kensington Palace, and continued to retain her even when Marlborough was temporarily sent to the Tower, suspected of high treason. When Sarah offered to resign, Anne responded with 'the greatest passion of tenderness and weeping it is possible to imagine', threatening to 'shut myself up and never see the world more'. The quarrel ended when Mary died of smallpox in 1694.

Seven years later the day came which Sarah and Anne had long hoped for, when William also died and Anne succeeded him. As Queen she promoted Sarah to Groom of the Stole, Mistress of the Robes and Keeper of the Privy Purse, with total salaries of £5,600, and appointed her Ranger of Windsor Forest with the right to live at Byfield House (now Cumberland Lodge) in Windsor Park. Sarah's two elder daughters she made Ladies of the Bedchamber with salaries of £1,000 each. Her husband she made a Duke and appointed him Commander-in-Chief of all English troops on the Continent.

But from this time onwards things between Anne and Sarah were not the same. Sarah began to live for long periods at Windsor, and her absences from court partly explain what happened. Her political opinions were more important. She had become a passionate Whig, while Anne, though she was often forced to appoint Whig ministers, was by instinct a Tory. Sarah not only continued to attempt to perform her court duties from a distance, but wrote 'very freely and very frequently to her majesty upon the subject of Whig and Tory'. By December 1706 she and Marlborough had persuaded Anne to appoint as a minister their son-in-law, the Earl of Sutherland.

It was only the following year, however, that Sarah discovered what she considered the real reason for the decline of her influence over the Queen: she had a rival. This was her own first cousin, Abigail Hill, a girl she had helped to become a Woman of the Bedchamber. Abigail, Sarah came to believe, had for four years been encouraging the Queen's Tory prejudices. She wrote to her husband warning him of Abigail's treachery, and to the Queen abusing Abigail. Later the same year two incidents persuaded her that Abigail was not merely a political rival. When Abigail married a Mr Masham without telling Sarah, Sarah discovered that Abigail and Anne had discussed with each other 'a hundred times' whether Sarah should be told; the Queen had even been present at Abigail's wedding. And on a day when Sarah entered the Queen's Bedchamber by a secret passage, Abigail also arrived, coming in 'with the boldest and gayest air possible; but upon sight of me, stopped, and immediately asked, making a most solemn curtsey, "Did your Majesty ring?"'

Sarah now began to accuse Anne of a homosexual relationship with Abigail, singing ballads on the subject to Whig ladies at their drawing-rooms, visiting Anne to read them to her; one, written for her by the playwright Arthur Maynwaring, included the verses,

> When as Queen Anne of great renown
> Great Britain's sceptre swayed,

Besides the Church she dearly loved
A dirty chamber maid. . . .

Her secretary she was not
Because she could not write
But had the conduct and the care
Of some dark deeds at night.

Back in London to carry out her duties as the Mistress of the Robes
for the public celebration of Marlborough's victory at Oudenarde,
Sarah noticed during the procession that the Queen was not wearing
the jewels she had arranged for her. A public quarrel began and was
still continuing when they reached the steps of St Paul's Cathedral,
where Sarah told the Queen to be quiet.

The following year, 1709, when the Queen was at Windsor they
quarrelled about the Queen's interference with the salaries and appointments which Sarah, as Groom of the Stole, considered to be her own
responsibility. When Sarah subsequently wrote claiming the right to
appoint a seamstress to replace the sick Mrs Rainsford, the Queen
replied, 'Rainsford is pretty well again and I hope will live a great
while. . . . If this poor creature should die . . . I shall then harken to
nobody's recommendation but my own.'

The Queen and Sarah met for the last time in April 1710, Sarah
promising that if Anne listened to her grievances, she need not answer.
The Queen took advantage of this condition and repeatedly replied to
Sarah's accusations and tears: 'You desired no answer and you shall
have none.'

Sarah now threatened to publish the letters the Queen had written
her unless Anne, as she had earlier promised, gave Sarah's own
positions at court to her daughters. Eventually Anne defied Sarah
and called for her unconditional resignation within two days. When
Marlborough brought Sarah this demand she threw her gold key of
office into the middle of the room and told him to take it to the Queen
at once. By the following year she had produced an early version of her
autobiography.

She was persuaded not to publish it, and instead spent the next
thirty years revising and improving her version of events. In 1742 (two
years before she died at the age of eighty-two) it was eventually
published, when it caused the sensation she had hoped for. By then the
Queen had been dead for twenty-eight years.

Sarah's other revenge was financial. During her period at court she borrowed £32,800 from the Privy Purse which there is no evidence that she ever repaid. She claimed that £18,000 was due to her as payment of a pension of £2,000 a year which she had in fact refused nine years earlier.

From the moment Sarah discovered that Abigail was her rival her behaviour is easily understood. She had been rejected and wished to recover her influence or be revenged. Earlier her feelings were probably more complex. Certainly she used her position for her own private and political purposes, but she was probably also flattered by Anne's friendship and had a certain affection for her.

Abigail Hill, Mrs Masham (d. 1734)

Abigail Hill, the woman who caused such an upheaval at court by displacing Sarah Jennings, Duchess of Marlborough, as Queen Anne's favourite, was Sarah's cousin. Her mother was Sarah's aunt. But Sarah had not met her cousin, and it was only when her uncle, Abigail's father, a merchant trading in the Levant, went bankrupt that Sarah gave the family money. And only when Abigail's parents both died in 1697 that Sarah persuaded Anne to employ Abigail and her sister Alice. Abigail was made a Woman of Anne's Bedchamber, a position she kept when, five years later, Anne became Queen.

It was a lesser one than that of Lady of the Bedchamber, given to persons of lower social standing. True, Lady Danvers, daughter of Lord Chandos, was a Woman of the Bedchamber, but only because she 'had lost the advantage of her birth by marrying a tradesman'.

Abigail described her duties:

The bedchamber-woman came in to waiting before the Queen's prayers which was before Her Majesty was dressed. The Queen often shifted in a morning: if Her Majesty shifted at noon the bedchamber-*lady* being by the bedchamber-*woman* gave the shift to the *lady* without any ceremony, and the *lady* put it on. Sometimes, likewise the bedchamber-*woman* gave the fan to the *lady* in the same manner; and this was all that the bedchamber-*lady* did about the Queen at her dressing.

When the Queen washed her hands, the page of the back-stairs brought and set down upon a side table the basin and ewer; then the bedchamber-*woman* set it before the Queen, and knelt on the other side of the table over against the Queen, the bedchamber-*lady* only looking on. The bedchamber-*woman* poured the water out of the ewer upon the Queen's hands.

The page of the back-stairs was called in to put on the Queen's shoes.

Though her position was inferior, Abigail soon began to take Sarah Jennings's place as the Queen's particular friend. Sarah (in her unreliable autobiography) dated this change from a visit to Bath in 1703. Abigail was at court, while Sarah was often absent at Windsor. She had another advantage over Sarah: she was a Tory. The Tory opinions she whispered to the Queen were those the Queen wished to hear, the Tory politicians she spoke for were those the Queen would have liked to employ.

Dean Swift, also a Tory, described her as 'a person of plain sound understanding, of great truth and sincerity without the least falsehood or disguise; of an honest boldness and courage superior to her sex, firm and disinterested in her friendship and full of love, duty and veneration for the Queen her mistress'. The Earl of Dartmouth gave a different picture. She was 'exceedingly mean and vulgar in her manners, of a very unequal temper, childishly exceptious [captious] and passion- ate'. The Queen suspected, he added, that Abigail and her sister listened at the door whenever he had a conference with Her Majesty. Swift agreed that Abigail was liable to 'give . . . a loose to her temper'. She played the harpsichord.

The Tory she particularly favoured was Robert Harley, a cousin. In 1710 she helped persuade the Queen to sack her Whig ministry and appoint instead a Tory one led by Harley. The following year her success seemed complete when, in January, Sarah was dismissed, and in December Marlborough was impeached. Abigail inherited Sarah's position as Keeper of the Privy Purse.

But Anne gave Sarah's other positions – Groom of the Stole and Mistress of the Robes – to the Duchess of Somerset who, like Sarah, was a Whig, even if a more ladylike one. Abigail and her Tory friends pressed the Queen to dismiss the Duchess, but she refused. Swift wrote a satirical poem accusing the Duchess of helping to murder her second husband (see below) and advising the Queen to, 'Bury those *carrots* [the red-headed duchess] under a *Hill*'.

When Abigail grew maternal she also displeased Swift. 'She is so excessively fond it makes me mad,' he wrote. 'She should never leave the Queen but leave everything to stick to what is in the interest of the public, as well as her own. This I tell her but talk to the wind.' And when her oldest son was so ill that Swift doubted if he would live, 'she stays at Kensington to nurse him which vexes us all.'

Perhaps Abigail's absences from court, like Sarah's in earlier years, helped to cool the Queen's feelings for her. When Harley needed twelve new peers to pass the peace treaty with France and planned to reward Abigail by choosing her husband, Samuel Masham, as one of them, the Queen objected. 'I never had the least intention', she wrote, 'to make a great lady of Abigail Masham; for by doing so I should lose a useful servant about my person, for it would give offence for a peeress to lie on the floor, and do all sorts of inferior offices.' She only agreed to Masham's peerage on condition that Abigail 'remained a dresser and did as she used to do'.

Abigail now began to intrigue with Harley's Tory rival, Henry St John, Viscount Bolingbroke. When peace was made with Spain, Bolingbroke helped Abigail (and himself) to monies from the 'South-Sea fund'. Abigail may have persuaded Anne to dismiss Harley, though Anne claimed she did so because he was so often drunk, ill-mannered and incoherent.

Abigail held her court offices till the Queen died, but grew anxious that she had not saved enough. When Anne fell into a coma Abigail was said to have left the Queen's bedside 'for three hours to go and ransack in St James's'. Though she and her sister Alice 'roared and cried enough whilst there was life . . . as soon as there was none they took care of themselves'.

The Mashams retired to Langley Marsh near Windsor, where they lived quietly for another twenty years, Abigail dying in 1734.

Elizabeth Percy, Duchess of Somerset (1667–1722) and Charles Seymour, 6th Duke of Somerset (1662–1748)

At the age of three Elizabeth Percy, only surviving child of the 11th Earl of Northumberland, inherited her family's vast possessions and titles, including the six ancient baronies of Percy, Lucy, Fitz-Payne, Poynings, Bryan and Latimer. When her mother remarried she became the ward of her grandmother. This dominating old lady first married her to Lord Ogle. Elizabeth was twelve, Ogle fifteen. He was a frail young man who died six months later. Dressed in mourning at the court of Charles II, Elizabeth became known as *la triste héritière*. She was red-headed but not beautiful.

Louise de Kéroualle, Duchess of Portsmouth, by Mignard

John Wilmot, 2nd Earl of Rochester, after Huysmans

She was next married, still only fifteen years old, to Thomas Thynne of Longleat in Wiltshire, 'a well-battered rake', known because of his great wealth as 'Tom of Ten Thousand'. Elizabeth at once fled to the Hague to stay with Lady Temple. Here a Swedish soldier, Count Charles Konigsmark, met her again and renewed his attempts to marry her. To remove the first obstacle to this plan (and because he had been told he could not marry the widow of someone he had killed in a duel), he hired three murderers who lay in wait for Thynne in Pall Mall, where one of them killed him with a blunderbus. Konigsmark fled the country, was captured, tried and acquitted by a corrupt jury, but died at the siege of Argos. Elizabeth, within three months of Thynne's murder, married the sixth Duke of Somerset, a man who possessed 'a greater share of pride than wealth'.

In 1694, at the height of Queen Mary's quarrel with her sister, Princess Anne, when Anne had been turned out of her Whitehall lodgings by Mary, Elizabeth and her husband supported Anne by leasing her Elizabeth's property of Syon House beside the Thames. Next year Elizabeth was chief mourner at Queen Mary's funeral, a position she took as wife of the first peer of the English royal blood, replacing Princess Anne who, aged thirty-one, was too fat and dropsical to walk.

Elizabeth was a Lady of the Bedchamber to Queen Anne from the start of her reign, and soon, like Abigail Hill, aroused the jealousy of Sarah, Duchess of Marlborough. According to Sarah, Elizabeth gained favour with the Queen by telling her every time she looked dull, 'My Queen, you must not think always of the poor prince' (her dead husband, Prince George of Denmark).

When the two duchesses went with the Queen to hear the trial of Dr Sacheverel they quarrelled openly. Since the Queen was *incognita* and watching from behind a curtain, Sarah obtained her permission to sit, but Elizabeth continued to stand all day, thus, in Sarah's opinion, insulting her.

When, in 1711, Elizabeth inherited Sarah's positions as Mistress of the Robes and Groom of the Stole, Tories realized what Sarah had been too jealous to see: that she and Elizabeth, as Whigs, were on the same side. Elizabeth was a life-long enemy of the house of Stuart, and therefore of the Tory party with its Jacobite sympathizers.

Swift, on Abigail Hill's advice, had suppressed his poem, 'The Windsor Prophecy', which suggested that Elizabeth had helped murder Thomas Thynne. But when he was being considered by the Queen for the position of Bishop of Hereford, Elizabeth showed her a copy of it, and she instantly withdrew her consent to Swift's appointment. Abigail watched this dramatic scene and reported it to Swift, who again revenged himself in verse.

> Now angry Somerset her vengeance vows
> On Swift's reproaches for her murdered spouse;
> From her red locks her mouth with venom fills,
> And thence into the royal ear instils. . . .

Elizabeth's third husband, Charles Seymour, Duke of Somerset, had inherited his title at the age of fifteen when his brother was murdered in Italy by a Genoese, Horatio Botti, whose wife he had insulted. In later life he was described as 'of middle stature, a very black complexion, of good judgment, but by reason of a very great hesitation in his speech, wants expression'. When recording this verdict by someone else, Swift added after the words 'good judgment', '(not a grain, hardly common sense)'.

The Duke's career at court spanned four reigns, but he was as ready to abandon his court appointments as to accept them. He was a Gentleman of the Bedchamber to Charles II, then first Lord of the Bedchamber to James II. In this position he was required to introduce the papal nuncio, d'Adda, to St James's, but refused, saying he would not take part in an illegal act. When James replied that, as king, he was above the law, Somerset said that this might be true, but he, Somerset, was not. As a result he lost his court position and his colonelship of the 3rd Dragoons.

His marriage to Elizabeth Percy brought him the vast possessions of the Northumberland family, including Alnwick Castle, Petworth, Syon House and Northumberland House. This was how he was able to give Princess Anne practical help in her quarrel with her sister, Queen Mary, by leasing Syon House to her. Like his wife, he was rewarded with a position at court when Anne succeeded to the throne, becoming Master of the Horse. He remained a favourite for some years, and joined the Tories when Marlborough refused him political promotion on the grounds that he would never employ someone so witless in anything of any consequence. The Tories, however, were suspicious of the Whig views of his wife and of her influence over the Queen, and had Somerset dismissed in the hope that she would follow her husband into retirement. She did not, but was still 'much the greatest favourite when the Queen died'.

George I reinstated Somerset as Master of the Horse, but he once more resigned when he was refused permission to bail his son-in-law, Sir William Wyndham, who was suspected of corresponding with the Jacobites. Such acts of principle earned Somerset the name of 'The Proud Duke'. It suited his character and his handsome figure that he played leading parts on numerous great state occasions. He was an important mourner at the funerals of Queen Mary, William III, Anne and George I, and he carried the orb at four coronations.

He was as arrogant in private life as in public. When he travelled he had servants sent ahead to clear the roads to protect him from the gaze of the vulgar public. When he had his afternoon sleep he required his two daughters to stand watch in turn by his chair. Discovering one of them sitting, he altered his will, deducting £20,000 from her inheritance for disobedience.

Elizabeth died in 1722, and Somerset married again. When his second wife tried to get his attention by tapping him on the shoulder with her fan he told her: 'Madam, my first duchess was a Percy and she never took such a liberty.'

He lived into a fifth reign, George II's, dying in 1748 at the age of eighty-six.

The Court of the House of Hanover

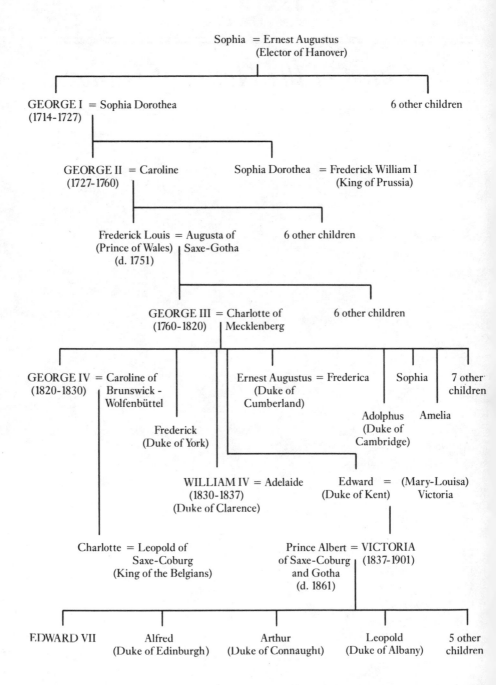

Sophia = Ernest Augustus
(Elector of Hanover)

GEORGE I = Sophia Dorothea
(1714-1727)

6 other children

GEORGE II = Caroline
(1727-1760)

Sophia Dorothea = Frederick William I
(King of Prussia)

Frederick Louis = Augusta of
(Prince of Wales) Saxe-Gotha
(d. 1751)

6 other children

GEORGE III = Charlotte of
(1760-1820) Mecklenberg

6 other children

GEORGE IV = Caroline of
(1820-1830) Brunswick -
Wolfenbüttel

Ernest Augustus = Frederica
(Duke of
Cumberland)

Sophia

7 other
children

Adolphus
(Duke of
Cambridge)

Amelia

Frederick
(Duke of York)

WILLIAM IV = Adelaide
(1830-1837)
(Duke of Clarence)

Edward = (Mary-Louisa)
(Duke of Kent) Victoria

Charlotte = Leopold of
Saxe-Coburg
(King of the Belgians)

Prince Albert = VICTORIA
of Saxe-Coburg (1837-1901)
and Gotha
(d. 1861)

EDWARD VII

Alfred
(Duke of Edinburgh)

Arthur
(Duke of Connaught)

Leopold
(Duke of Albany)

5 other
children

— 6 —

George I and George II

Events at court during the reigns of the first two Georges were
overshadowed by bitter quarrels between each king and his eldest son.
George I quarrelled with the future George II, and George II quarrelled
with Frederick, Prince of Wales, who would have succeeded him if he
had not died. One quarrel reached a climax at a baptism (see Pelham
Holles), the other at a birth (see Frederick, Prince of Wales). Both
sons were banished from the court of St James's, and both set up rival
courts which were livelier and attracted more interesting courtiers.
Both fathers and sons had disliked each other before these open breaks,
and continued to dislike each other even when they were nominally
reconciled.

There was another parallel between the courts of George I and
George II. For all but ten of the forty-six years which they reigned
there was no Queen. George I had left his divorced wife shut up in a
castle in Germany. George II's Queen Caroline died in 1737, leaving
him for twenty-three years a royal widower.

Not that queens had ever prevented English kings from taking
mistresses. Each had a succession, often finding them official positions
at court to justify their presences. Some of these ladies, like George I's
tall and scrawny Mme Schulenberg, Duchess of Kendal, were politically
active. Others, like George II's Henrietta Howard, Countess of Suffolk,
were quiescent. Most were rewarded with titles and comfortable
fortunes. George II's son, Frederick, Prince of Wales, continued the
tradition. There was no secrecy about these affairs. Queen Caroline
tolerated Mrs Howard in case the king should find someone more
intelligent and dangerous. Lady Archibald Hamilton, one of Frederick,
Prince of Wales's mistresses, was actively involved in the horrifying
delivery of the princess's first child.

George I's court was dull because George was dull. 'In private life
he would have been an honest blockhead,' Lady Mary Wortley Montagu
wrote. He disliked ceremonial and preferred to live privately. He knew
little English and never troubled to learn more. Sir Robert Walpole,
who became his Prime Minister, had to talk to him in Latin. He

brought with him a number of Hanoverian advisers, but Walpole managed gradually to manoeuvre them into the background. They could anyway hold no official positions at court, unless they became naturalized, and English aristocrats like the Duke of Newcastle (Lord Chamberlain) and the Duke of Somerset (Master of the Horse) occupied the most important ones.

The court was still divided into the Lord Chamberlain's department and the Bedchamber department (under the Groom of the Stole) above stairs; the Lord Steward's department below stairs; and the Stable department under the Master of the Horse. Though it had been reduced in numbers and many quaintly mediaeval positions been left vacant, it still numbered some 950. When the servants of these were included it formed a community of well over 1,000.

Almost the first thing that George II did when he succeeded to the throne was to destroy his father's will. The Archbishop of Canterbury produced this at the King's first council, George pocketed it and it was never seen again. But he disappointed opposition politicians by retaining his father's Prime Minister, Sir Robert Walpole.

During the next ten years Lord Hervey was by far the most interesting and important courtier. But for the accident that he was the Queen's favourite he would almost certainly have moved from the court into national politics, as courtiers like the Duke of Newcastle and Lord Chesterfield did, but Walpole kept Hervey in the comparatively unimportant position of Vice-Chamberlain because he needed him there to influence the Queen, who in turn controlled the King. By good luck, Hervey left memoirs which give one of the most vivid of all pictures of court life.

The rivalry between the King's court and the court of his son Frederick had begun before the Queen died and continued for another fourteen years – years which also saw the defeat of the Jacobite rising of 1745, and the appearance of George at Dettingen as the last British king to lead his troops in battle. But after Frederick died, unexpectedly young in 1751, the king continued to have domestic problems. Frederick's widow, the Dowager Princess Augusta, retained a rival court at Kew, where opposition politicians gathered. And there was trouble with Frederick's son, the future George III, when he refused to marry Sophia of Brunswick, the wife selected for him. Prince George's education was also the subject of controversy when Lord Harcourt and Bishop Hayter, his Governor and tutor respectively, tried to have their deputies dismissed, but failed and themselves resigned. In 1760, when George II died from a stroke in his lavatory, Prince George was still sufficiently under the influence of his mother, the Dowager Princess Augusta, to take seriously her well-known piece of advice, 'George, be a king'.

Melusina von der Schulenberg, Duchess of Kendal (1667–1743)

Melusina, daughter of Count Gustavus Adolphus of Schulenberg, was forty-six years old and had already been George I's mistress for twenty-three years when she came to England with him in 1714. She had begun life at the Hanoverian court as a Maid of Honour to his mother, the Electress Sophia. When the Electress once saw her at a ball she observed: 'Look at that mawkin and fancy her being my son's mistress.' According to Horace Walpole, who saw her when he was a young man, she was 'a very tall, lean illfavoured old lady ... by no means an inviting object'. The people of London called her 'the Maypole'.

She had at first refused to accompany George to England, fearing that the English, 'who, she thought, were accustomed to use their kings barbarously, might chop off his head in a fortnight'.

George soon gave her a cluster of Irish titles (Dundalk, Dungannon, Munster), and in 1719 made her Baroness Glastonbury, Countess of Faversham and Duchess of Kendal. Finally the Holy Roman Emperor, Charles VI, made her a princess. The English exchequer rewarded her with a pension of £7,500 a year.

She also made huge profits from the South Sea affair, and though, like George, she never learned to speak English, she intrigued at court to good effect, taking numerous bribes from politicians, including the enormous one of £11,000 from Bolingbroke's second wife. Louis XV believed she was an important influence on George (just as Louis XIV had believed in the influence on Charles II of his mistresses). His Ambassador, Count Broglio, reported that George visited Melusina every afternoon from five to eight, and it was then that she endeavoured 'to penetrate the sentiments of his Britannic Majesty'.

Commenting on her later on in life Horace Walpole said that she was 'no genius'; and his supposed father, Sir Robert, who knew her better though he spoke no German, said that her intellect was mean and contemptible. 'She would', he said, 'have sold the King's honour for a shilling advance to the highest bidder'. Just the same he used her to keep himself and his party in power (while his rivals relied less successfully on the Countess of Darlington – see below), and would refer to her as 'the good Duchess' and his 'fast friend'. If Lady Cowper was right he was wise. Schulenberg was, she wrote, 'as much Queen of England as ever any was'.

The Duchess seems not to have been deceived. According to Horace Walpole she hated Sir Robert. When the King and Sir Robert made a habit of dining together after shooting in New Park, she 'grew uneasy at these parties, and used to put one or two of the Germans upon the King to prevent his drinking' (very odd preventatives!).

She was rumoured to have gone through a ceremony of marriage with George's left hand. Certainly she and George remained attached to each other, perhaps from habit, long after he had dropped his younger mistresses, despite finding each other more and more boring. 'She was duller than the King', Lady Mary Wortley Montagu wrote, 'and, consequently, did not find out that he was so.' George would entertain himself while visiting her by cutting out paper shapes.

When George died (on a visit to Germany) she beat her breast, tore her hair and went into retreat for three months. Previously, according to Horace Walpole, George had promised that 'if she survived him, and it were possible for the departed to return to this world, he would make her a visit. The Duchess, on his death, so much expected the accomplishment of that engagement, that a large raven, or some black fowl, flying into one of the windows of her villa at Isleworth, she was persuaded it was the soul of her departed monarch . . . and received and treated it with all the respect and tenderness of duty, till the royal bird or she took their last flight.'

More usefully, George was said to have left her £40,000 in his will, but this was never confirmed.

Sophia Charlotte von Kielmansegge, Countess of Darlington (d. 1725)

Sophia Charlotte was one of the younger ladies who were rivals to Melusina, Duchess of Kendal, for George I's favours, though she was no chicken. She was forty when she arrived in England and was said to have already been his mistress, but she may alternatively (or additionally) have been his half-sister, since her mother and his father had had a long affair. George disapproved of her extravagance, and though he agreed to her accompanying him he did not offer to pay her debts. These almost prevented her coming, and she had to escape from Hanover and her creditors in disguise, then drive in a post-chaise through Holland to the boat.

She was as large as Melusina was scraggy, and in England called 'the Elephant and Castle'. Horace Walpole remembered being 'terrified by her enormous figure' which was

> as corpulent and ample as the Duchess of Kendal was long and emaciated. Two fierce black eyes, large and rolling beneath two lofty arched eye-brows; two acres of cheeks spread with crimson; an ocean of neck that overflowed, and was not distinguished from the lower part of her body; and no part restrained by stays; – no wonder that a child dreaded such an ogress.

Even when younger, according to Lady Mary Wortley Montagu, 'very bad paint' had left her without the charms which once attracted George. Attracted he was, however, perhaps because she had 'a greater vivacity in conversation' than Lady Mary had ever known in any German, male or female.

Like Melusina, Duchess of Kendal, she was given an Irish title (Leinster) then in 1722 made Baroness of Brentford and Countess of Darlington. Though for a time she was favoured by George, it was Melusina whose influence lasted to the end.

Thomas Pelham Holles, Duke of Newcastle (1693–1776)

Thomas Pelham Holles, who was eventually Prime Minister to George II and George III, began his career by spending about seven years as George I's Lord Chamberlain.

He had set out early in life to ingratiate himself with the Hanoverian House of Brunswick, and when still in his teens, during the last two years of Queen Anne's reign, had rented a mob to shout in its favour. George I soon gave him titles, and as a reward for helping to suppress the Jacobite rising of 1715 made him Duke of Newcastle. In 1717 he appointed him Lord Chamberlain, with a salary, pension and board wages which totalled over £4,000 a year. The position was not entirely a sinecure. The Lord Chamberlain was in charge of the whole of the above-stairs section of the royal household (apart from the Bed-chamber), and controlled directly or indirectly a staff of some six hundred and sixty. Though the Vice-Chamberlain (Thomas Coke, throughout the Duke's period at court, remembered for his gardens at Melbourne, Derbyshire) did routine administrative work, the Lord Chamberlain had to spend much time at court, either at St James's in winter or at Hampton Court or Windsor in summer. He was expected to entertain foreign ambassadors, and to play an important part on such grand ceremonial occasions as the King's birthday. Ceremonial was his special responsibility. Of all courtiers, the Lord Chamberlain was the most respected. George I's four Lord Chamberlains were all dukes.

He also had the right to censor plays, but in George I's reign this was disputed by Sir Richard Steele, a manager of Drury Lane Theatre, who claimed that Charles II's patent of 1660 made him independent of the Lord Chamberlain. Newcastle had a new patent issued which did not include Steele's name. This led to the Licensing Act of 1737, and to over two hundred years of increasingly resented court censorship of the theatre.

During his time as Lord Chamberlain, Newcastle was a central actor in the great court drama of the reign: the King's expulsion from St James's of the Prince of Wales. This occurred after the baptism of the Prince of Wales's child, at which the King had insisted that one of the godfathers should be the Lord Chamberlain. The Prince, who had wanted his uncle, the Duke of York, and particularly disliked Newcastle, kept his temper during the bedside ceremony, but then 'being no longer able to master his resentment, he came up to the Duke of Newcastle, and gave him some very injurious language'.

According to Horace Walpole, who was told the story by Henrietta Howard, Lady Suffolk, the words he used were: 'You are a rascal, but I shall find you.'

'What was my astonishment,' continued Lady Suffolk, 'when going to the Princess's apartment the next morning, the yeoman in the guard chamber pointed their halberts at my breast, and told me I must not pass. I urged that it was my duty to attend the Princess; they said, "No matter, I must not pass that way." In one word, the King had been so provoked at the Prince's outrage in his presence, that it had been determined to put a still greater limit on his Royal Highness. His threat to the Duke was pretended to be understood as a challenge, and to prevent a duel he had actually been put under arrest.'

Though the King released the Prince, he soon afterwards expelled him from court.

Few courtiers, let alone statesmen or Prime Ministers, have been so generally despised by their contemporaries as the Duke of Newcastle. Apart from his pomposity, verbosity, vanity, cowardliness, laziness and stupidity, they noticed his terror of catching cold. When he once visited Hanover with Sir Joseph Yorke, Ambassador at the Hague, Sir Joseph was disturbed in the night by one of the Duke's servants. Presently this man admitted that he had been sent to make sure Sir Joseph was using his bed, because the Duke planned to sleep in it when Sir Joseph had aired it.

Mohamet and Mustapha

George I brought to England with him two Grooms of the Chamber who caused astonishment. They were Mohamet and Mustapha, Turks whom he had captured in Hungary some twenty-eight years earlier when he was fighting for the Emperor against Turkey. At the Hanoverian court during these years they had westernized themselves. Mohamet had married into a well-off Hanoverian family and become a Christian, taking the Christian names of Ludwig Maximilian. He was eventually given by the Emperor the title of Ludwig von Königstreu. But he retained an exotic imagination, and in England would entertain fellow courtiers with his account of the poisoning of George I's sister, the Queen of Prussia. Diamonds had been used, he claimed, which had made her stomach so thin that he could poke his fingers through it at any point.

Mohamet was also George I's Keeper of the Closet, and in practice joint Keeper of the King's Privy Purse. The privy purse of £30,000 was vital to George I. Because its accounts were secret he could use it to pay the salaries of the Hanoverians he had brought with him, and so evade the Act of Settlement which prohibited the employment of foreigners. The Hanoverian treasurer paid these salaries, while Mohamet had charge of such things as tailors' bills and theatre subscriptions.

The king gave Mohamet rooms at court near his own, and provided for his mother who had come with him to England. Of all royal servants, Mohamet was perhaps the closest to the king. Count Broglio reported his political influence on George to the King of France. Mohamet used his position at court to enrich himself by selling offices.

When he died, a year before George, Mustapha took on his duties and was also well-favoured and rewarded.

Mary Bellenden, Mrs Campbell, Duchess of Argyll (d. 1736), and Colonel John Campbell, Duke of Argyll (c. 1693–1770)

Of the various pretty Maids of Honour who made the court of the Prince of Wales and Princess Caroline so appealing in the early years of the reign of George I, Mary Bellenden was the most beautiful and lively. A ballad of the day described her singing 'Over the Hills and Far Away', as she jumped downstairs. Horace Walpole remembered:

> Her face and person were charming, lively she was almost to etourderie. I never heard her mentioned afterwards by one of her contemporaries who did not prefer her as the most perfect creature that they knew. The Prince [the future George II] frequented the waiting-room, and soon felt a stronger inclination for her than he ever entertained but for his princess. The Prince's gallantry was by no means delicate; and his avarice disgusted her. One evening sitting by her, he took out his purse and counted his money. He repeated the numeration: the giddy Bellenden lost her patience and cried out, 'Sir I cannot bear it! If you count your money any more I will go out of the room.' The chink of gold did not tempt her more than the person of his royal highness.

Lord Hervey also considered her to have been 'incontestably the most agreeable, the most insinuating, and the most likeable woman of her time. . . . But', he continued, 'as she had to do with a man [the prince] incapable of being engaged by any charm but habit, or attached to any woman but his wife – a man who was better pleased with the air of an intrigue than any other part of it and who did not care to pay a valuable consideration even for that – she began to find her situation was only having the scandal of being the Prince's mistress without the pleasure. . . . She, therefore, very wisely, resolved to withdraw her own neck as well as she could.'

She was already in love, and when the Prince guessed this he promised to treat generously her future husband provided she revealed him before they were married. Mary promised to do this but broke her promise, marrying secretly a young Groom of the Bedchamber, Colonel John Campbell.

'The Prince never forgave the breach of her word; and whenever she went into the drawing-room, as from her husband's situation she was sometimes obliged to do, though trembling at what she knew she was to undergo, the Prince always stepped up to her, and whispered some very harsh reproach in her ear.'

According to Walpole, it was only when the Prince had been abandoned by Mary that he took Henrietta Howard, the future Duchess of Suffolk, to be his mistress. Previously the Maids of Honour had been in the habit of gathering in Mrs Howard's palace apartment. They called her the Swiss, and her rooms the Swiss Cantons, 'probably an allusion to the political neutrality she so wisely maintained at court'. When Mary left court, as she did soon after her marriage, she continued to correspond with Mrs Howard, telling her how dull she found country life. 'I wish we were all in the Swiss Cantons again,' she wrote in 1721.

Her uninhibited letter-writing style suggests that her character had not changed. From Bath she wrote, 'I do not know how your bills go in London, but I am sure mine are not dropped, for I have paid one this morning as long as my arm and as broad as my **.' From Coom-bank she wrote, 'I now take my leave, only adding one piece of advice, which is, take the utmost care of your *, for I left all the * in London in danger. If anybody inquires why I left town, pray satisfy them, that it was to save my *'. About the first, her editor (1824) wrote 'It is to be hoped, that Mrs Campbell's meaning will here escape the generality of readers.' About the second, 'What the danger was to which any part of the female person was at that time more particularly exposed, history does not inform us.'

Mary became the Duchess of Argyll when her husband inherited his title and had five children, before she died young in 1736.

Charles Howard, Earl of Suffolk (d. 1733) and Henrietta Hobart, Mrs Howard, Countess of Suffolk (1681–1767)

Henrietta Hobart, who became George II's mistress, was married to Charles Howard, third son of the Earl of Suffolk, when she was very young, during Queen Anne's reign. According to Walpole she was 'well made, extremely fair, with the finest light brown hair', but 'her mental qualifications were by no means shining'. According to Lord Hervey, Charles was 'wrong-headed, ill-tempered, obstinate, drunken, extravagant and brutal'.

Though Henrietta was also of a good family – her home was the great house of Blickling in Norfolk – she and Charles were at first 'almost in despair' about money and left England to 'seek their fortune' in Hanover. Here they continued to be poor and on one occasion she had to sell her hair to pay for a dinner party. But she obtained a job in the household of Princess Caroline (wife of the future George II) and in 1714, when George and Caroline came to England with his father, George I, Charles and Henrietta came too.

Charles was now appointed Groom of the Bedchamber to George I, and Henrietta Woman of the Bedchamber to Princess Caroline. They were thus in opposite camps when Prince George quarrelled with King George and Charles attempted to force Henrietta to leave Princess Caroline's service. He called on the Princess and threatened to remove his wife from the royal coach. The Princess told him to 'do it if he dare', though she was 'horribly afraid of him' as she 'knew him to be *so brutal* as well as a little mad and seldom quite sober'. She thought he might throw her out of the window, but manoeuvred herself out of danger and continued to defy him 'standing close to the door all the while to give me courage'.

A compromise was suggested by 'that old fool Lord Trevor', that the Princess should pay Charles £1,200 a year to let Henrietta keep her position, but the Princess 'pleaded poverty to my good Lord Trevor, and said I would do anything to keep so good a servant as Mrs Howard about me, but that for £1,200 a year, I really could not afford it.'

Good servant Henrietta may have been, but she could also be difficult and picked a quarrel with the Princess about the holding of a basin during the Princess's dressing ceremony, telling the Princess 'with her little fierce eyes and cheeks as red as your coat, that positively she would not do it'. Henrietta wrote to the ancient Abigail Hill, one time favourite of Queen Anne, now Lady Masham, and got an answer (quoted on pp.108–9) about the precise duties of Ladies and Women of the Bedchamber, after which she did what the Princess required.

Meanwhile she had become the mistress of Princess Caroline's husband, George, Prince of Wales, a deeply uxorious man, who had mistresses because he considered his honour demanded it rather than from desire or necessity. Caroline tolerated Henrietta because she felt that she was no threat, which a replacement might be. At first George was anyway more attracted to Mary Bellenden (see p.124) and as a result Henrietta was a poor third to the Queen and Mary. But when Mary wisely married Colonel Campbell, Henrietta moved up to second place which she held till 1734.

She was decently rewarded at £2,000 a year while George was Prince of Wales, and £3,200 when he became king. He also contributed £12,000 to a fine villa she had built at Marble Hill, Twickenham. And in 1731, when Charles became Earl of Suffolk, she was promoted to Groom of the Stole.

She was a woman of 'good sense, good breeding and good nature', and for many years the king spent 'every evening of his life, three or four hours in Mrs Howard's lodging'. But she was not over-faithful to him; she probably had an affair with Lord Peterborough, and was cultivated by a number of politicians who believed, wrongly, that she could influence the king. She had one serious social disadvantage; she was hard of hearing and became increasingly so.

But for George it was neither her unfaithfulness nor her deafness that was her fault but her honesty. 'The true reasons of her disgrace', Lord Hervey wrote, 'were the king's being thoroughly tired of her, her constant opposition to all his measures, her wearying him with her perpetual contradictions ...'. He showed his annoyance in public when, on several occasions, he snatched off the handkerchief with which Henrietta was dressing the Queen and told her 'because you have an ugly neck yourself, you hide the Queen's'.

In private, at Richmond, where the walls were thin and 'what is said in one room may often be heard in the next', Lady Bristol 'often heard the king talking there in a morning in an angry impatient tone', and on one particular morning regularly interrupting Henrietta, who always spoke in a low voice, with the words 'that is none of your business madam; you have nothing to do with that'.

Before she left court Henrietta demanded an interview with the Queen, which went on an hour and a half and much puzzled Lord Hervey, who could not imagine her going to the Queen and saying, 'Madam, your husband being weary of me, I cannot possibly stay in your house or your service any longer'. But this, it turned out, was more or less what she had said, at which the Queen had told her to 'take a week to consider this business, and give me your word not to read any romances in that time', and then think again about resigning.

Henrietta did not change her mind and a year later, her husband now dead, she married George Berkley. Since he was 'neither young, handsome, healthy nor rich' she was suspected of doing it from pique, but they seem to have been happy together.

Meanwhile Lord Hervey had spoken to Anne, the Princess Royal, about the danger to her mother, the Queen, that the King might take a more troublesome lover. Anne replied: 'I wish with all my heart, he would take somebody else, that mamma might be a little relieved from the ennui of seeing him for ever in her room.'

Henrietta lived till her eighties and despite her increasing deafness,

Horace Walpole remembered enjoyable autumn evenings of gossip
with her.

John Hervey, Baron Hervey of Ickworth (1696–1743), and Mary (Molly) Lepel, Lady Hervey (1700–1768)

John Hervey, courtier and politician, wrote memoirs which are not only
among the most vivid of all court memoirs but fill an important gap in
the history of the early years of George II's reign. About the Hervey
family in general Lady Mary Wortley Montagu wrote that God had
created men, women and Herveys. One of people who may have
belonged to the third category was Horace Walpole, nominally the son
of the Prime Minister, Sir Robert Walpole, but more probably the son
of John Hervey's half-brother, Carr, and therefore John's nephew.
There were many other Herveys. Carr had two sisters, and John
Hervey had six sisters, nine younger brothers and eight children.

He was sickly from childhood, suffering, to his embarrassment, from
recurring epileptic fits. These he tried to control by living on a daily
diet, described by one acquaintance as 'a small quantity of asses's milk
and a flour biscuit; once a week he indulged himself with eating an
apple'. Pope, during their great quarrel, described him as 'a mere
cheese curd of asses milk'. But he also drank quantities of tea, and his
father, Lord Bristol, a solid and respectable Whig, considered that his
ill-health was caused by 'that *vile and detestable plant*'.

He was good-looking, in an effeminate way. Before they quarrelled
Pope called him 'fair of face' and a ballad of the time described his
marriage to Molly Lepel in these lines:

> For Venus had never seen bedded
>   So perfect a beau and a belle
> As when Hervey the handsome was wedded
>   To the beautiful Molly Lepel.

Others were less flattering. When he was older, Sarah, Duchess of
Marlborough, wrote that he had 'a painted face and not a tooth in his
head', and Lord Hailes confirmed that he painted 'to soften his ghastly
appearance'. Whatever the truth, women loved him and he was regularly
unfaithful to his wife. Victorians attributed his amoral behaviour to
religious scepticism.

Hervey first moved in court circles during the reign of George I when his mother was a Lady of the Bedchamber to Caroline, Princess of Wales, and his brother, Carr, a Lord of the Bedchamber to the Prince. Their court was at Leicester House, and here Hervey met the people who were to be his friends and enemies for the rest of his life, including Pope, and the Maid of Honour he married.

When George I died, Hervey hoped to be rewarded with political office, but wasn't and went to Italy. He was at the time seriously ill, but caused surprise by returning to England in 1729 looking much recovered. He had met Stephen Fox, a young man of twenty-four, some eight years his junior, and, as his letters prove, fallen in love with him. 'I shall never cease to be yours,' he wrote. 'God forbid any mortal should ever have the power over me that you have.' He blushed when Fox's name was mentioned, 'just as I imagine your fondest mistress would have done.' Such comments suggest that in this relationship he thought of himself as the girl.

At court again, Hervey was rewarded by Walpole with the relatively minor post of Vice-Chamberlain. Here he formed a close relationship with another man: Frederick, Prince of Wales. When Hervey was recovering from one of his fits, he wrote that 'the Prince sat with me all yesterday and has promised to do so again today'. He also took as his mistress a girl named Anne Vane. When Anne became the Prince's mistress Hervey was angry – as most people believed, with Anne for deserting him for Frederick, but in reality with Frederick for deserting him for Anne. He never forgave Frederick, and one of his reasons for forgiving Anne and again taking her as his mistress was to use her as a spy on the Prince.

Around the same time Hervey became involved in a violent quarrel with Pulteney, leader of the opposition to Walpole, conducted by pamphlet, during which Pulteney called him 'half-man, half-woman'. Eventually, on January 25th 1731, they met in Upper St James's Park (now Green Park) behind Arlington Street to fight a duel. Each wounded the other and Pulteney was about to run Hervey through the body when his foot slipped and the seconds were able to stop the fight. Pulteney embraced Hervey and promised never to attack him again, but 'Lord Hervey made him a bow, without giving him any sort of answer'.

The reason for his quarrel with Pope is more obscure, but may have been rivalry for the friendship of Lady Mary Wortley Montagu. In a satire published two years after the duel, Pope attacked Lady Mary under the name of Sappho and Hervey as Lord Fanny. Pope's verse insults reached a climax in 1735 with twenty-five lines of rarely equalled abuse (part of 'Epistle to Arbuthnot') which began:

> Yet let me flap this bug with gilded wings,
> This painted child of dirt that stinks and stings!

and ended,

> Fop at the toilet, flatterer at the board
> Now trips a lady, and now struts a lord.
> Eve's tempter this the rabbins have express'd
> A cherub's face – a reptile all the rest!
> Beauty that shocks you, parts that none can trust,
> Wit that can creep, and pride that licks the dust.

Throughout these years Walpole kept Hervey in his insultingly minor court position because he was too important there to be promoted. He had acquired a controlling influence over Queen Caroline and this enabled Walpole via Hervey to control the King.

Writing of himself in the third person, he described how the Queen relied on him.

Lord Hervey was this summer in greater favour with the Queen, and consequently with the King, than ever; they told him everything, and talked of everything before him. The Queen sent for him every morning as soon as the King went from her, and kept him, while she breakfasted, till the King returned, which was generally an hour and a half at least. By her interest, too, she got the King to add a thousand pounds a year to his salary, which was a new subject for complaint to the Prince. She gave him a hunter, and on hunting-days he never stirred from her chaise. She called him always her 'child, her pupil, and her charge;' used to tell him perpetually that his being so impertinent and daring to contradict her so continually was owing to his knowing she could not live without him; and often said 'It is well I am so old, or I should be talked of for this creature.'

Lord Hervey made prodigious court to her, and really loved and admired her. He gave up his sole time to her disposal; and always told her he devoted it in winter to her business, and in summer to her amusement. . . .

In an earlier passage, at the time of Walpole's troubles with his Excise Bill, Hervey gives one of many examples of how keenly the Queen involved herself with the political events of the time.

'When Lord Hervey went up to the drawing-room, he saw her Majesty had been weeping very plentifully, and found her so little able to disguise what she felt, that she was forced to pretend headache and vapours, and break up her quadrille party sooner than the usual hour.'

Hervey apologizes for the 'unmethodised and often incoherent' nature of his memoirs, but their great merit is that he wrote them day by day, when the events they describe were fresh and accurate in his mind. As a result they are filled with living characters, as well as providing a unique picture of the way court life influenced national politics.

Hervey ceased to be useful to Walpole at court when the Queen died in 1737, but the Duke of Newcastle, who much disliked him, threatened to resign if he was promoted to the Cabinet, and it was only three years later that Walpole made him Lord Privy Seal. Next year, according to Horace Walpole, he was 'too ill to go to operas, yet, with a coffin-face, is as full of his little dirty politics as ever'. During the following eighteen months he deserted Walpole (when Walpole fell from power) but was nevertheless dismissed from office himself before he died in August 1743 at the age of forty-six.

In contrast to most other men who knew him, Hervey's father, the Earl of Bristol, was always his loyal supporter, referring to him as 'my dear and hopeful son', 'my kind and dutiful son', and 'my invaluable son'. Hervey and his mother did not appreciate each other. She deplored his marriage, and he called her 'Mount Vesuvius' because 'from her mouth came fire and rubbish'.

Since his father was still alive when he died Hervey never became Earl of Bristol and the title passed to his son, George William. It then passed to his second son, a naval officer, who was the proper husband of the bigamous Duchess of Kingston (see below.)

Molly Lepel, the Maid of Honour whom Hervey married, was the daughter of a German soldier and courtier, Nicholas Lepel, who had arrived in England as a Groom of the Bedchamber to Prince George of Denmark, the future Queen Anne's consort, become a naturalized Englishman and risen to the rank of Brigadier General. He was said to have made Molly a cornet in his regiment at birth. But eventually she was granted a pension instead, 'it being too ridiculous to continue her any longer an officer in the Army'. 'Into the bargain she was to be a spy,' wrote Sarah, Duchess of Marlborough, 'but what she could tell to deserve a pension I cannot comprehend'. The story can only be partly accurate since Molly's father was not commissioned to raise his regiment of foot till Molly was five years old.

Soon after George I's accession Molly joined the court of Princess Caroline, where she was one of a sextet of lively and pretty Maids of Honour, described as 'the maidens six without one virgin'. If Mary Bellenden was the most beautiful (see p.124), Molly was considered almost equally pretty. Pope was their particular friend and he gave a more respectable account of the sort of lives they led.

I met with the Prince, with all his ladies on horseback, coming from hunting. Mrs B[ellenden] and Mrs L[epel] took me into protection . . . and gave me dinner. . . . We all agreed that the life of a Maid of Honour was of all things the most miserable, and wished that every woman who envied it had a specimen of it. To eat Westphalia ham in a morning, ride over hedges and ditches on borrowed hacks, come home in the heat of the day with the fever and (what is a hundred times worse) with the red mark on the forehead from an uneasy hat. All this may qualify them to make excellent wives for fox hunters and bear abundance of ruddy-complexioned children. As soon as they can wipe off the sweat of the day they must simper an hour in the Princess's apartment: from thence (as Shakespeare has it) to 'dinner with what appetite they may', and after that, until midnight, work, walk or think as they please. I can easily believe no lone house in Wales with a mountain and a rookery is more contemplative than this Court: as a proof of it I need only tell you that Miss Lepell walked with me three or four hours by moonlight and we met no creature of any quality but the King, who gave audience to the Vice-Chamberlain, all alone, under the garden wall.

Molly left her court appointment after her marriage to John Hervey in 1720, but seems to have continued for a time to appear at court and use the rivalry between George I and the Prince of Wales to her advantage.

'King George the First', the Duchess of Marlborough wrote, 'used to talk to her [Molly] very much; and this encouraged my Lord Fanny [Lord Hervey] and her to undertake a very extraordinary prospect: and she went to the drawing-room every night and publicly attracted his Majesty in a most vehement manner, insomuch that it was the diversion of the town; which alarmed the Duchess of Kendal [Melusina von der Schulenberg] and the Ministry that governed her to that degree, lest the King should be put into the opposers' hands, that they determined to buy Lady Hervey off; and they gave her four thousand pounds to desist, which she did, and my Lord Fanny bought a good house with it, and furnished it very well.'

Molly's marriage was at first happy. 'They visited me twice or thrice a day', Lady Mary Wortley Montagu wrote, 'and were perpetually cooing in my rooms. I was complaisant a great while; but (as you know) my talent has never lain much that way. I grew at last so weary of these birds of paradise, I fled to Twickenham.' They had eight children; but Hervey became increasingly involved with his political intrigues and his mistresses at court and once described marriage as a 'shining stink'.

Molly survived Hervey by twenty-five years, and in later life continued to have admirers, including Horace Walpole, Edward Gibbon and Lord Chesterfield. Others were less kind. 'Nature took great care of her person,' Hanbury Williams wrote, 'but quite forgot her mind, which had this effect, that she was of the same mind with every person she talked to. If she did not understand 'em she still assented with a smile. In which she dealt much, but which in all the years I knew her never grew to a laugh.'

Anne Vane (1705–1736)

Anne Vane (not to be confused with her distant relative by marriage, the notorious Viscountess Anne Vane) became a Maid of Honour to Queen Caroline in the early years of George II's reign. Though she was described as a 'fat and ill-shaped dwarf' and Horace Walpole wrote that she 'had no other charms than of being a Maid of Honour, who was willing to cease to be so upon the first opportunity,' she was soon involved in affairs with at least three gentlemen at court. One of these was Frederick, Prince of Wales. When Anne became pregnant, the Queen, who knew about this affair with her son, told Anne she might leave court for good, but Frederick gave her a house in Soho Square and a pension of £1,600 a year. And when Anne's illegitimate son was christened in 1732 he was named Cornwell Fitz-Frederick Vane. As well as the Prince, however, both Lord Harrington and Lord Hervey told Robert Walpole the child was theirs, and the Queen believed it was Hervey's since one of Hervey's legitimate sons was like a 'twin-brother to little Fitzfrederick'. She anyway suspected the Prince of being incapable of fathering a child, but Hervey reassured her by quoting Anne's opinion that Frederick was 'in these matters ignorant to a degree inconceivable but not impotent'. Anne's affair with Lord

Hervey (Lord Fanny to Pope) was so public that Anne was known at court as Lady Fanny.

Hervey now quarrelled with Anne, blaming her for depriving him of the Prince's friendship. A couple of years later, however, they began a fresh affair. 'From ogling,' Hervey wrote, as always using the third person for himself,

> they came to messages, from messages to letters, from letters to appointments, and from appointments to all the familiarities in which they had formerly lived, both of them swearing that there never had been any interruption in the affection they bore each other. . . . The place of their meeting was an out of the way scrub coffee-house, little frequented, behind Buckingham House, where neither of them were known. Lord Hervey used to walk thither from Kensington in a morning after he was dismissed from the Queen, and Miss Vane could easily, under the pretence of walking in St James's for her health, slip out unobserved to this rendezvous, with a hat over her face, as guarding it from the sun. . . .

When the Prince gave Anne a house at Wimbledon, she would make weekly visits to her London house to meet Hervey,

> where she herself always opened the door to admit him after it was dark, on foot and wrapped in a cloak; and having but one servant in town it was easy for her to contrive to send that one out of the way at the hour she was to let her lover in or out. By these means they often passed the whole night together as free from apprehension as if they had been exposed to no danger. This was a great indiscretion in both, but much greater in the one than the other, as Lord Hervey on a discovery would only have been much blamed, whilst Miss Vane would have been absolutely ruined.

Hervey seems to have been genuinely fond of Anne, but he also used her as a spy on Frederick. At their meetings Anne would 'entertain him with the account of everything she learned from the Prince', with whom she continued to have a parallel affair.

By the summer of 1735 'the difficulty of getting tea, fruit, and supper' at Anne's house made them change their meeting place to Hervey's lodgings at St James's. Here one night Anne was taken suddenly with so violent a fit of the cholic that in a quarter of an hour she fell into convulsions. Lord Hervey, in vain to recover her, crammed cordials and gold powder down her throat; her convulsions grew stronger and at last she fell into a swoon that lasted so long he thought her absolutely dead.

What confusion and distress this put his Lordship into is easier to be imagined than described. He did not dare to send for any assistance, nor even to call a servant into the room, for not one was trusted with the secret. What to do he could not tell, nor what would or would not be said when it should come out, and to conceal it was impossible, that Miss Vane was found dead in his lodgings. Whilst he was agitated with these thoughts and apprehensions she came to herself, and by the help of more cordials, more gold powder, and hot napkins to her stomach, he got her up, dressed her, and led her to a chair in Pall–Mall. . . .

At this time Frederick wanted to drop Anne, for two reasons. His father had arranged his marriage to Princess Augusta. And he was anyway involved with a new and jealous mistress, Lady Archibald Hamilton. He therefore sent Anne a message that he would continue her pension of £1,600 a year if she lived abroad, leaving her son behind, but if not, not. Anne complained to Hervey, who composed a bitter letter for her to send to the Prince, threatening to expose their relationship. The Prince, furious with Anne and furious that he could not guess who had written the letter for her, showed it to 'his mother, his sisters, his servants and anybody he could get to read it'. Anne also showed it to everybody, and Hervey had the secret pleasure of seeing all approve of it (they suspected it was written by Pulteney) when they would have condemned it if they had thought it was Hervey's. There was much sympathy for Anne and condemnation of Frederick, with the result that Anne got her pension unconditionally.

She did not enjoy it long. Soon after retiring to Bath her son died, and she died a few weeks later. The Queen reported that the Prince was more distressed by the death of his supposed son than she had 'seen him on any occasion, or thought him capable of being'.

Philip Dormer Stanhope, Earl of Chesterfield (1694–1773)

'My great object', wrote Philip Stanhope, Earl of Chesterfield, to his son, 'was to make every man I met like me, and every woman love me. I often succeeded, but why? By taking great pains.' His ugliness may explain his desire to be liked. He was short, with a huge head. George I, according to Lord Hervey, called him a dwarf baboon. And he was not always successful. Apart from wanting to be loved, his own great love was for his illegitimate son, his great ambition was to be an orator and his great weakness gaming.

Early in the reign of George I (1715) he was appointed Gentleman of the Bedchamber to the Prince of Wales. In the same year he was elected to Parliament, though he was still under twenty-one and therefore should not have been entitled to sit. He began at once to speak impressively. Horace Walpole, who had heard all the great speakers of his time from Pulteney to Pitt, wrote that one of Chesterfield's speeches was the finest he ever heard. He had trained himself carefully, translating speeches he admired from Latin and French into English, and from English into French. But now he was warned by a political opponent that his age would be revealed if he voted as he had spoken, and he wisely went to live in Paris.

Here the French often paid him 'the highest compliment they think it in their power to bestow', by saying he could be a Frenchman. 'I shall only tell you,' Chesterfield wrote, 'that I am insolent; I talk a great deal; I am very loud and peremptory; I sing and dance as I walk along; and, above all, I spend an immense sum in hair-powder, feathers and white gloves!'

Back in England two years later, he was in difficulties with the King, because he belonged to the Prince's rival court at Leicester House, and with the Princess, who considered him too familiar with Henrietta Howard (later Countess of Suffolk), the Prince's mistress. But when the King and Prince were nominally reconciled, Chesterfield gave the King enough support in Parliament to be made Captain of the Yeomen of the Guard, a position in the Lord Chamberlain's department which brought him £1,000 a year, a gold-tipped ebony baton and a uniform.

He lost this position two years later for describing Sir Robert Walpole's newly revived Order of the Bath as 'one of the toys Bob gave his boys'. Soon afterwards his father died, he inherited his title and took his seat in the House of Lords, which he described as a hospital for incurables.

When George II came to the throne in 1727 he was confirmed as a

Gentleman of the Bedchamber to the King, but Walpole remained hostile, and he was soon sent to be British ambassador at the Hague. Here he lived in lavish style. To entertain the whole of the States-General as well as foreign ambassadors on the king's birthday he had a special banqueting hall built. 'I am at present over head and ears in mortar,' he wrote to his old friend, Henrietta Howard, 'building a room fifty feet long, and thirty-four broad'. 'He courted the good opinion of the Dutch people,' Horace Walpole wrote, 'by losing immense sums at play'. He courted especially a French woman living there, Mlle du Bouchet, and had by her the son to whom he wrote the letters which distinguish him from most other courtiers and politicians of the time.

When temporarily back in England in 1729 he was given another court appointment: Lord Steward of the Household, in charge of staff below-stairs. But now for several reasons he again fell from favour at court. Queen Caroline was confirmed in her dislike of him, according to Horace Walpole, when she discovered (as she thought) the degree of his intimacy with Henrietta Howard. 'The Queen', he wrote, 'had an obscure window at St James's that looked into a dark passage, lighted only by a single lamp at night, which looked upon Mrs Howard's apartment. Lord Chesterfield, one twelfth-night at court, had won so large a sum of money, that he thought it imprudent to carry it home in the dark, and deposited it with the mistress. Thence the Queen inferred great intimacy; and thenceforward Lord Chesterfield could obtain no favour at court.' Chesterfield's winnings that night were £15,000. But it was for his hostility in Parliament that Walpole had him dismissed in 1733 from all his court appointments.

He offended the King more seriously in September that year by marrying Petronilla Melusina Schulenberg, the King's illegitimate half-sister, daughter of George I by his mistress Mme Schulenberg, Duchess of Kendal. For Chesterfield the marriage was one of convenience: he hoped to get his hands on his bride's money. She had already been created Countess of Walsingham in her own right and granted an income for life of £3,000 a year from the Civil List. When her mother died, however, George II destroyed her will. At this, Chesterfield took the Crown to court, claiming his share of the £40,000 which it was supposed should have come to his mother-in-law if George II had not also destroyed George I's will. Chesterfield was paid £20,000 to drop the case.

After the death of Queen Caroline in 1737 Chesterfield tried to influence events at court by forming a friendship with George II's new mistress, Mme Walmonden, Countess of Yarmouth, but without much success. He held important ministerial offices but was never Prime Minister and, judging by events, was happier in perennial opposition. He helped Carteret to drive out Walpole, then helped to drive out Carteret. During the 1745 Jacobite rising he was Viceroy of Ireland. Even his enemies agreed that he was successful there, preventing an Irish rising by a mixture of tolerance and firmness, though the rumour, that during his administration no one was seen drunk in the Irish streets, stretches credulity.

He finally retired from politics in 1748. While in office he had apparently given up gaming, but the very next night he was back at the tables at White's Club in St James's Street.

His other memorable achievement was to help the Duke of Newcastle to persuade Parliament to pass the bill reforming the calendar – the Duke of Newcastle did not understand the bill. But Chesterfield was not forgiven by the public. At the famous Oxfordshire election of 1754 his candidate was harassed by the clamour of voters to, 'Give us back our eleven days'.

Apart from his letters to his son, which today seem delightfully free from hypocrisy, but in his own and Victorian times seemed Machiavellian, Chesterfield's reputation rests on his wit. Two of his enemies questioned this. Johnson found him not 'a lord among wits', but 'a wit among lords'. Horace Walpole, who disliked him for his hostility to his father, Sir Robert, wrote,

> It was not his fault if he had not wit: nothing exceeded his efforts in that point; and though they were far from producing the wit, they at least amply yielded the applause he aimed at. He was so accustomed to see people laugh at the most trifling thing he said, that he would be disappointed at finding nobody smile before they knew what he was going to say. His speeches were fine, but as much laboured as his extempore sayings.

His third great enemy, Lord Hervey, puts these words into George II's mouth. 'Chesterfield is a little tea-time scoundrel, that tells little womanish lies to make quarrels in families, and tries to make women lose their reputations, and make their husbands beat them, without any object but to give himself airs.'

Chesterfield was probably funnier, cleverer and pleasanter than such enemies allowed.

7

Frederick Louis, Prince of Wales

In Hanoverian tradition, George II strongly disliked his eldest son, Frederick. So did Queen Caroline, who once remarked, 'My dear firstborn is the greatest ass, and the greatest liar, and the greatest *canaille*, and the greatest beast in the whole world and I heartily wish he was out of it'. The boy was left in Hanover till he was twenty-one, and only then brought to England, partly to prevent him eloping with the King of Prussia's daughter, partly as a belated concession to the English who objected to their future king being brought up a German. George refused to pay the Prince's debts before he left Hanover, and thus gave his son a further reason for disliking his father. The debts were for gambling, a habit he had already acquired, as he had a mistress.

For a time there was peace between Frederick and his father, but from Frederick's marriage in 1737 to Princess Augusta of Saxe-Gotha, open warfare broke out. Now that Frederick was married he was more indignant than ever at the size of his allowance: only £50,000 out of a Civil List of £800,000, where his father had had £100,000 out of £700,000. When the King refused to increase it Frederick allowed Pulteney, who led the opposition to Walpole, to ask Parliament to make the Prince an allowance of £100,000 on its own account. Walpole was in a quandary. George II was ill and might not live. By defending the present king he might fatally offend the Prince who would soon become king. But he *did* defend the King, and the motion was defeated.

Soon afterwards Frederick gave calculated offence to his mother and father when his new princess became pregnant. The King planned to order the Princess to have the child at Hampton Court. Lord Hervey warned the Queen that even if this order was made Frederick would arrange for the birth to take place by accident somewhere else. The Queen replied that wherever it happened she would be present to make sure the child was genuine.

The Prince and Princess, as well as the King and Queen, were at Hampton Court when the Princess's labour began. At once Frederick, who was equally determined that his mother should *not* be present, ordered a coach to take the Princess to London. But,

> Her pains came so fast and so strong, that her water broke before they could get her out of the house. However, in this condition, M. Dunoyer, the dancing-master, lugging her down stairs and along the passages by one arm, Mr Bloodworth, one of the Prince's equerries, by the other, and the Prince in the rear, they, with much ado, got her into the coach, Lady Archibald Hamilton [the Prince's mistress] and Mr Townshend remonstrating strongly against this imprudent step, and the Princess begging, for God's sake, the Prince would let her stay in quiet where she was, for that her pains were so great she could not set one foot before the other, and was upon the rack when they moved her. But the Prince, with an obstinacy equal to his folly, and a folly equal to his barbarity, insisted on her going, crying 'Courage! Courage! ah, quelle sottise!'

By the time they reached London,

> Notwithstanding all the handkerchiefs that had been thrust one after another up Her Royal Highness's petticoats in the coach, her clothes were in such a condition with the filthy inundations which attend these circumstances that when the coach stopped at St James's the Prince ordered all the lights to be put out that people might not have the nasty ocular evidence which would otherwise have been exhibited to them of his folly and her distress. When they came to St James's, there was no one thing prepared for her reception. The midwife came in a few minutes; napkins, warming-pan, and all other necessary implements for this operation, were sought by emissaries in different houses in the neighbourhood; and no sheets being to be come at, Her Royal Highness was put to bed between two table-cloths. At a quarter before eleven she was delivered of a little rat of a girl, about the bigness of a good large toothpick case.

Meanwhile, astonishingly, the King and Queen had gone to bed at Hampton Court 'without hearing one single syllable of the Princess's being ill, or even of her not being in the house'. It was half past two before the Queen reached St James's. Though angry, she was satisfied the child was genuine, telling Lord Hervey, 'I had my doubts upon the road that there would be some juggle; and if, instead of this poor, little, ugly she-mouse, there had been a brave, large, fat, jolly boy, I should

not have been cured of my suspicions; nay, I believe . . . I should have
. . . gone about his house like a madwoman, played the devil, and
insisted on knowing what chairman's brat he had bought.'

Just as George I had banished George II from court when he was
Prince of Wales, so George II now banished his own son Frederick. 'I
am weary of the puppy's name,' he said, 'I wish I was never to hear it
again, but at least I shall not be plagued any more with seeing his nasty
face.' Frederick went first to Kew, then established a rival court at
Norfolk House in St James's Square. The king also banned from St
James's anyone who visited the Prince and Princess, and warned foreign
ambassadors against visiting them. Just as George II had made Leicester
House a centre of opposition to George I, so Frederick now made
Norfolk House a centre of opposition to George II. And in much the
same way the Prince's court was lively and popular, while the King's was
dull. The Prince courted popularity much like a modern parliamentary
candidate, walking about the streets of London with only a couple of
servants, and in the country 'conversing with the humblest labourer or
mechanic; making himself at home in their cottages, and occasionally
becoming a partaker of their humble fare'.

In 1742 Walpole tried to tempt Frederick into a reconciliation by
offering to get the King to pay his £200,000 of debts, but Frederick
disliked Walpole even more than the King and rejected the idea. Five
weeks later, when Walpole resigned, the King and Frederick were
temporarily reconciled, but soon 'relapsed into their former feelings of
antipathy and disgust'.

It was partly Frederick's interest in the arts and sciences that made
his circle of friends more entertaining than his father's. They included
members of the notorious Hell-fire Club, to which he belonged. Also
Viscount Cobham, creator of the great gardens at Stowe, William Pitt,
Earl of Chatham, and the Grenvilles, one of whom, George, was the
Prime Minister who helped to start the American War of Independence.
Most eccentric was Budd Doddington, who joined the Prince when
Walpole refused him a peerage, and played the roles of money-lender
and court buffoon.

Gambling remained one of the Prince's passions, and according to
Walpole he was a cheat. He would also amuse himself by attending
'bull-baits' at Hockley-in-the-Hole in disguise; and Doddington
describes an afternoon he spent hunting for a gypsy fortune-teller.

After Anne Vane (see p.133) and the jealous Lady Archibald
Hamilton, Lady Middlesex became his mistress. She was 'very short,

very plain, and very yellow; a vain girl, full of Greek and Latin, and music and painting, but neither mischievous nor political'.

Frederick was so sure he would soon succeed his old father that by 1751 he had already chosen the members of his first ministry and settled their policies. He died that year – in the arms of the same dancing-master who had helped with the Princess's delivery, who had been playing the violin to him. His doctors diagnosed suffocation caused by the breaking of 'an imposture in his breast', this the result of a blow 'received either at tennis or cricket'. They also found when they opened him 'another large bag of matter . . . on the right side which is supposed to have been of long standing'. His father, George II, lived another nine years.

George Budd [Doddington], Baron Melcombe (1691–1762)

George Budd Doddington was a man of such extraordinary conceit that his contemporaries found him a joke. In 1749, when he had once again deserted George II to attach himself to Frederick, Prince of Wales, but to his alarm was required to appear at court next day to kiss the King's hand, the King neither scowled nor abused him but 'burst out laughing in his face'.

He had been born George Budd, son of one Jeremias Budd, a chemist of Carlisle (also described as an Irish fortune-hunter), who had successfully married a sister of one of the richest commoners in England, with vast estates in the West Country.

George was soon elected to a seat in Parliament and had also been a diplomat in Madrid by the time, in 1720, his uncle died and he inherited his fortune. It was then that he added his uncle's less ridiculous name to his own and became George Budd Doddington.

He now performed a succession of political desertions remarkable even for the time. These years included his first period as friend, adviser and court buffoon to Frederick. It was a strange country, Frederick remarked, where Doddington was considered a clever man but had just lent him £5,000 which he had no chance of ever seeing again. For the Prince's amusement Doddington once allowed himself to be rolled up in a blanket and trundled downstairs.

But it was for the tawdry magnificence of his dress and of his two great houses that his contemporaries particularly laughed at him. At Eastbury in Dorset 'he slept in a bed encanopied with peacocks' feathers'. At Hammersmith 'round his state bed he displayed a carpeting

Frederick, Prince of Wales, by Mercier

Elizabeth Gunning, Duchess of Hamilton
and of Argyll, by Cotes

of gold and silver embroidery' which clearly showed that it had come from the tailor's shop floor by its 'pockets, button holes and loops'. To travel to and from Town he used what had probably been his ambassadorial coach in Madrid, 'drawn by six fat unwieldy black horses, short-docked, and of colossal dignity'.

For dress he kept a wardrobe 'loaded with rich flaring suits' these also dating from his time in Spain. 'In the meantime his bulk and corpulency gave full display to a vast expense and profusion of brocade and embroidery.'

Around him he kept three of his own buffoons, his heir, Mr Wyndham, the Keeper of the Privy Purse, Sir William Breton, and Dr Thompson, described as 'a misanthrope, a courtier and a quack'. He called his Dorset house 'La Trappe' and these three his monks. Friends, however, found him genuinely witty. He was in the habit of falling asleep after dinner. When one of his guests, Lord Cobham, challenged him to repeat what he had just been saying, Doddington perfectly retold Cobham's story. 'I went to sleep,' he added, 'because, about this time of day, I knew you would be telling that particular story'.

During his last period at the court of Frederick, Prince of Wales (1749–1751), Doddington was given the position of the Prince's Treasurer of the Chambers. He then kept the diary which, in Walpole's words, showed 'the wonderful folly of the author, who was so fond of talking of himself, that he tells all he knew of himself, though scarce an event that does not betray his profligacy'. It was with Doddington that Frederick drew up precise plans for who was to form Frederick's first ministry when the King died and Frederick succeeded him. The great disaster of Doddington's life was that Frederick, not the king, died.

Nine years later when George II finally did die, George III's favourite, Bute, at last gave Doddington the honour which he had been hoping for all his life and which Frederick had promised him: a peerage. The day before the new king's coronation, Lord Melcombe, as Doddington now became, was seen 'before a looking glass in his new robes, practising attitudes and debating within himself the most graceful mode of carrying his coronet in the procession'. Doddington died the next year, but survived long enough to be presented to the new Queen, a ceremony at which his breeches 'broke from their moorings in a very indecorous manner'.

Elizabeth Chudleigh, self-styled Duchess of Kingston (1720–1788)

Elizabeth Chudleigh was the only child of West Country parents who had both been born Chudleigh. Her father died when she was six and she was brought up in the country, but came to London with her mother at the age of twenty, at the suggestion of William Pulteney, later Earl of Bath. Pulteney had met her while shooting, been charmed by her beauty and wit, and now tried to educate her. When this failed, he obtained an appointment for her as Maid of Honour to Augusta, Princess of Wales.

At court she was admired by, among many others, the Duke of Hamilton, then nineteen (who later married the younger of the two beautiful Gunning sisters – see p.146). But Hamilton went on the Grand Tour, and his letters to Elizabeth were intercepted by an aunt who either disliked him or favoured a rival. The rival was Lieutenant Augustus John Hervey R.N., second son of Lord Hervey, (see p.128), whom Elizabeth had met at the Winchester races. She took offence at Hamilton's apparent neglect and in 1744 secretly married Hervey at Lainston in Hampshire.

Their wedding night was such a failure that they parted, Hervey in a ship for the West Indies, Elizabeth for London, saying that she never wanted to see him again. Two years later, however, he returned, jealous of her success at court, and had a violent interview with her behind locked doors at his apartment. The following year she gave birth to a child. It died soon afterwards, and she kept it secret, pretending she had been ill, but it was widely suspected. 'The world says I have had twins,' she complained to Lord Chesterfield. 'I make a point of believing half what it says,' Lord Chesterfield replied.

Elizabeth now became the most admired of all the Maids of Honour at the Prince of Wales's court. Her clothes were magnificent, her entertainments extravagant, her presumed lovers numerous from the Prince of Wales downwards. Her most notorious appearance was at a masked ball at Somerset House. 'Miss Chudleigh's dress, or rather undress, was remarkable,' Lady Mary Wortley Montagu wrote. 'She was Iphigenia for the sacrifice, but so naked the high priest might easily inspect the entrails of the victim. The Maids of Honour (not of maids the strictest) were so offended they would not speak to her.' The Princess of Wales protected her by throwing a veil over her.

A fortnight later Horace Walpole reported that George II had given 'Miss Chudleigh, the Maid of Honour, with whom our gracious monarch has a mind to believe himself in love', a watch worth 35 guineas, and in December the same year that he had made her mother housekeeper at Windsor. In 1760, to celebrate Prince George's birthday, she gave the most fantastic of all her entertainments: a two-hour firework display in Hyde Park, which the guests watched from a darkened room before a sumptuous supper. Her current lover, the Duke of Kingston, presided.

Meanwhile Hervey had continued to pester Elizabeth, threatening to disclose their marriage. To protect herself, Elizabeth went to Lainston and, while a friend distracted the clerk, tore the record of her marriage out of the parish register. In 1759, however, Hervey's brother seemed about to die, thus making him Earl of Bristol, and Elizabeth, regretting what she had done, went to the clergyman who had married her and persuaded him to reinsert the marriage in the register.

But now the Duke of Kingston offered to marry Elizabeth and she wished she had left what she had done alone. The alternative was a divorce, but Hervey would only agree to this if she admitted her adultery, which she refused to do. Eventually, however, when Hervey himself wished to remarry, they colluded to get their marriage annulled on the grounds of non-consummation. In February 1769 the court declared Elizabeth a spinster, and less than a month later she married the Duke of Kingston.

All might have been well for Elizabeth. The Duke died five years later, leaving her the whole of his real estate for life. But the Duke's nephew, Evelyn Meadows, had been accidentally passed over in the subsequent descent of the Duke's property, and now began proceedings against the Duchess on the evidence of a servant who claimed that her original marriage had been real.

When the Duchess heard of this she was in Rome, spending her late husband's money, but for some reason her bank manager would not provide her with what she needed to travel home. She obtained it by drawing two pistols on him.

The trial for bigamy took place in the House of Lords in 1776 and the Duchess was found guilty. As a peer she was now freed (she could otherwise have been punished by burning her hand), and before a writ could be issued to forbid her to leave the country she fled to Dover where the captain of her yacht took her to Calais in an open boat. Meadows' attempt to have the Duke's will declared invalid also failed, leaving Elizabeth in possession of his large fortune.

This she spent on buying enormous continental estates, including one near St Petersburg for the manufacture of brandy, one at St Assise with a three-hundred-bedroom château, and one at Montmartre. She was invariably cheated and brought a suit against the vendor of the Montmartre estate. When she was told one day at dinner that this had failed she suffered a minor stroke. A few days later she insisted on two glasses of mid-morning madeira, lay down on her bed again and was soon found to be dead.

Maria Gunning, Countess of Coventry (1733–1760), and Elizabeth Gunning, Duchess of Hamilton and of Argyll (1734–1790)

Maria and Elizabeth Gunning were Irish daughters of an aristocratic family, but so poor that they had to borrow clothes from an actress, Mrs Woffington, to be presented to the Lord-Lieutenant. They thought of going on the stage.

Instead, in 1751, they came to London, where they were at once considered outstandingly beautiful. Maria was more so than Elizabeth, but the remarkable thing, according to Walpole, was that they were *both* so beautiful. In London they were followed by admiring crowds. But they were naïve. At Hampton Court, when the housekeeper offered to show them 'the beauties', meaning the room containing Kneller's portraits, they were furious, understanding her to mean some kind of peep-show.

At court they were admired by George II, among others, now in his seventies. He took it as a joke when Maria one day told him she longed to see a coronation. When she was mobbed in Hyde Park he gave her the protection of two sergeants of the guards in front and twelve soldiers behind. With these she paraded for two hours one Sunday summer evening.

Meanwhile she had been pursued by other admirers, including the young and sober Earl of Coventry, a Lord of the Bedchamber, but he only found courage to marry her when the Duke of Hamilton gave him an example by impetuously marrying her younger sister, Elizabeth.

Maria's marriage was not a success. She took no particular interest in the great house and grounds which Capability Brown had built for Coventry at Croome in Worcestershire, quarrelled with Coventry when they visited Paris (where she was considered uncivilized for not knowing French) and at court conducted a notorious affair with Lord Bolingbroke.

The Duke of Hamilton's pursuit of Elizabeth had reached a climax at midnight on February 13th/14th 1752, when he demanded to marry her instantly, sent for a priest and had the ceremony carried out at a

Mayfair chapel at twelve-thirty a.m., using for a ring one from his bed curtains. At Elizabeth's subsequent presentation 'the noble mob in the drawing-room' was so keen to see her that it 'clambered upon chairs and tables to look at her'.

When Hamilton died six years later Elizabeth was briefly engaged to the Duke of Bridgewater, but the younger Duke is said to have refused to marry her unless she gave up seeing her sister, who was misbehaving so publicly with Lord Bolingbroke. Since Elizabeth refused, Bridgewater went to Lancashire to build canals (and became known as the 'father of inland waterways'); and Elizabeth married John Campbell, who was to make her a Duchess for the second time when in 1770 he became Duke of Argyll. (His mother was Mary Bellenden, the gay young Maid of Honour of the Prince of Wales's court in George I's reign).

Next year Maria died. When she grew ill, to prevent visitors seeing her she would have no light in her bedroom except the lamp for her tea-kettle. Tuberculosis may have caused her death, or perhaps lead-poisoning from the white lead which was generally used as make-up at the time to produce a becoming blush.

Elizabeth also became ill with suspected tuberculosis, but was well enough to go with Lord Harcourt and a shipload of noble ladies to fetch Princess Charlotte, George III's future queen, from Mecklenberg, and accompany her on her stormy voyage to England. She was made one of the Queen's Ladies of the Bedchamber.

From 1763 Horace Walpole regularly commented in his letters on her changed looks, but others disagreed 'Even when far advanced in life', Sir N. Wraxall wrote, she remained beautiful, and 'seemed composed of a finer clay than the rest of her sex'. She was not that far advanced, and only fifty-five or fifty-six when she died in 1790.

George III

When George III came to the throne in 1760 he was young, immature and priggish. By 1820 when he died he had for nine years been apparently mad. During the intervening years his supposed attempts to rule personally (in fact a myth invented by the Whigs) often made him unpopular, but gradually he had matured into an endearing eccentric who enjoyed designing his own uniforms and taking clocks to pieces. He would write letters under a false name to the *Annals of Agriculture*, and because of his interest in the subject became known as 'Farmer George'.

One of his earliest acts was to issue a proclamation 'for the encouragement of piety and virtue, and for the preventing and punishing of vice, profaneness and immorality' especially among those employed near the 'royal person'. As a result his court became a dull place. Gaming died out and even the Sunday Drawingrooms of previous reigns were abandoned. Lord Harcourt, Lord Bruce and Lord Ashburnham were typical of the respectable but unexciting aristocrats who became his courtiers. Formidable and respectable German ladies like Mme Schwellenberg, or equally respectable English ladies like Fanny Burney served the Queen, holding positions often previously held by royal mistresses. When the King used monies which had once made such mistresses rich to buy political support, politicians led by Edmund Burke had their revenge. In 1781 a bill was passed which abolished many ancient and quaint court positions.

The King was not uninterested in women. In his teens he had an affair with Hannah Lightfoot, known as the fair Quakeress. Half a dozen scandalous accounts of this affair suggest among other things that the King (as Prince of Wales) actually married Hannah, that the children she had by him were the true heirs to the throne and that he went through a second ceremony of marriage to Queen Charlotte after Hannah had died. A more probable version of the story is that a man named Axford was persuaded to marry Hannah, on condition he then left her to George, precisely to prevent her children later making inconvenient claims to be the King's heirs.

Soon after he came to the throne George was infatuated with Lady Sarah Lennox. But after Princess Charlotte had been brought from Mecklenberg in 1761 to be his Queen he had no more affairs and grew fond of this not very lovely girl. He was even fonder of their fifteen children, and when St James's Palace became too small, bought and expanded Buckingham House to accommodate his large family. In the summer he presently began to use Windsor Castle, neglected by George I and George II, as his country palace.

So it was ironic that members of the royal family themselves continued to provide most of such scandal as occurred at court. Though the King did not quarrel so openly with his eldest son (the future George IV) as George I and George II had quarrelled with *their* eldest sons, he disapproved of Prince George's extravagant and dissolute way of life; he would have disapproved more strongly if he had known that the Prince had secretly married Mrs Fitzherbert, so offending against the Royal Marriage Act which forbade members of the royal family to marry commoners without royal permission.

His favourite daughter, Princess Amelia, also married secretly, something he was only told after she had died at the age of twenty-seven. His son, the Duke of York, Commander-in-Chief of the Army, was accused of promoting officers at the suggestions of his mistresses. His fifth son, the Duke of Cumberland (the future King of Hanover), was involved in a still more sinister scandal, being strongly suspected of murdering his Corsican valet.

But it was the madness of the King himself which caused the greatest public stir. In 1762 and 1765 he had attacks of fever, but these were not generally known about and there is no contemporary evidence that delirium was one of the symptoms. In 1788, when he *did* seem to go mad, this could not be concealed. A succession of doctors was called before he ended in the hands of Dr Frances Willis, an old clergyman who, with his son, ran a private madhouse in Lincolnshire.

The optimistic Willises became the government doctors, predicting the recovery which Pitt, the Prime Minister, hoped for, while Drs Baker and Warren were the opposition doctors, exaggerating the king's illness for the benefit of the Prince of Wales who wished to be appointed Regent. The Willises' cures were the standard ones of the time (emetics, quinine, cupping, blooding and a low diet) but put special emphasis on the straight waistcoat in which the king was regularly tied so that Dr Francís Willis could establish a domination over him and correct his mad delusions. These included the idea that he was really married to Lady Pembroke, a beautiful Lady-in-Waiting of his younger days, now fifty. Despite his treatments which exacerbated his illness the king eventually recovered.

In 1801 and 1804, however, he had further serious attacks, and in the opinion of his doctors needed always to be protected from things which would over-excite him. His final decline in 1810 they attributed to the death of his daughter and the scandals in which his two sons had become involved. But for the last nine years of his life when he seemed entirely mad, he was probably merely senile. He grew a white beard behind which he lived in a private world. His belief that he was married to Lady Pembroke grew stronger, and he thought that his daughter, Amelia, was still alive, living in Hanover. Sometimes he believed that he himself was dead, and would dress in mourning 'in memory of George III, for he was a good man'.

For a hundred and forty years the king's madness was no better understood than it had been during his lifetime, but it is now thought to have been porphyria, a hereditary disorder from which several of his relatives and descendants also suffered, though less severely.

Simon Harcourt, 1st Earl of Harcourt (1714–1777)

Simon Harcourt, First Earl of Harcourt, was described by Lord Waldegrave as 'an honest, worthy man but whose heart was better than his head'. And by Horace Walpole as a marvel of pomposity and propriety.

He became a Lord of the Bedchamber to George II in 1735 and was with the King at the Battle of Dettingen. In 1751, after the death of Frederick, Prince of Wales, he was appointed Governor to George, Frederick's son, the future George III. George was backward. At the age of eleven he could not read. Harcourt did not improve matters. He was said to have been satisfied that he had done his duty if he taught the Prince to turn out his toes.

George's tutor, appointed at the same time, was Thomas Hayter, Bishop of Norwich, the bastard son of a former Archbishop of York. Soon Harcourt and Hayter charged the Prince's sub-governor, Andrew Stone, with being a secret Jacobite, drinking the health of the Pretender and teaching the young Prince to follow the principles set out in Bolingbroke's *Patriot King*. Bolingbroke maintained that a king should not place 'himself at the head of one party in order to govern his people', but 'put himself at the head of his people in order to govern ... all parties'. As applied to England this would have meant no longer automatically choosing Whigs for his ministers, as English sovereigns had for most of the century. When the charges were twice dismissed, Harcourt and Hayter both resigned.

Harcourt remained in royal favour, however, and in 1761 he was sent by George, now King, to bring back his future queen from Mecklenberg. '*If he can find it*', Walpole commented. As the King's proxy he had to make twelve formal applications for the Princess's hand before she could accept him. He wrote home about her: 'She is no regular beauty; but she is a pretty size.' Protocol satisfied, they set sail, accompanied by two duchesses and a countess, on the royal yacht which had been renamed *Charlotte* in the Princess's honour, and repainted. Wouldn't the smell of paint turn the Princess's stomach? Walpole was asked. 'If her head is not turned,' he replied, 'she may compound for anything less.'

Though the voyage was a stormy one and the Duchesses of Ancaster and Hamilton were violently sick, the Princess was 'only slightly indisposed. . . . While the other ladies were crying, she was undaunted; consoled them, prayed, sang Lutheran hymns, and, when the tempest a little subsided, played "God save the King" to her guitar'.

The yacht tried for ten days to reach Greenwich, before abandoning the attempt and docking at Harwich, so disappointing the waiting crowds on the banks of the Thames. Three days later Harcourt was made Master of the Horse to the new queen, and in 1763 her Lord Chamberlain.

But after five years at court he went abroad to be Ambassador in Paris, then Viceroy of Ireland. He is best remembered today for the house he began at Nuneham Courtenay, one of the first in England to be sited for its view. To build it he had to bring stone down the Thames from his family home at Stanton Harcourt, because the nearby quarries were too busy supplying the Duke of Marlborough. He also removed the old village of Nuneham, which was inconveniently near his new house, to its present position along the Oxford to Wallingford road, an act of social vandalism which inspired Goldsmith's poem, 'The Deserted Village'.

In 1777 Harcourt retired to enjoy the delights of Nuneham, but he only enjoyed them for nine months. In September that year he was found drowned in his own well. The incident so excited Horace Walpole that he described it in different words in seven different letters. 'Lord Harcourt was missing t'other day at dinner time', he wrote to one correspondent, 'at last he was found suffocated in a well with his head downwards . . . an odd exit for the governor of a king,

Ambassador and Viceroy.' Harcourt had been trying to rescue his small dog.

John Stuart, Earl of Bute (1713–1792)

John Stuart, Earl of Bute, was described by Horace Walpole as a Scotchman who 'at five-and-thirty had fallen in love with his own figure, which he produced at masquerades in becoming dresses'. His pride in 'a leg of unrivalled symmetry' became well known. So did his pompousness. Though vain, Bute was an educated man with wide interests. An acquaintance, M. Dutens, wrote that 'his knowledge was so extensive, and consequently his conversation so varied, that one thought one's self in the company of several persons' at the same time.

Bute first became involved with royalty when he met Frederick, Prince of Wales, at the Egham races, where the royal party had been delayed by a shower and he was called into its tent to make a fourth at whist. It was a shower that had an important influence on English history. In 1750 Frederick made Bute a Lord of the Bedchamber at his court at Leicester House.

When Frederick died next year Bute went through four years of obscurity. But in 1755 he returned to favour there and in the following years his influence on Frederick's widow, the Dowager Princess Augusta, became enormous. At the famous masked ball at Somerset House, when she threw a veil over her Maid of Honour, Elizabeth Chudleigh (see p.144), who had appeared nearly naked as Iphigenia, Miss Chudleigh told the Princess, '*Votre Altesse Royale sais que chacune a son But*'. In fact Bute owed his influence at Leicester House not to the Princess's love but to the adulation of her son, the young Prince George.

'The Princess Dowager and Lord Bute', Chesterfield wrote, 'agreed to keep the prince entirely to themselves ... except at levees ... he saw nobody and none saw him'. As part of this process she and Bute frustrated the old king's attempt to marry Prince George to the German princess of Brunswick-Wolfenbuttel whom he had selected.

When the young prince came of age George II and his ministers tried to extract him from the influence of Bute by offering him accommodation at St James's Palace, but Prince George replied that parting with his mother would cause him much distress. The King's ministers gave way, afraid of the consequences of opposing their future king, and agreed that Bute should be made the Prince's Groom of the

Stole. George II was angry, and refused personally to hand Bute the gold key of office, but gave it to the Duke of Grafton who 'slipt [it] into Bute's pocket'. Bute in practice became George's Governor, and it was now that George's letters to Bute began to contain the most exaggerated expressions of gratitude, admiration and self-deprecation.

Instead of 'My Dear Lord', they would begin with 'My Dearest Friend'. 'I have had the pleasure of your friendship during the space of a year,' he wrote in 1756, 'by which I have reap'd great advantage, but not the improvement I should if I had follow'd your advice.' Two years later he wrote that if Bute should ever set him adrift he would not accept the crown but 'retire to some distant region where in solitude I might for the rest of my life remain,' and the same year, 'the more I consider how I have thrown away my time the more I am surprised at the greatness of your indulgence'. By 1759 George was claiming to value Bute's friendship 'above every mortal joy'. 'If I say things you think improper,' he wrote the same year, 'impute them to the violence of my love'.

Soon after George succeeded his grandfather, becoming George III, Bute was appointed the King's Groom of the Stole and First Gentleman of the Bedchamber. An astonishing few months followed in which Bute, a courtier with no seat in the House of Commons nor in the Cabinet, was in practice Prime Minister. Bute and George III now set about bringing the war to an end, and in the process driving out of power the Whig politicians who had held it for so long. Within three years they had achieved peace, but Bute had made himself more unpopular than any Prime Minister before or since. 'No Petticoat Government' was the cry against Princess Augusta, who was generally believed to be Bute's mistress. When the King went to visit his mother, members of the crowd would shout to ask if he was going to suck. 'No Scotch Favourite' was the cry against Bute. The London mob would burn (or carry about suspended from gallows) a petticoat representing the Princess and a jack-boot representing John (Jack) Bute.

In April 1763 Bute resigned from office, but he continued to be the King's friend and adviser. Various politicians tried to end this connection and George Grenville who became Prime Minister in 1765 forced the King to promise that in future Bute 'should never directly or indirectly, publicly or privately, have anything to do with his business, nor give advice upon anything whatsoever'. But George and Bute only finally ceased to correspond in July 1766.

Bute lived for another twenty-six years, employed Capability Brown to landscape his fine gardens at Luton Hoo and privately printed at the cost of £12,000 an edition of only twelve copies of a nine-volume work on British flora.

Henry Herbert, 10th Earl of Pembroke (1734–1794), and Elizabeth Spencer, Countess of Pembroke (1737–1831)

Henry Herbert, 10th Earl of Pembroke, was the son of Lieutenant General Herbert, the 9th Earl, and went into his father's regiment as a cornet at the age of eighteen. Four years later he was appointed a Lord of the Bedchamber to the Prince of Wales, the future George III. The same year he married Elizabeth Spencer, daughter of the Second Duke of Marlborough and thus great grand-daughter of the famous duke. She was a girl of beauty and elegance. At George III's coronation in 1760 Horace Walpole noted that 'Lady Pembroke, alone, at the head of the countesses, was the picture of majestic modesty'. In the early years of the new reign Pembroke fought abroad, but then resumed his court duties, and after George III's marriage to Queen Charlotte, Elizabeth became one of her Ladies of the Bedchamber, which she remained for many years.

Her husband's career was less straightforward. In 1762 Horace Walpole reported that Lord Pembroke, 'Earl, Lord of the Bedchamber, Major-General, possessed of ten thousand pounds a year, master of Wilton, husband of one of the most beautiful creatures in England, father of an only son' had eloped with a certain Miss Hunter, daughter of a Lord of the Admiralty, who was 'silly and in no degree as lovely as his own wife who has the face of a Madonna and . . . is dotingly fond of him'. Pembroke had left letters saying that he had 'long tried in vain to make [his wife] hate him'.

The couple were intercepted in the North Sea and Miss Hunter taken in a privateer to the Netherlands, where Pembroke followed her in a cod-fishing-boat, but her father let it be known that he 'desired no such recovery', and they remained abroad. A month later, according to Walpole, Pembroke was 'doing nothing but write tender and mournful letters to his charming wife which . . . are intended to draw money from her'.

Miss Hunter had a child by Pembroke but eventually they parted, she to marry a future Field Marshal, he to return to court, be reunited with his wife and in 1769 reappointed a Lord of the Bedchamber.

Next year he again fell into disfavour when he voted in the House of Lords for an independent enquiry into public expenditure, but was again restored, and re-appointed Lord Lieutenant of Wiltshire two years later.

In the 1780s the Pembrokes took their daughter to Nice in an attempt to cure her of consumption. The attempt failed, but before the girl died Pembroke had fallen in love with an Italian singer and gone with her to Florence.

Early in his military career Pembroke had published *Method of Breaking Horses*, a manual on which British cavalry-training was based from then onwards, and which remains a classic description of the art of dressage. He compiled it from his experience with the 15th Hussars (Eliott's Horse) of which he had been Lieutenant Colonel.

Meanwhile his wife had pursued her blameless career at court, only becoming retrospectively interesting because of the King's belief that she was his wife and the proper queen. He first imagined this during his madness of 1788–89; after 1810 it became a continuous delusion. In 1811 he told his youngest son, 'Is it not a strange thing, Adolphus, that they still refuse to let me go to Lady Pembroke, although everyone knows I am married to her? But what is worst of all is, that infamous scoundrel Halford [Sir Henry, a royal doctor] was by at the marriage, and has now the effrontery to deny it to my face.' There is no evidence that the King had ever done more than desire 'Queen Esther'.

Thomas Bruce Brudenell, Lord Bruce, Earl of Ailesbury (1729–1814)

While still a schoolboy Thomas Bruce Brudenell was chosen by his childless uncle, Charles, Earl of Ailesbury, to inherit the wardenship of Savernake Forest, which he did when he was only seventeen. As a fourth child he would have been without a title, but his uncle secured an additional one, with remainder to Thomas, who now became Lord Bruce. Early in George III's reign he was appointed one of the King's Lords of the Bedchamber.

He was a correct and elegant courtier (an abusive anonymous letter told him, 'nor dont my Lord stand so much like a monkey with that poor spindle shank pushed forward in the silly affected attitude which makes you the laughing stock of the whole drawing-room'), but a fussy man, continually writing anxious letters from court to his Wiltshire steward. Here he employed Capability Brown for some ten years to redesign the grounds of his great house, Tottenham Park.

In 1776 he was made Earl of Ailesbury and appointed Governor to the Prince of Wales, the future George IV, but he soon resigned the post. He may have been persuaded to do this by his wife, a sickly lady, daughter of Henry Hoare, the creator of the great garden at Stourhead, who complained that she was left alone at home so much. But, according to Thackeray, Bruce resigned in a huff when Prince George corrected his Greek pronunciation.

Some seven years later, when his wife and eldest son had both died, Bruce returned to court, first as Queen Charlotte's Chamberlain, then as her treasurer. Meanwhile, in gratitude to George III he erected a tall obelisk in Savernake Forest, obtaining it secondhand from the grounds of the late George Budd Doddington's Hammersmith house (see p.142).

He entertained the King twice at Tottenham. The first time he was embarrassed when neither he nor any retainer could blow King John's hunting-horn, with which the warden should traditionally have welcomed the King. Fanny Burney came with the King and Queen on the second occasion. She was so short-sighted that she thought Tottenham was set in an entirely flat landscape, but observed that: 'The good lord of the mansion put up a new bed for the King and Queen that cost him £900.' (If agricultural wages are taken as a base, the equivalent of about £250,000 in 1986.)

Frances [Fanny] Burney, Madame d'Arblay (1752–1840)

Fanny Burney was the third of six children of an organist, Dr Burney, who was living at King's Lynn, Norfolk, when she was born. She was a backward child. When, at the age of eight, she and her family moved back to London she could neither read nor write, and was known as 'the little dunce'. Her brother James would pretend to teach her with the book upside-down.

She was also shy, and so silent and serious in front of visitors that she became known before she was eleven as 'the old lady'. In private, and when playing parts, she was less shy. After going to the theatre she would 'take the actors off and *compose* speeches for their characters, for she could not read them'. She and her sisters would play in the garden behind their London house with the daughters of their neighbour, a 'hair-merchant'. 'One day, the door of the wig-magazine being left open, they each of them put on one of those dignified ornaments of the head and danced and jumped about in a thousand antics, laughing till they screamed.' When a 10-guinea wig fell into a water butt and the owner was furious, Fanny told him, 'The wig is wet, to be sure; and the wig was a good wig, to be sure; but 'tis of no use to speak of it any more, because *what's done can't be undone.'*

She continued to have no formal education. Two of her sisters were sent to school in Paris, but Dr Burney kept Fanny at home, afraid that she was too fond of her maternal grandmother who might persuade her to turn Roman Catholic. On the other hand he had many literary and artistic friends, the actor David Garrick among them, who would come to tea in his Poland Street home. These, together with Dr Burney himself who wrote musical history, were an important influence on Fanny. As soon as she could write 'she began to scribble, almost incessantly, little poems and works of invention'.

Her stepmother, however, 'inveighed very frequently and seriously against the evil of a scribbling turn in young ladies – the loss of time, the waste of thought, in idle, crude inventions . . .' and when she was fifteen Fanny 'made over to a bonfire . . . her whole stock of prose compositions, while her faithful sister, Susanna, stood by weeping. . . .'

But she continued to expand in her head one of the stories she had burned, and when this was complete, wrote out two volumes in a disguised hand and offered them anonymously to a publisher. A second publisher took them, and in 1788 published the book as *Evelina; or, A Young Lady's Entrance into the World*. Dr Burney discovered his daughter's work and told Mrs Thrale (whose daughter he taught music); Mrs Thrale told Dr Johnson; Dr Johnson learned it almost by heart and imitated the characters with roars of laughter. Burke sat up all night reading it, and so did Sir Joshua Reynolds, who also read it at table, where he became so absorbed that someone had to feed him. Fanny, hearing some of this news when visiting Dr Crisp, an old friend of her father's, ran into the garden and danced round its mulberry tree.

She was soon introduced to the Thrales and became a friend of the family, often staying with them in Streatham. During the next five years she met most of the literary celebrities of the period. She was much liked by Dr Johnson, and Sheridan offered to accept a play from her without seeing it. Macaulay reported that her second novel, *Cecilia*, was awaited as impatiently as any by Scott, and when this was published it led to meetings with Burke and the celebrated blue-stocking, Mrs Elizabeth Montagu.

Fanny also met Mrs Delany, and in her house at Windsor first came into contact with the royal family. This she hoped might lead to an appointment for her father. When the Master of the King's Band died and the position was vacant, she and her father were advised not to apply directly, but to walk about on the terrace of Windsor Castle where George III might see them and take the hint. The hint was too subtle. The King bowed to Dr Burney but spoke only to Fanny, who soon afterwards was invited to become Second Keeper of the Robes to the Queen.

Life at court left her no time to write novels (of which the Queen disapproved), but fortunately she continued to keep the journal which she had begun the same year that she burned her juvenilia. It gives an unrivalled picture of court life. The people whose names Fanny changed have been easily identified. La Guiffardière, the Queen's French reader, who frequently pestered Fanny, becomes Mr Turbulent. Miss Gunning is Miss Fuzilier.

Fanny was not a happy courtier. She was easily insulted, but easily gave insults herself, often because she was short-sighted and prohibited by court etiquette from wearing glasses. The work she did was menial and lasted from six in the morning till midnight. She disliked her superior, 'Mrs' Schwellenberg, a bad-tempered German woman, who forbade Fanny to entertain friends, lived in greater style than the Queen and had her rooms so placed that she could bar the way to the royal apartments.

Fanny was forced to spend long evening hours with this lady, submitting to insults or playing piquet with her, according to her whim. Here she met the two pet frogs which Mrs Schwellenberg kept in glasses for fondling, and heard her describe them to Mrs Delany. 'A commendation ensued, almost ecstatic, of their most recreative and dulcet croaking and of their amiable ways of snapping live flies.' They were trained to croak, Mrs Schwellenberg explained on another occasion. '"I only go so to my snuff-box, knock knock knock, they croak all I please."'

'"Very pretty, indeed!" exclaimed Colonel Goldsworthy.

'"I thought to have some spawn," she continued; "but Lady Maria Carlton . . . came and frightened them. I was never so angry!"

'"I am sorry for that," cried the Major, very seriously, "for else I should have begged a pair."'

While she was a courtier Fanny was given tickets by the Queen for the impeachment of Warren Hastings, and she wrote vivid descriptions of Burke's great prosecuting speeches.

When he narrated, he was easy, flowing, and natural; when he declaimed, energetic, warm, and brilliant. The sentiments he interspersed were as nobly conceived as they were highly coloured; his satire had a poignancy of wit that made it as entertaining as it was

Fanny Burney by Edward Francis Burney

George III by Zoffany

penetrating; his allusions and quotations, as far as they were English and within my reach, were apt and ingenious; and the wild and sudden flights of his fancy, bursting forth from his creative imagination in language fluent, forcible, and varied, had a charm for my ear and my attention wholly new and perfectly irresistible.

But the great event of Fanny's time at court was the King's madness. On one occasion she accidentally met him when he was being exercised in Kew Gardens by his two doctors. Fanny fled. 'Heavens how I ran. . . . My feet were not sensible that they even touched the ground.' The King ran after her and when the alarmed shouts of the doctors at last made her stop, he put both arms round her shoulders and kissed her cheek.

He then insisted on walking with her and telling her 'everything that came uppermost in his mind. "Never mind her!" he said about Mrs Schwellenberg, "don't be oppressed – I am your friend! don't let her cast you down! I know you have had a hard time of it. . . ."'

He next 'gave me a history of his pages, animating almost into a rage, as he related his subjects of displeasure with them, particularly Mr Ernst. . . .' Presently he turned to Handel, and 'ran over most of his oratorios, attempting to sing the subjects of several airs and choruses, but so dreadfully hoarse that the sound was terrible.' Returning to his staff, he told her that he was 'very much dissatisfied with several of his state officers, and meant to form an entire new establishment. He took a paper out of his pocket-book, and showed me his new list. "When I once get away," he added, "I shall rule with a rod of iron".' By this time his doctors were 'quite uneasy at his earnestness and volubility' and managed to end the interview.

In spite of the King's offer of support, Fanny continued to find court life under Mrs Schwellenberg hard to bear. She grew ill, her friends protested, and finally in 1791 she obtained with difficulty permission to resign. Her pay of £200 a year was reduced to a pension of £100.

She retired to her sister's house at Mickleham, where in 1793 she met and married the French refugee, General d'Arblay. She was forty-one. At first they lived on nothing but her pension, then a new novel, *Camilla*, enabled her to build 'Camilla Cottage' nearby. When the General made his peace with the French government they settled in France and lived for ten years at Passy. And in 1815 when Napoleon fell her husband was made a General once more. Fanny had an adventurous time in Brussels during the battle of Waterloo, while the general was kicked by a horse and never able to serve actively again. He died three years later.

Fanny now returned to England where she lived from then on, writing among other things a pompous memoir of her father, 'singularly vague in dates'. She was eighty-eight when she died in 1840. Though her novels are now little read, the earlier ones had an important influence on Jane Austen, who took her title, *Pride and Prejudice*, from the final pages of *Cecilia*. Her journal, the major part of which appeared two years after her death, is as fresh today as when it was published. Her somewhat obsequious comments on the King, Queen and Princesses are interspersed with observations of disarming frankness.

Rev. Francis Willis (1718–1807) and his sons, Dr John Willis (1715–1835), Rev. Thomas Willis (1754–1827), and Dr Robert Darling Willis (1760–1821)

Francis Willis, a seventy-year-old clergyman, who also held a medical degree, was first summoned to attend the apparently mad King George III early in December 1788. By this time the King's principal doctor, Sir George Baker, had called in at least four other doctors to help him, but had realized that they neither understood the King's illness nor knew how to treat it.

Willis was sent for because he specialized in lunacy. Though Willis's father had made him take holy orders he had always been interested in medicine, and achieved some remarkable cures in his Lincolnshire parish. When called to read the 'departing prayer' to a shepherd named Isaac he had instead told the man's wife to 'give him a clyster . . . , apply a blister to his back and head', and give him 'a paper of Dr James's powder' (the aspirin of the eighteenth century). As a result Isaac brought up three worms, one a foot long, and after two more doses, two more worms. Four days later Willis saw Isaac in a market, seven miles from home, very well, selling sheep. Willis's successes had led to an appointment at a Lincoln hospital, where he took a special interest in mad patients. Presently he set up a private lunatic asylum near Stamford.

His early methods were standard for the time (purges, bleeding, low diet), but included establishing a domination over his patients by staring at them. 'His piercing eye seemed to read their hearts and divine their thoughts as they formed and before they were even uttered. In this way he gained control over them which he used as a means of cure.'

The King was temporarily lucid on the day Willis arrived, and showed that he well understood the significance of his being transferred from normal doctors to a lunatic doctor. 'He told one of his pages, that as Dr Willis was now come, he could never more shew his face again in the country that he would leave it for ever, and return to Hanover.'

By now the two best known incidents of the King's first madness had already occurred. During one he left his carriage in Windsor Park to hold a conversation with an oak tree, believing it was the King of Prussia. During the other he pulled the Prince of Wales from his chair and flung him against a wall. He was also violent to his pages, kicking one and pulling his hair, and was regularly delirious. His doctors had treated him with James's powder and 'Bark' (quinine). When violent they had tied him to his bed.

Willis's treatment was more of the same, with the addition of massive doses of tartar emetic, blistering and the straight waistcoat. He told the King's equerry, Robert Fulke Greville, that he 'broke in' his patients like 'horses in a manège'. When he arrived with his son, John, who was also a doctor, they brought with them three 'physical assistants.' That evening, after the King had obstinately refused to abandon some of his delusions, they put him into the waistcoat. From then onwards the King 'repeatedly said that he would never more wear the crown, and desired that his eldest son might be sent for'.

To others the Willises seemed very different in character. Fanny Burney wrote that they were 'most incomparable people. They take a pleasure, that brightens every particle of their countenances, in communicating what is good, and they soften all that is bad with the most sedulous kindness.'

Such optimism was what the Prime Minister, the younger Pitt, needed, to prevent the passing of a Regency Bill which would give power to the Prince of Wales (the future George IV) who would then replace Pitt's Tory ministry with a Whig one. As a result the Willises became the government doctors and Francis Willis was described as 'Pitt's Poodle'. He was said to have written letters to Pitt which Pitt read to other MPs, 'giving assurances of the King's great amendment and of his immediate recovery, and this on days when [the King] had been in a straight waistcoat'. The opposition's doctors, Sir George Baker and Richard Warren (Doctor to the Prince of Wales), were as pessimistic as the Willises were optimistic.

Soon the Willises had taken complete charge of the King. One of them was constantly with him, whereas Dr Warren's visits would only last fifteen minutes. 'My father', John Willis wrote in the family journal,

'stuck up a paper in the pages room containing the following words,
"No one is to be suffered, except the pages, to go into his majesty's
room, unless introduced by, or with the leave of the Dr Willis'".'
Warren was deeply offended, considering himself 'the highest authority
. . . as the first physician'. Francis Willis was not even a member of
the Royal College of Physicians, and his son merely a graduate of
Edinburgh.

The rival doctors quarrelled about the words of the bulletins they
issued. When Warren wanted the King's night to be described as
'good', Willis insisted on the words 'very good'. They could not even
agree about the King's pulse, Warren on one occasion recording 106,
Willis 96. And they disagreed openly in front of one of several
Parliamentary committees of inquiry about who had been responsible
for having the King's legs blistered.

They were agreed that the result of this had been unfortunate, but
the Willises continued the practice, as they did the straight waistcoat.
Six more physical assistants were recruited, and in January 1789 Dr
Willis had a special chair made in which to confine the King. When
the King first saw it he 'eyed it with some degree of awe'. Afterwards
he would call it his 'Coronation Chair'. Six days later 'Dr Willis had
the King confind to his chair . . . and gave him a severe lecture on his
improper conversation, Eliza, etc [his delusion that he was really
married to Lady Elizabeth Pembroke]. H[is] M[ajest]y becoming more
loud and impatient under this lecture, Dr Willis ordered a handkerchief
to be held before his mouth, and he then continued and finished his
lecture.'

By now the Willises, father and son, had been reinforced by a second
son, Thomas Willis, rector of St George's, Bloomsbury. Thirteen years
later this clergyman, though never a doctor, was to play a more
important part in the King's second attack of madness.

Gradually, despite the Willises' treatment, the King recovered. By
March 1789, the nine physical assistants had been sent away. Many of
his pages had also been dismissed, nominally because they had 'obtained
a sort of familiarity' with the King 'which would not be pleasing to
him', but in fact because they were suspected of acting as spies for the
Prince of Wales. The Willises also left. Dr John was given a pension of
£650 for life, and Dr Francis a pension of £1,000. Francis had believed
he would get £1,500, but he more than made up for this disappointment
soon afterwards with payments of £20,000 for treating the mad queen
of Portugal. Of the three Willises the King preferred the Revd Thomas,

telling Pitt that he should be given the first vacant prebendary of Worcester, though he never was.

Thomas Willis continued to be a friend of the King's, and happened to visit him at Buckingham House in February 1801 when his second attack was beginning. Three weeks later he was asked to send for his brother, Dr John, and within two days for Dr Robert Darling, their youngest brother, as well as for four keepers from a private madhouse. Francis, the old father, was not recalled. 'He is eighty-three,' Addington, the current Prime Minister, explained, 'but he is also rough and violent'.

During the next months the Willises gained even more complete control of the King; they alone could visit him, and if Acts of Parliament had to be signed, they took them to him. Addington even asked Thomas Willis's advice about whether or not the King would agree to peace with France, and Thomas Willis's answer led to negotiations, then the Peace of Amiens. Again the Willises gave the government support by their optimistic reports on the King's chances of recovery. For the March 26th 1802 they arranged a royal Drawingroom, suggesting how recovered he was, then blistered his legs so severely at breakfast and lunch that he could not attend and reveal symptoms of madness.

As the King genuinely improved, he began violently to dislike the three brothers. Afraid of losing their power, they used a classic Catch-22 argument: his dislike of them showed that he *must* still be mad. Dr John 'assured the King that . . . abuse of men who had brought him out of very severe and dangerous fever was a proof of a remnant of the disorder'.

Nevertheless the King continued to grow better and on Sunday April 18th they saw him, without their permission, riding down the Mall on his way to Kew. The Willises set out in pursuit, in order to 'take him anew' or more simply to kidnap him. At seven o'clock next morning they and their four physical assistants laid an ambush for him outside Kew House where they expected him to call to take his son, Prince Adolphus, riding. When he failed to arrive they went to find him at the Prince of Wales's house.

'Sire, I will not forgive you whilst I live,' the King told Thomas Willis, and tried to escape, but found John Willis and his four physical assistants waiting for him outside the door. They took him to Prince Adolphus's house where for a month they kept him prisoner. He had to smuggle one note to Adolphus in an official envelope addressed to Lord Hawkesbury, and one to the Queen in the drawer of a desk which he sent her. Again, despite massive doses of tartar emetic, cupping and bleeding, the King recovered. The three Willises were rewarded with £5,000 (Dr John), £3,000 (Dr Robert) and £2,000 (the Revd Thomas).

When, in 1804, the King had a further relapse, Addington once more sent for the Willises, providing them with an order from the Cabinet office which gave them total charge, but this time they found the Dukes of Kent and Cumberland at the King's door, blocking their way. The dukes told the Willises that they had promised the King that if he were ever ill again they would 'use every means in our power to prevent any one of the Willis family from having a place about him'. The King recovered without the Willises.

Astonishingly, however, in 1810, at the start of his final madness, Perceval, the Prime Minister, once again summoned Dr Robert Darling Willis. By June 1st 1811, he was in complete charge; that day the Queen's Council ordered that 'nobody be suffered to communicate with the King but with the consent of Dr Willis and in his presence'. Later the same year Dr John Willis reappeared, and in November the Archbishop of Canterbury went in person to Windsor to see that the order giving the Willises total control of access to the King was being observed. For the next nine years, until the King's death, the Willises remained in charge of his case, his physicians only allowed to treat or speak to him if a Willis was present.

It was not till 1966 and 1968 that two articles in the *British Medical Journal* attempted any scientific posthumous diagnosis of the King's illness. In 1969 Ida Macalpine and Richard Hunter expanded these articles into their convincing book, *George III and the Mad-Business*. The King was not 'mad', they argue, but suffering from the hereditary condition known as porphyria. Not only do all the more obvious symptoms of his case (initial infection of the upper respiratory tract, later paralysis, delusions and agonizing pains) 'read like a textbook case' of porphyria, but on six occasions his urine was described as 'dark', 'bilious' or 'bloody', symptoms of the condition from which it takes its name.

— 9 —

George IV and William IV

George, Prince of Wales (the future George IV), eldest son of George III, first held court at Carlton House. This large house covered the area now occupied by Wellington Place, the Athenaeum Club, the Institute of Directors and part of Carlton House Terrace. It had a fine garden, laid out by William Kent in the 1730s when it had been owned by an earlier Prince of Wales, Prince George's grandfather, Prince Frederick. Now, in 1783, it was given to Prince George at his coming of age, thus at last releasing him from Buckingham House, as part of an arrangement which also settled his debts of £29,000 and gave him an income of £62,000. North, the Prime Minister, had asked for £100,000, but George III had had it reduced to this inadequate amount.

From his childhood Prince George and his father did not agree. The Prince later claimed that, 'The King hates me, he always did from seven years old,' and Lord Brougham considered the King's hatred of the Prince 'scarcely betokening a sound mind'. He was consistently mean to his son when he was a child on the principle that 'persons should feel their situation will *by degrees improve* [author's italics], and particularly young persons'. And he became increasingly dismayed not only by the Prince's debts but by his love life.

This had begun when Prince George fell passionately in love with a young Maid of Honour, Mary Hamilton. He sent her a description of his own looks which included 'fine teeth, a tolerable good chin, but the whole countenance is too round. I forgot to add very uggly ears. . . .' and of his character which ended: 'Now for his vices, or rather let us call them weaknesses – too subject to give loose or vent to his passions of every kind, too subject to be in a passion . . . he is rather too fond of Wine and Women.'

Before the year was over he had abandoned Miss Hamilton in favour of 'Perdita' Robinson, an actress who would drive about in her carriage dressed as an Amazon. When this passion also cooled George III had to spend £5,000 buying back from Mrs Robinson the many indiscreet love letters which the Prince had sent her.

Soon after Prince George moved into Carlton House he further infuriated his father by openly supporting the Whigs against Pitt in the general election of 1784. In its gardens he gave a fête with nine marquees and four bands to celebrate the personal victory of Charles James Fox, his own great friend and Pitt's enemy. But it was not till later the same year that the Prince embarked on his best known act of parental provocation, his long affair with Mrs Fitzherbert.

She was a respectable, twice-widowed Roman Catholic. The husband from whom she took her name had died of a chill caught while taking a bath after he had overheated himself when helping to suppress the 'No Popery' riots led by Lord George Gordon. Prince George was so besotted with Mrs Fitzherbert that he would go to Fox's mistress, 'tell her of his love, cry by the hour, beat his brow, tear his hair, roll on the floor and fall into fits of hysterics'. On December 15th 1785 he and Mrs Fitzherbert were secretly married. 'It was at the Prince's own earnest and repeated solicitations,' Lord Holland wrote, 'not at Mrs Fitzherbert's request, that any ceremony was resorted to. She knew it to be invalid in law; she thought it nonsense and told the Prince so.' Though Mrs Fitzherbert was right – the Royal Marriage Act forbade any member of the royal family to marry a commoner without royal consent – the Prince did not consider it nonsense as later events showed. When his debts soon afterwards grew too serious he closed Carlton House, sold his carriages and horses, sacked his servants and went with Mrs Fitzherbert to Brighton. Here he built the Royal Pavilion, with a house for her in its grounds. Here for the best part of eight years they lived in modest domesticity.

In 1793, however, the Prince's debts (now £370,000) forced him to do what his father had long wanted: agree to a legal marriage. Next year he ended his affair with Mrs Fitzherbert. But he had already begun to live with a new mistress: Lady Jersey. And he chose the wife he was being forced to take with 'childish petulance. . . . He had to marry: he did not care: he would take the first and most obvious frump from the serried frumpish ranks of German Princesses.'

Princess Caroline of Brunswick, though short, was not a total frump. Her looks were pleasant and she had piled-up long fair hair. But the Prince asked for a glass of brandy when he first saw her, and when he had left the room the Princess told Lord Malmesbury that she found the Prince 'très gros'. (He weighed seventeen stone). At their wedding he 'looked like death and full of confusion', and he probably only slept with her for the single night during which their daughter Charlotte was conceived. Soon they were occupying separate apartments at Carlton House and communicating by letter. Within six months the Prince –

who was anyway aggrieved that, in spite of his marriage, his debts had not been fully settled – was living again with Lady Jersey, and by 1800 he was being seen with Mrs Fitzherbert at the opera (she had taken the precaution of getting the Pope's permission.)

If the Prince's treatment of his wife was ruthless, for a total of twenty-five years he suffered the consequences. When he became Regent in 1811 Whig politicians, disappointed that he had not called them to office, used his behaviour towards her to rouse general anger with him. Largely as a result of their propaganda he became one of the most unpopular of all royal figures, often not daring to appear in public for fear of hooting mobs. For a hundred years historians agreed with the Whig verdict, treating the Princess as victim and the Prince as villain. But after his initial rejection of her, the Princess was equally provocative. According to Lady Douglas she was soon claiming to have a son living with her who might be hers by the Prince, and thus heir to the throne. This child was found by a committee which conducted what was known as the Delicate Investigation to have been adopted by the Princess from a woman who had called at her door to ask for work for her husband. William Austin, as the boy was named, died in 1849 in a lunatic asylum. On one well-reported occasion when the Prince was entertaining the Tsar and the King of Prussia at the opera, the Princess appeared suddenly in a neighbouring box. And in 1814 she went abroad where she spent five years travelling the courts of Europe and the Middle East, publicly advertising her rejection.

With her went one Pergami, a good-looking Italian who had changed his name from Bergami because Pergami sounded more aristocratic, whom she had promoted from servant to Chamberlain and lover. In spite of this, when her husband became George IV she returned home to claim her rights as queen. The King postponed his coronation in order to have a bill passed which would dissolve the marriage, but when this failed he held the ceremony without her. At five-thirty that afternoon she arrived at Westminster Abbey, but was refused entry at each of its doors because she had no spectator's ticket.

Even when dead she continued to persecute him. The London mob took charge of her funeral coach and coffin and drew it through the city instead of letting it be taken down the Thames, cheering it like an election float.

Meanwhile George had not been celibate. Apart from his long-standing mistresses, eleven others are known by name. When he finally left Mrs Fitzherbert he continued to favour middle-aged or elderly aristocrats, first Lady Hertford, then for the rest of his life Lady Conyngham.

The Prince's supposedly scandalous life took from him the credit of standing at the country's head during a period of great national success, in particular the victorious conclusion of the Napoleonic Wars. Nevertheless whenever there was an excuse he organized lavish celebrations at Carlton House. In 1811, theoretically in honour of the Bourbons, but in fact to celebrate the Regency, he entertained two thousand guests there to a sumptuous all-night banquet. In 1814 he not only organized an even more splendid feast at Carlton House but a public fête which spread over St James's Park, Green Park, Hyde Park, and included Mr Sadler's ascent by balloon (he was picked up on the Essex coast) and a re-enactment of the Battle of Trafalgar on the Serpentine.

George IV's love life, his personal grossness and his indulgence in cherry brandy continue to make him easy to laugh at. He was also wildly extravagant, though wrongly accused of heavy gaming. Only when he succeeded to the throne were his extravagances brought under control and his debts liquidated by that mysterious figure, surgeon-turned-courtier, Sir William Knighton. Even his acknowledged talent for collecting seems to have been in part pathological. When he died, five hundred of his pocketbooks were found around his palaces, all containing small sums of money which in total made £10,000. But his passion brought the country important benefits. Books and pictures he collected form the basis of the British Library, the National Gallery and the Wallace Collection. As for his building, Buckingham Palace and Windsor castle as we know them today were remade for him, and but for modern philistinism London would have at least one fine street, Nash's great avenue leading from Carlton House to Regent's Park. Less often remembered in his defence is his personal charm which so impressed all who knew him. He was an inspired mimic, his subjects ranging from Dr Johnson's black servant to his own mad father.

'King George had not been dead three days before everybody discovered that he was no loss, and King William a great gain,' Greville wrote. The new king 'proposed to all the household . . . to keep their places. . . . He soon afterwards, however, dismissed most of his equerries, that he might fill their places with members of his own family.' These were the FitzClarences, his nine illegitimate children (called by Greville 'the bastards') mothered for him by the successful actress, Mrs Jordan, with whom he had lived at Bushey Park for twenty years. He had only left her because he was short of money and needed a richer woman.

Before that, for the whole of his early life, the Duke of Clarence, as he had then been, was a seaman: and in 1827 he had been made Lord High Admiral of the Fleet. But since he had by then been ashore for almost forty years the appointment was meant to be honorary. This was not what the Duke understood, and the following year on his own authority he took the Channel Fleet to sea. Soon he was forced to resign but not before he had 'distinguished himself by making absurd speeches . . . and by a general wildness that was thought to indicate incipient insanity'.

When he succeeded to the throne he behaved with similar good-natured irresponsibility. He had been King for less than a month when he set out on his own for 'a ramble' about the streets. Outside White's in St James's Street a woman recognized and kissed him. A mob soon gathered and he had to be rescued by two Privy Councillors 'who got shoved and kicked about to their inexpressible wrath' but managed to get him back to the palace 'amid shouting, bawling and applause'.

And he continued to make long, rambling and often embarrassing speeches – thirty years earlier he had given the House of Lords a succession of lectures on the wickedness of adultery, in the presence of his brothers, all of whose private lives were notorious. It was largely for his speechmaking that he became known as 'Silly Billy'. But by accident, or because of an underlying good sense which his manner did not suggest, he handled the great political crisis of his reign, the Reform Bill of 1832, wisely, agreeing to make as many peers as necessary to enable the House of Lords to pass it, but writing a letter to the individual lords which made this unnecessary.

Family quarrels were the most dramatic events at court during his seven-year reign. Towards the end of the previous reign his younger brother, the Duke of Cumberland, had taken charge of the two regiments of Horse Guards. The Duke of Wellington had realized how inappropriate this was during the Catholic Emancipation disturbances when the Duke of Cumberland had been 'organising mobs to go down to Windsor to frighten Lady Conyngham and the King' but had also been in charge of the Horse Guards 'who would naturally have been called out to suppress any tumult'. Together, William and Wellington forced the Duke of Cumberland to resign his command.

The King had a confirmed hatred for his brother Edward's widow, Victoria, the Duchess of Kent. At his birthday dinner at Windsor in 1836, with more than a hundred guests present, and the Duchess sitting next to him, he made a speech which told her what he thought of her. 'I trust to God,' he said, 'that my life may be spared for nine months longer, after which period, in the event of my death, no regency would take place. I should then have the satisfaction of leaving the royal authority to the personal exercise of that young lady (pointing to the Princess [her daughter, the future Queen Victoria]), the heir presumptive of the Crown, and not in the hands of a person now near me, who is surrounded by evil advisers and who is herself incompetent to act with propriety in the station in which she would be placed. . . .' 'Princess Victoria burst into tears,' Greville continued, 'and the whole company were aghast . . . the Duchess announced her immediate departure and ordered her carriage. . . .'

But the King's life was spared long enough to thwart the Duchess. Princess Victoria came of age on May 24th next year and William died four weeks later.

Frances Twysden, Countess of Jersey (1753–1821)

Frances Twysden, Countess of Jersey, was forty and a grandmother when she became the mistress of George, Prince of Wales, the future George IV. She was the daughter of an Irish bishop, and perhaps for that reason always referred to the Prince as 'the Primate'. At this time (1793) the Prince was still involved with Mrs Fitzherbert. Two years later when he married Princess Caroline, Lady Jersey was appointed one of her Ladies-in-Waiting.

Lady Jersey was a skilled player of the harp. She and her husband, who was seventeen years her senior, were both keen performers in amateur theatricals. Queen Charlotte described her as 'little and bewitching'. Robert Huish (when she was safely nine years dead) was less polite. She might, he wrote, 'be considered in the human race, as the type of the serpent – beautiful, bright, and glossy in its exterior – in its interior poisonous and pestiferous'.

He first tells how she employed a youth to trail the Prince to a house on the road to Lewes where he was conducting an affair with a beautiful young rival by the name of Lucy Howard. The Prince, he writes, found the boy in the garden and beat him so severely that he was a cripple for life.

He then suggests that Lady Jersey played a key part in destroying the Prince's marriage, by extracting from the Princess the admission that she was in love with a certain Prince of Brunswick and 'loved one little finger of that individual far better than she should love the whole person of the Prince of Wales'. This she passed on to the Prince. Though this story can be faulted in detail, Lady Jersey was doubtless jealous, and may well have told tales to the Prince which made him feel morally justified in rejecting a wife he found physically repulsive. In mitigation, Huish claims that Lady Jersey believed that the Prince had made an arrangement by which, if he married, she should remain his accepted mistress.

Lady Jersey came with the Prince and Princess on their honeymoon, and during its second part, which they spent at Kemshott House near Basingstoke, was the only other woman in the party. Soon afterwards Lady Jersey is said to have stolen letters which Princess Caroline had given her for forwarding to Germany and passed them to the Queen, well aware that one of them contained offensive comments on the Queen.

Once the Prince and Princess had parted, as they did soon after their honeymoon, his connection with Lady Jersey became open, and at the Princess's request she ceased to be one of her Ladies-in-Waiting. In the autumn of 1796 the Prince and Lady Jersey spent several weeks at Bognor. That October she wrote that he was 'going to fly round Dorsetshire, make a nest for me and my young ones and perch in London'. In Dorset he found Crichel House and here they spent the winter together. Within two years, however, he had grown tired of her and returned to Mrs Fitzherbert.

Colonel Sir John MacMahon (d. 1818)

In 1812 Colonel John MacMahon, the bastard child of an Irish butler and a chambermaid, was appointed Paymaster of the Widows' Pensions, a position which carried a salary of £2,000 a year, but which involved no work and was described as 'one of the snuggest sinecures in the gift of the Crown'. It was due to have been abolished on the death of the previous holder. About MacMahon, Thomas Raikes wrote in his journal that MacMahon was an obsequious little man with a red pimpled face, always ready to perform any commission however complicated, for his master, the Prince Regent. Robert Huish called him 'perveyor general of female beauty to the royal harem'. 'The military exploits' of this 'panderer to [the Prince's] worst passions . . . could be contained in a single page' and his 'actual service' had consisted entirely of 'putting on and putting off his uniform'.

When members of Parliament objected to MacMahon's appointment, MacMahon, who was himself an MP, said he had fought for seven years in the American War of Independence, and would be a Lieutenant General if he had not been forced by ill-health to retire. Moreover his job was not a sinecure for he had 'the affairs of sixteen hundred widows to attend to'. In answer to this Mr Whitbread 'archly declared that if the gallant colonel could produce a voucher from the ladies, that he had performed his duty to their entire satisfaction' he would think MacMahon deserved his salary, and the House of Commons at a second reading deprived him of it. Two months later the Prince appointed MacMahon his private secretary, at the same salary. Since he was also Keeper of the Privy Purse to the Prince at £1,000 a year, auditor of the Duchy of Cornwall at £1,000 a year and secretary to the Prince as a duke at £500 a year, he was receiving an annual total of £4,500.

As an example of MacMahon's usefulness to the Prince Huish gives a long and circumstantial account of his management of the seduction of the two daughters of a country clergyman. MacMahon first met them when they joined the coach to Bath, and soon charmed father and daughters with his 'easy familiarity', his eyes meanwhile 'feasting on the youthful beauty so unexpectedly presented to his view'. From Bath he wrote to the Prince:

> ... I hasten to inform your Royal Highness, that chance has thrown me into the company of two most lovely girls, the daughters of an indigent curate, and who, from their apparent simplicity and ignorance of the world, may be soon brought to comply with the wishes of your Royal Highness. I shall immediately devise some plan by which they may be induced to visit the metropolis, and the remainder of my task will then not be difficult of execution. The prize is too valuable to be lost sight of ... from the knowledge which I possess of your royal taste, the elder will be the object of your choice.

MacMahon first lured father and daughters to London with the promise of a nearby vicarage, then provided them with temporary lodgings at the house of Mrs Hamilton, a well-known procuress, in Gloucester Place, New Road. To Mrs Hamilton's came many well-bred gentlemen, among whom was a mysterious Colonel Fox. They were naïve enough to fail to notice that he either came on his own or accompanied at most by MacMahon.

One morning MacMahon arrived unexpectedly to tell Mrs Hamilton that she must visit her attorney to discuss important business. He would stay with the younger girl while she went with the elder. On the way Mrs Hamilton made an excuse to call at Taylor's shoe shop in Bond Street, 'that infamous resort of titled demireps and fashionable prostitutes'. Here by coincidence, who should they meet but Colonel Fox, who gallantly offered to protect the girl while Mrs Hamilton went to see her lawyer. 'In this hour rang the knell of her maiden innocence,' Huish wrote, and concluded: 'We will draw a veil over the remaining part of this tragical story.'

When his wife died, MacMahon took to drink and retired to the country, dying soon afterwards worth £90,000. According to Creevey he earned £10,000 of this in a single payment from Lady Beaumont, for having her husband made an earl.

Ellis Cornelia Knight (1757–1837)

Cornelia Knight was a learned spinster of forty-eight when, in 1805, she was appointed to the household of King George III's, Queen Charlotte. Her father, an admiral, had died when she was eighteen and she had spent the next twenty-five years travelling around Europe with her peevish mother. They dressed in drapery, suggesting to Mrs Thrale statues which had stepped off their pedestals. The high point of this long tour was a period at Naples where Miss Knight was known to the officers of the Mediterranean Fleet as 'the charming poet-laureate', and became a good friend of Nelson and Lady Hamilton.

She published two novels, set in Roman times, which were admired but made little money. Of the first, *Dinarbas*, Fanny Burney wrote that the principles it recommended were 'both pure and lofty. It is not a work which you will read quickly through, or with ardour, but it is one, I think, of which you will not miss a word.' Fanny (who was the Queen's Second Keeper of the Robes at this time) was sure that the princesses 'could read nothing more chastely fitted for them'. Miss Knight's second novel, *Flaminius* was admired in manuscript by Horace Walpole and dedicated to him. She also began the journal on which she later based the autobiography for which she is remembered.

Her third book, *A Description of Latium, or La Campagna di Roma*, appeared in 1805, the year in which Queen Charlotte (either because the first had been dedicated to her or because she remembered how Fanny Burney had admired it) recruited Miss Knight. Cornelia Knight thus became the second lady novelist to attend on the Queen. Her appointment was more of a success than Fanny's had been, perhaps because its conditions were more generous. She was paid £300 a year (Fanny got £200), was lodged at Windsor in a house of her own, and had no 'particular employment' except to be present at the Queen's 'evening parties, when invited, and always on Sundays and red-letter days, and be ready to attend upon her in the morning when required to do so'. But Miss Knight, like Fanny, became discontented. 'Perhaps . . . my pride had been somewhat hurt', she wrote 'by the Queen not always . . . feeling properly my situation'. She also wished 'for a more active and more important employment than that which I had at Windsor, dull, uninteresting and monotonous'.

She was in this frame of mind when she was offered a position with the seventeen-year-old Princess Charlotte, daughter of the Prince Regent. For five pages Miss Knight describes how she attempted to get the Queen positively to order her to accept this offer, so that she would not be blamed for taking it. Her manoeuvres included numerous interviews and the exchange of many letters with the princesses, the old King's doctor and the Prince Regent, and one fit of hysterics. In the end she achieved precisely the opposite of what she wanted, by tactlessly pointing out to the Queen that the Queen would be £300 better off by not having to pay her salary and by being free to let her house. What was more, to help the Queen out of her financial difficulties 'in respect of Frogmore and the Farm', she would lend the Queen £1,000 free of interest. Hardly surprisingly, the Queen was deeply offended and wrote a letter which made Miss Knight ill for two days. But she accepted the appointment, writing to the *Morning Post* when it was announced to point out that she was not to be the Princess's 'sub-governess' but one of her 'ladies companions'.

About Warwick House, where Miss Knight now went to keep the Princess company, she wrote: 'Nothing could more resemble a convent'. Everything done there was to promote the sending of the Princess 'back to the nursery'. The Prince Regent told Miss Knight that while he lived Princess Charlotte must 'be subject to me as she is at present, if she were thirty, or forty, or five-and-forty'. On another occasion he talked to Miss Knight for a long while against his wife, 'and the little regard she had shown Princess Charlotte when a child, and how by her negligence there was a mark of the small-pox on the Princess Charlotte's nose, having left her hands at liberty, whereas *he* used continually to watch beside her cradle. He said very severe things of the Princess of Wales in every way, and even accused her of threatening to declare that Princess Charlotte was not his daughter.'

George IV by Wilkie

Queen Victoria, 1840, by Hayter

As the year passed Miss Knight began to accompany the Princess on more exciting occasions. At the opening of the new Military College at Sandhurst, 'when the Queen was about to depart, the Prince Regent was not to be found, and we afterwards learned that he, with the Duke of York, Prince of Orange (father), and many others, were under the table. The Duke of York hurt his head very seriously against a wine cellaret. In short, it was a sad business.'

But the great drama of Miss Knight's time with Princess Charlotte centred around the Princess's engagement to the Hereditary Prince of Orange. The Prince Regent told Miss Knight of this when it was still secret, asking her to remain with the Princess until the marriage and give the Princess 'good advice, particularly against flirting'.

Read on its own, Miss Knight's account of what followed suggests that the engagement failed because the Princess wished the Prince of Orange to promise that under no circumstances would he force her to live in Holland. But this hardly accounts for the Prince Regent's actions when the engagement was broken off, when he dismissed Miss Knight along with all the Princess's other ladies and ordered the Princess to be confined to Cranbourne Lodge, a remote building in Windsor Forest. Nor perhaps for the Princess's escape that night from Warwick House and attempt to reach her mother, which failed when she was pursued and brought back by the Bishop of Salisbury.

Other evidence strongly suggests that the engagement failed because Princess Charlotte had fallen in love with an obscure member of the Prussian royal family, Prince Frederick Augustus, with whom she had had secret meetings at Warwick House which had been connived at and perhaps arranged by Miss Knight.

In disgrace, but as always considering herself ill-used, Miss Knight returned to the continent, where Sidney Smith once visited her in Paris, and found her 'a very disagreeable affected woman, living up two pairs of stairs and looking very ugly'. She died in 1837, the year in which Princess Charlotte, her one-time royal mistress, would have become Queen of England had she not died in childbirth.

Sir William Knighton (1776–1836)

William Knighton was the best-mannered doctor Prince George (the future George IV) had ever met, the Prince said when explaining why he had given Knighton a baronetcy. Knighton had been recommended to the Prince by the Marquis of Wellesley. He came from Devon where he had studied medicine, been appointed an assistant surgeon at the Royal Naval Hospital, Plymouth, and married the daughter of a naval captain. Since then he had also practised in London as an accoucheur (his enemies called him the man midwife) and in Edinburgh before returning to London in 1809 to become one of the Prince's doctors.

Prince George was still more pleased with Knighton when Knighton came into possession of compromising papers which had belonged to the Prince's pimp, Col. John MacMahon, and instead of selling them had handed them to the Prince. Soon afterwards he promoted Knighton to be auditor of the Duchies of Cornwall and Lancaster, and, in the second year of his reign, to be his private secretary and Keeper of the Privy Purse.

When Knighton received these appointments Wellington warned him never to interfere in politics. Publicly Knighton took the Duke's advice, but for five years he went on secret missions to the continent for George. Exactly what these were is not certain since his widow burned his papers, but Knighton was probably redeeming the King's many IOUs and settling affairs with ex-mistresses.

Knighton's function at court is clearer. He controlled the King's extravagance. As early as 1823, according to Wellington, he was 'getting [the King] out of debt very quickly'. The King presently agreed that 'no goods were to be supplied or work done on account of the privy purse except upon Knighton's orders, given in writing'.

But as well as coming to depend on Knighton, the King, like a naughty wife, enjoyed being mischievous when he wasn't there. At a dinner at the Royal Lodge, Windsor, in July 1827, Greville reported that 'While the Tyrolese were dancing and singing, and there was a sort of gay uproar going on, with which the King was greatly delighted, he said, "I would give ten guineas to see Knighton walk into the room now", as if it were some master who was absent, and who should suddenly return and find his family and servants merrymaking in his absence; it indicates a strange sort of power possessed by him.'

Eighteen months later the King had grown violently resentful of this power. According to Greville he now abhorred Knighton 'with a detestation that could hardly be described. He is afraid of him, and that is the reason he hates him so bitterly. When alone with him he is more civil, but when others are present (the family, for instance) he delights in saying the most mortifying and disagreeable things to him.'

Mont Charles had told Greville that the King's

language about [Knighton] is sometimes of the most unmeasured violence – wishes he was dead, and one day when the door was open, so that the pages could hear, he said, 'I wish to God somebody would assassinate Knighton'. In this way he always speaks of him and uses him. Knighton is greatly annoyed at it, and is very seldom there. Still it appears there is some secret chain which binds them together, and which compels the King to submit to the presence of a man he detests, and induces Knighton to remain in spite of so much hatred and ill-usage.

Successful as Knighton was in managing the King's monies, he knew that there was one extravagance the King would not abandon: his mistress, Lady Conyngham. In May of 1829 Greville noted that 'the influence of Knighton and that of Lady Conyngham continue as great as ever; nothing can be done but by their permission, and they understand each other and play into each other's hands. Knighton opposes every kind of expense, except that which is lavished on her.'

Just how irksome Knighton secretly found this concession is suggested by his behaviour as soon as the King was dead, when 'by the vigilant watch he kept over the property of various kinds [he] prevented the pillage Lady Conyngham would otherwise have made'.

Once the dead King's affairs had been settled Knighton retired to the country, dying six years later. Throughout his time at court he took no private advantage of his power over the King, accepting no more than his baronetcy in honours and accumulating no private fortune.

Henry, 1st Marquess of Conyngham (1766–1832), and Elizabeth Denison, Marchioness of Conyngham (1770–1861)

Exactly when Lady Conyngham replaced Lady Hertford as George IV's favourite matronly aristocrat is not certain, but the fact was well known by 1820. This was the year in which Queen Caroline returned from abroad to claim her rights as queen, and be greeted by the London mob with wild enthusiasm. 'It is odd enough,' Greville wrote, 'Lady Hertford's windows have been broken to pieces and the frames driven in, while no assault has been made on Lady Conyngham's. Somebody asked Lady Hertford', Greville continued, '"if she had been aware of the King's admiration for Lady Conyngham", and "whether he had ever talked to her about Lady C." She replied that "intimately as she had known the King, and openly as he had always talked to her upon every subject, he had never ventured to speak to her upon that of his mistresses".'

The King's passion for his new mistress had been so intense that he was said to have lost thirty pounds in dieting to make himself more attractive. Lady Conyngham was no sylph herself but a plump lady in her late forties with five children. As long as she was his mistress, a contemporary ballad said, he would 'never need *pillows* to keep up his head'.

From 1821 the influence of the Conyngham family at court was supreme, their only rival Sir William Knighton, Keeper of the Privy Purse. The Marquess was made a Privy Councillor and Lord Steward of the Household. During a dinner one night Greville noted that 'Lady Conyngham had on her head a sapphire which belonged to the Stuarts', which the King had recovered from Prince Leopold, the widower of his dead daughter Princess Charlotte, on the grounds that it was a crown jewel. The same year, at the Royal Pavilion, Brighton, when Lady Conyngham herself gave orders for the saloon to be lighted, the King told her, 'Thank you, thank you, my dear; you always do what is right, you cannot please me so much as by doing constantly everything you please, everything to show that you are mistress here.'

The Conynghams took full advantage of their position. In London they lived in a royal house in Marlborough Row where they were 'supplied with horses, carriages etc., from the King's stables,' and where Lady Conyngham behaved 'entirely as mistress of the house'. When the King visited them there and went in to dinner he took Lady Conyngham on one arm and her daughter Elizabeth on the other. Both received 'magnificent presents ... particularly the mother has strings of pearls of enormous value'.

Eight years later Greville wrote that

The wealth she has accumulated by savings and presents must be enormous. The King continues to heap all kinds of presents upon her, and she lives at his expense; they do not possess a servant; even Lord Conyngham's valet de chambre is not properly their servant. They all have their situations in the King's household, from which they receive their pay, while they continue in the service of the Conynghams. They dine every day while in London at St James's, and when they give a dinner it is cooked at St James's and brought up to Hamilton Place in hackney coaches and in machines made expressly for the purpose.

Lady Conyngham caused a particular scandal by trying to force Lord Liverpool, the Prime Minister, to give her son's tutor, a curate named Sumner, a canonry at Windsor. Liverpool refused, so, to please her, the King appointed Sumner a Domestic Chaplain.

In 1829 Knighton, according to Greville, persuaded Lady Conyngham not to leave Windsor when the King was ill. 'At that time she was in wretched spirits and did nothing but pray from morning till night. However her conscience does not seem ever to have interfered with her ruling passion, avarice, and she went on accumulating. During the last illness wagons were loaded every night and sent away from the Castle, but what their contents were was not known, at least he did not say. All Windsor knew this.' When the King died Knighton prevented further pillaging, but by this time Lady Conyngham had accumulated a satisfactory fortune (estimated at half a million) on which she lived for another thirty-one years, dying near Tunbridge Wells at the age of ninety-one. Her husband had resigned his court positions on George IV's death, and himself died two years later.

Ernest Augustus, Duke of Cumberland, King of Hanover (1771–1851), Mr J. Sellis (d. 1810), Lady Lyndhurst and Lord Graves

At half past two in the morning of May 31st 1810 George III's fifth son, Ernest Augustus, Duke of Cumberland, was asleep in his apartments at St James's Palace when he was woken by two blows to his head. For a moment he believed he was being attacked by a bat, then he saw light glinting on a sabre (it was his own, which had been recently sharpened by his valet, a Corsican named Sellis), and realized that someone was murdering him. He tried to ring his night bell but found the bell-rope missing. Leaping from his bed, he ran towards the room of his other valet, crying 'Neale, I am murdered', receiving other blows on the head and thigh as he went – a total of seventeen, he later claimed. By the time Neale arrived with a poker the murderer had escaped and the Duke had collapsed into a chair, one thumb almost cut off where he had tried to grasp the sabre, his brain visibly pulsing through a gash in his head.

Neale and other servants now went to fetch Sellis, but found his door bolted on the inside. When they reached the second door to his room they heard curious gurgling noises inside. Entering, they saw Sellis sitting half-dressed on his bed, smiling in a benign way, his throat cut from ear to ear. Beside him was a cut-throat razor and a bowl of water tinged with blood.

The jury at the inquest on Sellis was largely composed of Whitehall and Charing Cross tradesmen, headed by Francis Place, a tailor and radical propagandist. They were therefore ill-disposed towards the Duke. He was a man of remarkable ugliness, his looks not improved by the loss of his left eye in hand-to-hand conflict at the first battle of Tournay. He had been intended from birth by his father to command the Hanoverian army, and his bravery and military abilities were well known. He had once lifted a French dragoon bodily from his horse and carried him back to camp as a prisoner. His political opinions, however, were highly reactionary; since his return to England he had been active in the House of Lords where he had violently opposed any reform of the laws against Roman Catholics. Furthermore, at the inquest on Sellis a physician gave evidence that Sellis's throat had been cut from left to right, that is, if Sellis had done it, with the razor in his right hand; but Sellis was known to be left-handed.

None the less, the jurors, after a four-hour hearing and four hours of consideration, accepted the Duke's account of the incident, and found that Sellis had committed suicide. He was buried in 'the high road' in Scotland Yard. Their verdict was based on the presumption that Sellis had tried to murder the Duke then killed himself when he had failed. Colonel Willis, Comptroller of the Household to the Prince of Wales, suggested an explanation. 'I strongly suspect,' he wrote, 'that the motives which activated Sellis . . . were the taunts and sarcasms that the Duke was constantly, in his violent, coarse manner, lavishing on Sellis's religion, who was a catholic.'

This was not the end of the matter. 'It was the fashion', wrote Miss Knight, the Queen's literary companion, 'to go and see the Duke's apartments, which for several days were left in the same state as when he was removed. The visitors discovered traces of blood, etc.' And the public continued to believe, as it had done from the start, that Sellis had been murdered by the Duke. He was said to have been found in bed with Mrs Sellis, or alternatively to have made homosexual advances to Sellis, so enabling Sellis to blackmail him. In 1813 one Henry White was fined £200 and imprisoned for fifteen months for publishing stories of this sort, but they continued to appear, and another pamphleteer was sent to prison for the same reason in 1832. In the 1930s a supposed confession of the Duke to his secretary, Captain Charles Jones, was deposited in the Royal Archives at Windsor, but the weight of contemporary evidence suggests that this is not genuine.

Meanwhile the Duke had been the subject of scandalous rumours of another sort. In 1829 a Captain Thomas Garth claimed that he held documents which proved that he had been fathered by the Duke and mothered by Princess Sophia, the Duke's sister. That Princess Sophia was Garth's mother there is no doubt. She had delivered him in the reign of George III, though the King never knew it. He was told that she was suffering from dropsy, and had been cured by roast beef, a story he would often repeat in front of those who knew the truth. But the courtier, Christopher Papendiek, was another possible father, and General Garth, an aged equerry of George III's, a still more likely one. The Princess had been infatuated with General Garth, and he was known to have had the opportunity of sleeping with her just nine months before the child was born. The only improbability in this story was, as Greville wrote, that 'he was a hideous old Devil, old enough to be her father, with a great claret mark on his face'. But this was no argument, Greville added, 'for women fall in love with anything'.

If the Duke was innocent in these two cases, he was not when, the same year, he attempted to assault Lady Lyndhurst, wife of the Lord Chancellor. Lady Lyndhurst reported the incident to Greville whom she happened to meet next day on Wimbledon Common. Although she had escaped (by ringing the bell for a servant) the Duke had stayed in her house for two or three hours, abusing the government and threatening to destroy her and her husband.

Six months later, in 1830, public opinion convicted the Duke, untried, of a second murder. The supposed victim was Lord Graves, a Lord of the Bedchamber to William IV, who was found dead with his throat cut. A number of recent newspaper articles had reported that the Duke was having an affair with Lady Graves, and though Graves had written a letter claiming to believe his wife to be innocent, it was generally supposed that the Duke had killed him from ill-defined motives of jealousy. As with Sellis, it is more likely that Graves committed suicide, even though rumours of his wife's seduction by the Duke were the underlying cause.

Next year two young ladies claimed that they were strolling beside the Thames near Hammersmith one evening when they were almost ridden down by the Duke as he galloped past along the tow path. Tom Moore's poem on this subject was published by *The Times*:

> The Duke is the lad to frighten a lass,
>   Galloping dreary Duke
> The Duke is the lad to frighten a lass,

He's an ogre to meet and the Devil to pass:
  With his charger prancing,
  Grim eye glancing,
  Chin like a mufti
  Grizzled and tufty
Galloping dreary Duke

Ye Misses, beware of the neighbourhood
  Of this galloping, dreary Duke
Avoid him all, who see no good
In being run o'er by a Prince of the Blood.
  And as no nymph is
  Fond of a grim phiz
  Fly ye new married,
  For crowds have miscarried
At sight of this dreary Duke.

The Duke maintained that he had been at Kew at the time of the incident, shooting wild duck.

During the last years of William IV's reign radical journalists began openly to suggest that the Duke would like to succeed to the throne, and that he might find it convenient to remove his niece, Princess Victoria, the heir apparent, in the way he had removed Sellis and Lord Graves. Though nothing of the sort happened, the Duke did in 1837 become King of Hanover, where by Salic law a woman could not reign. A fierce quarrel with Queen Victoria followed, in which the Duke insisted that he, as the male heir, should have inherited certain royal diamonds, and the Queen insisted on keeping them and ostentatiously wearing them. The matter was only settled twenty years later, by arbitration, which gave the then King of Hanover most of what he claimed. Meanwhile in Hanover the Duke abolished the constitution and for fourteen years ruled as an autocrat, surviving in a period during which more liberal sovereigns lost their powers or their thrones.

About his younger brother, George IV said, 'there was never a father well with his son, or husband with his wife, or lover with his mistress or a friend with his friend, that he did not try to make mischief between them'. And William IV said: 'Ernest is not a bad fellow, but if anyone has a corn he is sure to tread on it.'

Queen Victoria

Queen Victoria – who was just eighteen years old in 1837 when she succeeded her uncle, William IV – quickly showed that she meant to be queen without the help of her mother, the Duchess of Kent. The help she did accept came from her old governess, Baroness Lehzen, from Baron Stockmar, her uncle King Leopold's close adviser, and from Lord Melbourne, the Prime Minister. When Stockmar refused, as a foreigner, to be her Private Secretary, Melbourne nominally undertook the job, but the work was in practice done by Lehzen.

The Queen, Melbourne and Lehzen were together responsible for the earliest public scandal of the reign: the suspecting of Lady Flora Hastings of pregnancy when in fact she had a liver tumour. At court there were also less public scandals. Both the Lord Chamberlain, Lord Conyngham (son of George IV's mistress, Lady Conyngham), and the Lord Steward, Lord Uxbridge, installed their mistresses as servants at Buckingham Palace. Lord Uxbridge was a Paget, Lord Conyngham married a Paget and there were so many other members of the Paget family at court that it was sometimes described as 'the Paget Club'.

The Queen almost lost Lord Melbourne in 1839, but when Peel, who would have replaced him as Prime Minister, asked that her exclusively Whig Ladies-in-Waiting should be adulterated by a few Tory ones, the Queen refused and Melbourne struggled on for two more years. Even after he had resigned they continued to write to each other.

Meanwhile the Queen had married her first cousin, Prince Albert. At first she excluded him from her official work, but gradually he asserted himself, his most important early victory being the sacking of Baroness Lehzen. The next twenty years were happy ones for Victoria in which she came to rely wholly on Albert, he in turn relying on Stockmar. Albert reorganized the royal residences, selling the Royal Pavilion, Brighton, and buying new houses at Osborne on the Isle of Wight and Balmoral in Scotland. And he systematized the Queen's household, placing the traditional upstairs and downstairs indoor departments under a single 'Controller of the Household'.

The Queen was forty-two and Albert the same age when, in December 1861, he died of typhoid. She proceeded to use the rituals of mourning to institute a twenty-year sulk with God. 'He gave me great happiness,' she wrote in her journal, 'and He took it away leaving me alone to bear the heavy burden in very trying circumstances'. She met no one except her family, members of her household and occasional visiting Cabinet ministers, and even ordered the railway stations to be cleared of people when the royal train took her from Windsor to the Isle of Wight. During the whole of the rest of her reign she only spent twenty nights at Buckingham Palace. When signing informal letters she invariably described herself as 'unhappy'. At the signing of state papers she is said to have looked towards Albert's marble statue to ask for its approval.

Court life as a result became exceedingly dull. One Cabinet minister described Balmoral as a convent. Inmates met for meals then retired to their cells. The Queen's liking for cold rather than heated rooms added to the convent atmosphere. The public disapproved and the press agreed with it; when *The Times* published a particularly hostile article, she wrote defending herself. It was only very gradually that her popularity returned, helped by spontaneous sympathy when an Irish youth tried to shoot her in the grounds of Buckingham Palace, and when her son, the Prince of Wales, fell seriously ill with typhoid. Disraeli, a late replacement for Melbourne, amused her and she would occasionally meet the outside world when she took tea with the Dean of Westminster. Eventually when sixty she began to dance again, an amusement she had once much enjoyed. 'I am agreeable to see', a visiting Danish prince wrote, 'that the queen dances like a pot'.

But it was less for any change in the Queen's behaviour than because of the country's imperial position and the people's general sense of well-being that they grew to appreciate her again, recognizing how hard she worked and sympathizing with her isolated widowhood. By 1887, the year of her fiftieth jubilee, she was highly popular, and remained so till she died in 1902.

Typical of the reliable and respected members of her court during the second half of her reign were Sir Henry Ponsonby, her Private Secretary from 1867 to 1895, and Lady Antrim, her tall and elegant Lady-in-Waiting. More curious were the Munshi, the promoted Indian servant who tried to teach her Hindi, and, before him, John Brown, the Highland gillie, who became a close personal attendant. About a proposed parliamentary bill Disraeli remarked that he must first consult the two J.B.s: John Bull and John Brown.

The Queen was less successful as a mother to her eldest son. It is surprising that her stern and unimaginative attempts to fit him to follow her produced in the end a reasonably wise and successful King.

Sir John Conroy (d. 1854)

During the first two years of her reign Queen Victoria hated Sir John Conroy more violently than any other person – with the possible exception of her mother, the Duchess of Kent. Conroy was her mother's Comptroller. The Queen's many descriptions of him in her journal ranged from 'a certain wicked person' to 'that monster and demon incarnate'. Both the Duke of Wellington and Greville believed that the Duchess of Kent was Conroy's mistress. 'I said I considered he was her lover,' Greville told the Duke in 1831, 'and he said, "I suppose so"'. According to the Duke the Queen's hatred of Conroy and her mother was 'unquestionably owing to her having witnessed some familiarity between them'. The Queen read Greville's journal when she was older and professed to be shocked by such suggestions, but by then she was anxious to show respect for her dead mother.

Conroy's family came from Ireland where he owned a small estate. He had a boisterous Irish charm which his enemies disliked though some were reluctantly complimentary. 'Such an extraordinary character one will not easily find again,' King Leopold of the Belgians wrote after Conroy's death. 'What an amazing scape of a man he must have been,' Lord Melbourne said, 'to have kept three ladies at once in good humour'.

After the Duchess of Kent among Conroy's ladies came Princess Sophia, sister of George IV and William IV. Sophia also employed Conroy as her Comptroller, while he described her as his spy at court, bringing back to Kensington Palace, the residence of the Duchess of Kent, news of events at Buckingham Palace. Conroy's third supposed lady was Flora Hastings.

His aim, apart from making his fortune, was to have the Duchess of Kent made Regent whether or not her daughter, Victoria, had come of age by the time William IV died. He could then become the young Queen's Private Secretary, and incidentally get his daughter, Victoire, a position at court. He therefore tried to keep Princess Victoria apart from her uncle, William, to spread the idea that she was a sickly child who would never manage to be queen without her mother's help, and to extract promises from her that she would favour a regency and give him the offices he wanted.

In the autumn of 1835, when Victoria was ill with typhoid at Ramsgate, he brought her a document by which she promised to make him her Private Secretary. The Duchess as well as Conroy tried to force her to sign, but, supported by Baroness Lehzen, she refused.

Meanwhile the King grew increasingly angry at the way in which the Duchess and Conroy were keeping Victoria from him. He made a violent attack on them at his birthday dinner of 1836, and in May 1837 offered her £10,000 a year in her own right, her own privy purse and the right to appoint her own Ladies-in-Waiting. Conroy forced her to send a reply which accepted the money but asked for it to be paid to her mother since she wanted to remain 'in every respect as I am now'. Melbourne, for the King, offered a compromise: £4,000 for Victoria, £6,000 for the Duchess, but the Duchess and Conroy rejected this without consulting Victoria.

By June 15th negotiations had returned to the question of Conroy's future position at court. Lord Liverpool offered him the Privy Purse, but Victoria told Liverpool that she could never accept someone who had been so offensive to her. This was the situation when, five days later, William IV died. The new queen at once dismissed Conroy from her own household.

In compensation Conroy asked for £3,000 a year, the Grand Cross of the Bath, a peerage and a seat on the Privy Council. 'This is really too bad!' Melbourne told Baron Stockmar. 'Have you ever heard of such impudence!' But he advised the Queen to pay the pension and promise an Irish peerage as soon as one became vacant. In later years Conroy complained bitterly that he never received this.

Though the Queen had dismissed Conroy herself, he remained the Comptroller and close adviser of her mother, and as a result provoked Victoria into her mishandling of the Flora Hastings affair (see p.88). It was not till 1839 that the Duke of Wellington persuaded Conroy to retire from the Duchess of Kent's household and go abroad.

The Duchess's new Comptroller eventually discovered that for nine years Conroy had kept no household or private accounts for her. £50,000 given her by King Leopold was missing, and so was £10,000 from King William. Of Princess Sophia's monies, which should have been considerable, there remained only a bank credit of £1,608.

Charles Cavendish Fulke Greville (1794–1865)

Charles Greville, the diarist, was known to his friends as 'Punch' or 'Gruncher' because of his taciturn manner. One acquaintance called him 'crosser than any pair of tongs'. When old he is said to have 'wept bitterly' because he wasn't given the piece of a chicken which he fancied. Another acquaintance said: 'He would go from London to Berwick to serve a friend, but no power on earth would induce him to get out of an arm chair he had selected.' He had a long nose and a receding forehead, and kept himself scrupulously clean.

He was first introduced to royalty when he became a page at the court of George III. There were other courtiers in his family, for example Fulke Greville, an Equerry to George III often mentioned in Fanny Burney's journal. But the relation who helped him most was his maternal grandfather, the Duke of Portland, twice Prime Minister, one of the most powerful Whig aristocrats. The Duke arranged for his grandson while still a child that he should in due course acquire two well-paid government jobs. One was Secretary to the Island of Jamaica. This post became Greville's in 1828. He never went to Jamaica and paid someone else to do the work but was left with a useful £1,700 a year. He had already in 1821 become Secretary to the Privy Council, bringing him £2,500 a year.

He held both these positions till he died and they gave him an income just about sufficient to maintain him in the society which he enjoyed, though he was always in debt. More important, the second of them, Secretary to the Privy Council, prevented him from ever becoming an active politician and at the same time gave him the opportunity to know all the important politicians and courtiers of his time.

His chief recreation was horse racing. He regularly attended meetings, owned several famous horses and lost largish sums of money backing them. For a time he managed the horses of the Duke of York (brother to George IV). But he equally regularly disparaged himself in his memoirs for this frivolous occupation. How could he read a book with proper attention, he wrote, when 'the mind is far away on Newmarket Heath'?

His other preoccupations – politics and people – are what make his memoirs the most interesting source for some forty years of English political history (1820–1860), rivalling in importance those which Lord Hervey wrote a hundred years earlier. Like Hervey's, Greville's are misdescribed since they are more in the nature of a journal or diary, and consist of entries made day by day when the events were fresh. If

Greville discovered that what he had written was false he would sometimes add a note, but he did not remove his earlier entry. On August 6th 1821 he wrote, 'For ever be this day accursed which had been to me the bitterest of my existence. The particulars will remain too deeply engraved on my memory to need being written down here.' Fifteen years later in February 1836 he added, 'The devil take me if I have any idea to what this alludes.'

Greville remained a bachelor all his life. There is no suggestion that he was homosexual – he had a number of mistresses and one illegitimate son – but he had an old-womanly delight in gossip. At the same time he wished what he wrote to be as accurate as possible. His memoirs make it clear that he was a person in whom all who knew him liked to confide. At such moments he can be pictured as he was once described, his eyes 'lit up with intelligence and interest'. The final verdict of Lytton Strachey, who with Roger Fulford edited the eight volume definitive edition of Greville's *Memoirs*, was that Greville was 'not exactly a gossip, nor a busy body', but 'an extremely inquisitive person'.

Lady Flora Hastings (1806–1839)

In January 1839 Flora Hastings, a Lady of the Bedchamber to Queen Victoria's mother the Duchess of Kent, returned from a holiday in Scotland looking suspiciously pregnant. The Queen was one of the first to notice this and mentioned it obliquely to Lord Melbourne, her Prime Minister and Private Secretary. Meanwhile Lady Flora, feeling unwell, had gone to the court physician, Sir James Clark, who had prescribed '12 rhubarb and ipecacuanha pills and a liniment of camphor, soap and opium' for what he described as a derangement of the bowel, pain in the left side and a protuberance of the stomach, though he had further suspicions. Who it was who first spread such suspicions around the court is uncertain – possibly Clark, possibly Queen Victoria's confidante and ex-governess, Baroness Lehzen – but by the end of the month they were general, and the Queen wrote in her journal, 'We have no doubt that she is – to use plain words – *with child!!* Clark cannot deny the suspicion: the horrid cause of this is the monster and demon incarnate whose name I forbear to mention, but which is the 1st word of the 2nd line of this page.'

The first word of the second line was J.C., standing for Sir John Conroy, Comptroller to the Duchess of Kent. Conroy, it was thought, had shared the coach which had brought Lady Flora back to London.

Underlying the whole scandal was the Queen's desire to think the worst of her mother's Comptroller, and of Lady Flora, her mother's Lady-in-Waiting.

Sir James Clark, who was still treating Lady Flora, now asked if he might examine her 'without her stays'. She refused. A few days later he suggested that she must be secretly married and should see a second doctor. When she refused his suspicions seemed confirmed.

By February 16th the Duchess of Kent had been told and Lady Flora had been forbidden to wait. At this she changed her mind and agreed to be examined by Sir James Clark, together with Sir Charles Clarke (no relation) her family doctor. After the examination she wrote to her uncle, 'I have the satisfaction of possessing a certificate, signed by my accuser, Sir James Clark and also by Sir Charles Clarke, stating as strongly as language can state it that "there are no grounds for believing pregnancy does exist or ever has existed".' Queen Victoria sent Lady Flora an apology.

The Queen soon began to wonder whether she had been right, because the doctors were less than certain that they believed their own certificate. 'Sir C. Clarke', Victoria wrote to her mother, 'had said that though she is a virgin still that it might be possible and one could not tell if such things could not happen'. On February 23rd she visited Lady Flora who seemed to be genuinely ill, but rumours continued to circulate and in March Lady Flora's mother and brother demanded that Sir James Clark, who had started 'this atrocious conspiracy' should be dismissed. Soon afterwards *The Examiner* published Lady Flora's letter to her uncle, describing her examination and her certificate of innocence. She was now cheered whenever she appeared in public while the Queen and Melbourne were hissed.

At the beginning of April Lady Tavistock, the Lady-in-Waiting who at an early stage had told Lord Melbourne of Sir James Clark's suspicions, heard that Lady Flora's brother, Lord Hastings, planned to challenge her husband to a duel. She was persuaded to try to prevent this by seeing Lady Flora, but though she pursued her round the palace Lady Flora would not speak to her. Both Lady Flora and the Duchess of Kent now cut Lady Tavistock and the Queen again began to cut Lady Flora. These palace dramas were fully reported in the press, which also at this time published Lady Flora's mother's earlier correspondence with Melbourne.

'It is unaccountable', Greville wrote, 'how Melbourne can have permitted this disgraceful and mischievous scandal, which cannot fail to lower the character of the court in the eyes of the world.' Throughout,

Melbourne's advice had been to do as little as possible and hope that everything would go away. He continued, however, to believe that Lady Flora was pregnant and that he would be proved right. As late as June 7th, when he was told that Lady Flora was too sick to wait, he commented, '"Sick" with a significant laugh.' It was the Queen, not Melbourne, who finally decided that she must again visit Lady Flora, as she did on June 26th. Two weeks later Lady Flora was dead. A postmortem found a tumour on her liver.

Stones were thrown at the coach which the Queen sent to the funeral, the Tory MP for Canterbury fought a duel with the Whig MP for Cockermouth, and two months later Lord Hastings provided the press with a fresh batch of letters which helped to make the young Queen still more unpopular.

Louise Lehzen, Baroness (1784-1870)

Louise Lehzen (created a Hanoverian baroness by George IV in 1827) was an important figure at court during the first years of Queen Victoria's reign, when in effect she acted as the Queen's Private Secretary because Lord Melbourne, who nominally held this position, was too busy or too lazy. She had been Victoria's governess since the Princess was five, had helped her to make and dress a hundred and thirty-two period dolls and had encouraged her to be interested in history. It was Lehzen who had engineered the well-known scene in which Victoria is supposed to have learned for the first time that she would probably be queen. Lehzen had slipped into one of Victoria's history books a genealogical table. Victoria studied it, burst into tears, then announced, 'I will be good.'

Lehzen's father was a clergyman of Coburg. Here his daughter had acquired the lifelong habit of chewing caraway seeds. She treated Victoria with upright sternness. The Queen responded by loving her governess, and it was years before she realized what an inadequate education she had given her. But Lehzen deserved some of Victoria's gratitude. She had been her ally against Sir John Conroy, her mother's Comptroller, and had been present during Victoria's typhoid attack at Ramsgate, when Conroy had tried to force the Princess to promise him the position of her Private Secretary.

On the evening of the day when William IV died Victoria wrote in her journal: 'My *dear* Lehzen will *always* remain with me as my friend.' She created for Lehzen the position of Lady Attendant on the Queen.

At Buckingham Palace where she soon moved she had a new door made between her bedroom and Lehzen's. By the spring of the following year she was writing in her journal of 'my ANGELIC, dearest mother, Lehzen, who I do so love! . . . the most estimable and precious treasure I possess and EVER SHALL POSSESS.' Lehzen's notepaper carried at its head the picture of a little golden train, with the caption, 'I am coming'. Whenever Victoria called she came.

As long as Melbourne was Prime Minister he, Lehzen and the Queen formed an inner council, Melbourne managing the country, Lehzen the court. In Greville's opinion it was Victoria's fear that she would lose Lehzen which caused the so-called bedchamber crisis, in which the Queen refused to let Peel replace any of her Whig Ladies-in-Waiting with Tory ones. It was probably Lehzen who encouraged the Queen to believe that Lady Flora Hastings was pregnant, suspecting that it was her enemy, Sir John Conroy, who had deflowered her.

Even when Victoria married Prince Albert, Lehzen at first retained her power, Albert keeping his feelings about Lehzen from Victoria. The real cause of these was the way in which Victoria would exclude him from matters of state which she discussed with Lehzen and Melbourne. 'Rested and read despatches, some of which I read to Albert,' the Queen wrote in her journal, and on another occasion, 'Albert helped me with the blotting paper when I signed'. In letters to his adviser, Baron Stockmar, Albert described Lehzen as 'the house dragon spitting fire' and 'the yellow lady', a reference to her frequent attacks of jaundice. And he complained to Melbourne when he learned that, in an attempt to keep the Whigs in power, Lehzen had spent £15,000 in bribes at the 1841 general election. But it was only when Victoria had had their first child that he risked an open attack on her, accusing her of mismanaging the nursery and making the Princess Royal seriously ill. Lehzen had allowed Sir James Clark to put the child on a diet of nothing except chicken soup and asses' milk, meanwhile poisoning her with calomel. 'I shall have nothing more to do with it,' Albert wrote to Victoria. 'Take the child away and do as you like and if she dies you will have it on your conscience.' To Stockmar he wrote, 'Lehzen is a crazy, common, stupid intriguer, obsessed with lust of power . . . There can be no improvement till Victoria sees Lehzen as she is.'

When Stockmar threatened to resign, Victoria gave way and Albert arranged for Lehzen to go to Germany. She left without saying goodbye to Victoria. But they continued to write to each other, and they met twice abroad. 'Saw my poor old Lehzen,' Victoria wrote in 1862, 'she is grown so old'.

Christian Frederick Stockmar, Baron (1787–1863)

Christian Frederick Stockmar, a native of the small German state of Coburg, trained in medicine, and first came into contact with Coburg's rulers during the last years of the Napoleonic Wars when he was an army doctor. At this time he so impressed Prince Leopold, brother of Ernest the reigning duke, that Leopold made him his doctor. In 1816 when Leopold became engaged to the Prince Regent's daughter, Princess Charlotte, he summoned Stockmar to England, and Stockmar was with the Princess the following year when she died in childbirth. She spoke her last words to him: 'Stocky, they have made me drunk.'

Leopold now promoted Stockmar to be his Secretary, Keeper of the Privy Purse and Comptroller, and for the next fourteen years he was the Prince's closest adviser, helping him to decide against accepting the throne of Greece and in favour of becoming King of the Belgians. Leopold then made Stockmar a baron, but Stockmar decided that, as a foreigner, he should not hold official positions in Leopold's new Belgian court. However, he remained with Leopold in Brussels and was responsible for bringing Leopold's nephew, the future Prince Consort, to study there. Already he and Leopold were probably planning a marriage between this nephew and Leopold's niece, the future Queen Victoria.

In 1837 Stockmar came to England to give Victoria advice during the traumatic last days of William IV's reign, when Sir John Conroy was plotting to have his employer, the Duchess of Kent, made Regent. It was because of Stockmar's help in defeating this plot that Victoria ever afterwards trusted him. He stayed for a year and she would have liked to make him her Private Secretary, but again as a foreigner he refused.

He returned in 1840, however, in time for her marriage to Albert, and for the next seventeen years he was the grey eminence behind the English throne, remaining the Prince Consort's closest friend, and, once Lord Melbourne and Baroness Lehzen had gone, becoming the Queen's most influential adviser. Though he had a wife and daughter in Coburg, he spent the greater part of most years in England, arriving in the autumn and not leaving till the spring. At Buckingham Palace,

Windsor Castle and Osborne he had his own rooms reserved for him and he moved as the court moved.

One of the jobs Albert gave him was to report on the organization of the royal household. He found chaos: colossal overmanning, petty theft of many kinds and the complete absence of any proper chain of responsibility.

'The housekeepers, pages, housemaids, etc., are under the authority of the Lord Chamberlain', he wrote, 'all the footmen, livery-porters, and under-butlers, by the strangest anomaly, under that of the Master of the Horse . . . and the rest of the servants, such as the clerk of the kitchen, the cooks, the porters, etc., are under the jurisdiction of the Lord Steward. Yet these ludicrous divisions not only extend to persons, but they extend likewise to things and actions. The Lord Steward, for example, finds the fuel and lays the fire, and the Lord Chamberlain lights it.' Stockmar described what happened if a scullery window or cupboard door needed mending: 'A requisition is prepared and signed by the chief cook, it is then counter-signed by the Master of the Household, thence it is taken to the Lord Chamberlain's Office, where it is authorised, and then laid before the Clerk of the Works, under the office of Woods and Forests.

'As neither the Lord Chamberlain, nor the Master of the Horse, have a regular deputy residing in the palace,' Stockmar continued, 'more than two thirds of all the male and female servants are left without a master in the house. They can come on and go off duty as they choose, they can remain absent for hours and hours on their days of waiting, or they may commit any excess or irregularity: there is nobody to observe, to correct or to reprimand them.'

When an intruder broke into the palace – as a boy named Jones had done in 1840, being found at one o'clock in the morning under a sofa in the room next to the Queen's – Stockmar showed that there was no courtier or servant who could be held responsible.

His solution, which the Prince Consort accepted, was to promote the resident Master of the Household and persuade the heads of the other three departments to delegate to him the charge of their palace staff.

In general Stockmar's aim was to increase the power of the English monarchy by turning it into a constitutional one, no longer aligned to a particular party. In this he was not proposing a return to tradition. There was no precedent among Victoria's immediate predecessors, William IV, George IV or George III, let alone her more remote ones, for her acting as an impartial political umpire. Stockmar's instrument for transforming her role was the Prince Consort. 'Be you therefore the constitutional genius of the Queen,' he wrote to Albert. To Stockmar, as much as to anyone, we owe the constitutional monarchy we have today. By persuading Victoria to abandon obvious political interference, he opened the way for her successors to give up all except nominal power.

The insular English press disliked Stockmar, describing him typically as 'intriguer Stockmar, the agent of Jesuit Leopold'. And Gladstone called him 'a mischievous old prig'. But Sir Robert Morier, a distinguished diplomat, considered that Stockmar's was 'the noblest and most beautiful political life which this century has seen'.

William Lamb, 2nd Viscount Melbourne (1779–1848)

'Melbourne too idle', was Charles Greville's opinion of William Lamb, Lord Melbourne, when Melbourne was Home Secretary during the public disturbances of the early 1830s. It is a verdict which historians have generally supported. Certainly when Victoria came to the throne and Melbourne agreed to be her Private Secretary (after Baron Stockmar had refused) he left the practical work to Victoria's ex-governess, Baroness Lehzen. In his defence he could claim that he was overworked since by then he was also Prime Minister.

In the earlier years of the century Melbourne had been a Whig Member of Parliment of no great distinction. In 1829 he had moved to the House of Lords when he inherited his title. His private life had been less conventional. He had parted from, then divorced his bad-tempered wife, Caroline, and subsequently been twice named as co-respondent in divorce cases, the second time by the husband of the early feminist, Caroline Norton. Despite his denials, Melbourne certainly had a long affair with Mrs Norton.

He became Prime Minister for the first time in 1834, and was again Prime Minister in 1837 when William IV died. It was now that he took upon himself the responsibility of guiding the young Queen Victoria. He first called on her at Kensington Palace at nine a.m. on June 20th, the same morning that her uncle had died. From then onwards he saw her at least twice a day, wrote to her or received letters from her two or three times a day and dined with her three or four times a week. When she moved to Windsor he often came there to stay. Lord David Cecil calculated that 'in these first years of her reign Melbourne spent four or five hours of every day talking or writing to his royal mistress'. 'I hope you are amused at the report of Lord Melbourne being likely to marry the Queen,' Lady Grey wrote to Creevey.

In fact this was never likely. Their relationship was that of benevolent uncle and admiring niece. 'When he is with her he looks loving, contented, a little pleased with himself; respectful, at his ease, as if accustomed to take first place in the circle, and dreamy and gay, all mixed up together,' Princess Lieven wrote. At her coronation the Queen herself wrote that Melbourne gave her '*such* a kind, and I may say, *fatherly* look'.

She also believed that he had 'such a strong feeling against immorality and wickedness'. Her journal is full of similar comments, suggesting that Melbourne, whose views were cynical and who had a particular reputation for swearing, was acting a part when with the Queen. But it was a part which he enjoyed, since behind it there lay a genuine desire to teach her political tolerance. And if the Queen often missed the irony in his advice, she was also often aware that he was being funny and mildly naughty. Some of his aphorisms which she solemnly recorded have an Oscar-Wilde-like flavour. 'If you have a bad habit,' he told her, 'the best way to get out of it is to take your fill of it'. And, 'For recruiting the spirits there is nothing like laying a good while in bed'.

Melbourne failed the Queen in the two great scandals of the early years of her reign: the Flora Hastings affair, and the so-called Bedchamber crisis. They both occurred in the early months of 1839. He failed about Lady Flora partly because he could not control the Queen's moral indignation, coupled with her suspicion that it was her great enemy, Sir John Conroy, who had got Lady Flora with child; and partly because his own cynical view of human nature made him suspect, till only a few weeks before Lady Flora died, that she might indeed be pregnant.

He failed over the Bedchamber crisis because he had been too successful an uncle to Victoria. It was the thought of losing him (as well as her ex-governess, Baroness Lehzen) and having Peel instead that lay behind her refusal to let Peel replace some of her Whig Ladies-in-Waiting with Tory ones. When she thought that Melbourne might have to resign they had a dramatic farewell, the Queen in floods of tears, Melbourne holding her hand. Three days later, when he had been mistakenly persuaded to stay, she wrote to him with satisfaction, 'As the negotiation with the Tories is quite at an end ... the Queen hopes Lord Melbourne will not object to dining with her on Sunday?' For two more years Melbourne was again her guide and protector,

remaining so even when she married early in 1840, and only finally
resigning when defeated in Parliament in mid-1841. Once more the
Queen cried when they parted, but not so violently.

Melbourne and the Queen gave up their connection reluctantly. In
October she again asked him to dinner, she continued to write to him
and he continued to answer. They had come to rely on each other too
much to realize how improper it was that the Queen should be taking
regular advice from the Leader of the Opposition.

Baron Stockmar, Prince Albert's *éminence grise*, understood, and
wrote Melbourne a stern memorandum. 'This is a most decided
opinion indeed, quite an apple-pie opinion,' Melbourne said about it.
But it was only after Stockmar had visited Melbourne and written him
another long memorandum that Melbourne ceased to include political
advice in his letters to the Queen.

Sir Henry Frederick Ponsonby (1825–1895)

As a young Grenadier Guards officer Henry Ponsonby was nine years
an ADC to various Lords-Lieutenant of Ireland before, in 1856, he
was appointed Equerry to the Prince Consort. When the Prince died
he became an extra Equerry to Queen Victoria, and nine years later
succeeded Lord Grey as her Private Secretary. His appointment was
opposed. He had published articles and written letters to the press
under a pseudonym (on subjects like military history and pheasant
shooting). His wife, Mary Bulteel, had the dangerous reputation of
being clever. The Duke of Cambridge considered that he had 'extreme
radical tendencies on military and other matters'. Though the Queen
disregarded such opposition, Ponsonby received a letter from her
containing 'a hint . . . to be cautious in expressing my opinions and not
to permit my wife to compromise me in her conversation'. For twenty-
five years Ponsonby was so cautious and skilful in handling the Queen
(no easy matter) that he had only one serious difference with her. After
eighteen years he also became her Keeper of the Privy Purse.

Of the enormous mass of letters and papers which Ponsonby left
(twelve bound volumes and a hundred and seventeen boxes containing
a hundred and fifty to two hundred letters each) the fullest series was
written to his wife from Balmoral. Here he invariably attended the
Queen for many months each year, but was only once allowed to bring
his wife, and was forbidden to buy or rent a nearby house for her in
case she distracted him from his royal duties.

In part Ponsonby's correspondence became so vast because of the Queen's habit of always communicating with everyone by letter. It was a habit which the household at Balmoral imitated, with the result that this cold ugly palace was filled with people in separate rooms writing notes to each other, only meeting for formal meals. Ponsonby regularly reported to his wife on the boringness of these occasions.

Queen's dinner was painfully flat partly I think because she had a cold, partly because she sat between Leopold who never uttered and Gainsborough who is deaf ... there were prolonged silences broken by the Queen, Leopold and C.'s respectable coughs, Crowley's deep cough and S.'s gouty cough and all the servants dropping plates and making a clatteration of noises.

When the Queen didn't have a cold she would 'prattle and talk away on minor topics', but she alone could start a conversation and politics were forbidden.

In dealing with the Queen Ponsonby had often to modify (or send back) violently worded letters which he received for her, or rewrite the violent letters she herself wrote. She would have periods of calm, then he would report, 'Yesterday the Queen was on the rampage' (1873), or 'The Queen full of business and sending ticklers all round' (1893).

'The fact is that any advice I give HM must be given in a most gingerly way,' he wrote, and described how he did it. 'When she insists that 2 and 2 make 5 I say that I cannot help thinking they make 4. She replies that there may be some truth in what I say, but she knows they make 5. Thereupon I drop the discussion.' Ponsonby believed that the Queen's ultimate good sense would argue his case better than he could.

In his early years with the Queen he tried, none too effectively, to make her understand how unpopular her prolonged mourning for Albert was making her. He was more effective in preventing her from publishing a ghosted life of John Brown, the Highland gillie who had subsequently been her close companion for over twenty years.

His one serious difference with the Queen concerned his support for Gladstone's attacks on Turkey for its Bulgarian atrocities. The Queen considered Disraeli was right in ignoring these because it was more important to support Turkey against Russia. It required numerous letters and memos for Ponsonby to persuade the Queen that his support for Gladstone on this question did not affect his loyalty to her. Even then she continued to suspect him of dangerously radical opinions and in writing to him would describe the liberal politicians she feared as 'your friends'.

Some of her later notes suggest the tact which, as a liberal, he must have needed in dealing with her. In 1892, when Gladstone was likely to become Prime Minister once more, she wrote, 'The Queen and many *still hope* the Queen *and the country* may not be exposed to such a misfortune as to be in the hands of *such* dangerous and reckless people as Mr Gladstone and his crew . . . the idea of a deluded excited man of 82 trying to govern England and her vast empire with the miserable democrats under him is quite ludicrous. It is like a bad joke.'

Ponsonby's humour was deadpan. In his son's words, it consisted 'in making without a smile or in writing some serious or even solemn remark which summed up the situation exposing its ridiculous aspect'. He had 'two ways of laughing: an excellent laugh aloud, quite hearty, which he called "my coachman's laugh," completely satisfied the recorder of the joke, but was really an actor's laugh. When he was genuinely tickled, he was absolutely silent, his face grew very red and the tears streamed down his cheeks.'

The novelist, A. C. Benson, remembered him as 'without any exception, the most perfectly and beautifully courteous man I have ever seen, so unembarrassed, so resourceful, so entirely natural that for a time one hardly realised what a triumph of art, in a sense, his manner was'. And the Queen's Assistant Private Secretary, Colonel Arthur Bigge, called him 'one of, if not the greatest gentlemen I have known: the entire effacement of *self*: the absolute non-existence of conceit, side or poise: the charming courtesy to strangers old, young, high, low, rich, poor. His extraordinary wit and sense of the ridiculous, his enormous powers of work – too much – it killed him, but I never heard him say he was hard-worked or had too much to do . . .'

On the door of his palace room he had painted, 'Don't knock. Come in.'

John Brown Esq. (1826–1883)

Already by 1868 John Brown's curious relationship with Queen Victoria had become such a scandal that an American visitor heard the Queen constantly called Mrs Brown. He was told among other things that 'the Queen was insane, and John Brown was her keeper' and that 'the Queen was a spiritualist and John Brown was her medium'. Slightly more accurately, he heard that the Queen had been forbidden to hold a review in Hyde park because the Prime Minister, Lord Derby had objected to Brown appearing with her. Lord Derby had indeed protested, knowing that there was 'an organisation getting up to hoot J.B.' and the Queen had agreed to leave Brown out, but she was planning to change her mind when by good luck the news arrived that a relative of hers, Maximilian, Emperor of Mexico, was likely to be executed and Derby could reasonably cancel the review.

By this time the Queen had known Brown for almost twenty years, since, in 1849, he had been given a job as a royal gillie at Balmoral. He was no penniless Highland boy but the second of six children of a modestly prosperous local farmer. The same year he was promoted to under-groom to ride on the box of the Queen's carriage, and two years later made the permanent leader of the Queen's pony on her Highland expeditions. He was an honest, independent young man of fine build. The Queen probably noticed this – others certainly did. Eleanor Stanley, a Maid of Honour, called him 'the most fascinating and good-looking young highlander'. At the annual gillies' ball she danced with Johnny Brown.

In 1858 Brown received his most important promotion, to replace Prince Albert's special stalker. Brown now came with the royal pair on their deer stalking expeditions. While Albert stalked, Brown kept the Queen amused. 'There could not be a nicer, better, or handier servant,' she wrote to her daughter, the Princess Royal. Brown 'had charge of me and all, on all those expeditions, and therefore I settled that he should be specially appointed to attend on me (without any title) and have a full dress suit . . . He was so pleased when I told him you had asked him to dinner.'

Two years later, when Prince Arthur, her third son, wanted to borrow Brown, she replied, 'Impossible! Why what should I do without him? He is my particular gillie.' To uncle Leopold, King of the Belgians, she wrote that Brown 'takes the most wonderful care of me, combining the offices of groom, footman, page and maid, I might almost say, as he is so handy about cloaks and shawls'. Next year Brown and another servant came with the Queen and Albert on the first of what she called her 'Great Expeditions' when the royal couple travelled about Scotland incognito as Lord and Lady Churchill, and though at Grantown the two servants were unfortunately unable to serve the Queen and Albert in their hotel room, being 'bashful', a Scottish euphemism for drunk, the Queen's infatuation with Brown was clearly well-established by this time, well before Albert died, as he did in December 1861.

Back at Balmoral in 1863, the Queen's carriage overturned, the Queen was thrown out, landing on her face, and Brown was thrown off the box, injuring his knee. But he gallantly raised the Queen, borrowed a pony for her and led her home. Brown was now, she decided, also needed at Osborne on the Isle of Wight and he began to attend her there in 1864. In 1865 he was given an official position as The Queen's Highland Servant, with a salary of £120 (soon doubled), and a definition of his duties, which ended: 'He is to include as before cleaning her boots, skirts and cloaks unless this proves too much.' It did, and before long he had a servant of his own.

For the next eighteen years Brown virtually ran the Queen's household at Balmoral. After breakfast and lunch he would attend on her for orders which he would then pass to other members of the household, who increasingly resented this. In the billiard room one morning, Lord John Manners, who was on a visit, was amazed when Brown looked round the door and called out, 'All what's here dines with the Queen' – his method of inviting her guests for the evening.

In any dispute the Queen supported Brown. When Brown's youngest brother, Archie, who had been appointed valet to Prince Leopold, the Queen's fourth son, complained that the Prince's newly appointed governor, Lieutenant Walter Stirling, had treated him badly, Stirling was dismissed. Archie was not the only one of Brown's five brothers to profit by Brown's success. Two others came hurrying back from New Zealand and Australia to be made a Balmoral shepherd and Keeper of Her Majesty's Kennels at Windsor respectively. A fourth was made Keeper of the Queen's Lodge at Windsor, and though the fifth remained a farmer, the Queen gave him his own farm. She also settled more comfortably in life a number of other Brown relatives.

To justify Brown's elevation the Queen had her factor, Dr Andrew Robertson, prepare Brown's pedigree. Robertson concentrated on Brown's grandmother, Janet Shaw, and managed to connect her with good Jacobite ancestors and the leaders of the great Highland clans. Though the Queen had the result widely circulated among her household and relations, it did not prevent growing public criticism of Brown. Typically, the London correspondent of *John O'Groats Journal* reported that Brown had been sacked for drunkenness, *Tomahawk* published a cartoon entitled 'A Brown Study', showing Brown standing beside an empty throne, and *Punch* satirized a Court Circular (the official daily report on the Queen's movements) as follows:

Balmoral, Tuesday
Mr John Brown walked on the slopes

He subsequently partook of a haggis
In the evening Mr John Brown was pleased to listen to a bagpipe
Mr Brown retired early.

Unrepentant, the Queen wrote of Brown in her book, *Leaves from the Journal of Our Life in the Highlands*, that Brown had 'all the independence and elevated feelings peculiar to the Highland race, and is singularly straightforward, simple-minded, kind-hearted, and disinterested; always ready to oblige; and of a discretion rarely to be met with'. When Prince Arthur refused to speak to Brown she insisted that he must (though the Prince asked for her Private Secretary, Henry Ponsonby to be a witness at the subsequent interview). And, according to Edith Sitwell, when Brown fell down drunk in the Queen's presence one day she remarked that she had felt a slight earth tremor. But it was only on the day of celebration for the recovery of the Prince of Wales from typhoid, when an Irish youth penetrated the grounds of Buckingham Palace and threatened the Queen with a pistol which Brown grabbed, that Brown was transformed into a public hero.

Vindicated, the Queen rewarded Brown with the Devoted Service Medal, specially invented for him and called by some 'The Greater Order of Brown', and officially made him John Brown Esq. She raised his salary to £400, and built for him at Balmoral a fine stone house. During the 1870s he began to come with her on foreign tours. In Coburg, the German state from which her mother came, when the band's drums played too loudly, Brown intervened to protect the Queen's ears, ordering the commanding officer: 'Nix boom boom.'

Rumours then and since have suggested that Brown was either the Queen's lover or secretly married to her. It would explain the rough and familiar way in which he often spoke to her, calling her 'woman'. Where so many have been keen to believe these stories, the strongest evidence that neither of them is true is that there is no positive evidence to support them. Balmoral was a small enclosed community in which such things could not have been totally hidden.

In the 1870s Brown became unwell. Already in *Leaves* Queen Victoria had made so many references to his poor legs that a seventy-page pamphlet, published in 1881, was entitled *John Brown's Legs, or Leaves from a Journal in the Lowlands*, dedicated 'To the Memory of those extraordinary Legs, poor bruised and scratched darlings'. The pamphlet described how the Queen ordered Tennyson to write a sonnet in their honour, for 'no nobler theme ever inspired the pen of genius'. Now

Brown developed severe attacks of erysipelas, and this was what he died from at Windsor in 1883.

Here his body lay in state for six days before it was taken to be buried at Balmoral. On his tomb the Queen had inscribed, from St Matthew's Gospel, 'Well done, good and faithful servant; thou hast been faithful over a few things, I will make thee ruler over many things: Enter thou into the joy of the Lord.' Nineteen years later, as soon as Edward VII became king, he had Brown's room at Windsor turned into a billiards room, his photos and busts burned or smashed and the life-size bronze figure of Brown which the Queen had placed beside her summer cottage at Balmoral removed to a distant hillside.

Meanwhile the Queen had wanted to have published a memoir of John Brown as part of a second book about the Highlands. It required all the skill of Sir Henry Ponsonby to dissuade her. To the Queen he wrote, 'as Sir Henry proceeds he becomes more bold and asks the Queen's forgiveness if he expresses a doubt whether this record of Your Majesty's innermost and most sacred feelings should be made public to the world . . .' The project was abandoned.

Ponsonby's is probably the fairest verdict on Brown. 'He was the only person who could fight and make the Queen do what she did not wish. He did not always succeed nor was his advice always the best. But I believe he was honest, and with all his want of education, his roughness, his prejudices and other faults he was undoubtedly a most excellent servant to her.'

The Munshi Abdul Karim

'Abdul is most handy in helping her when she *signs* by drying the signatures,' Queen Victoria wrote in 1887. If she had known how historians would pick out her similar comment made almost fifty years earlier on the help the Prince Consort gave her with the blotting paper she might have chosen a different example.

It was in 1887 (four years after the death of John Brown) that Indian servants had arrived at Balmoral. At first, wrote Sir Henry Ponsonby, her Private Secretary, 'the Queen was merely excited about them as a child would be with a new toy . . . their picturesque costumes gave a ceremonial reminder that she was Empress of India'. But soon she picked out the Munshi and another named Mahomet for their special helpfulness. The court grew apprehensive and Major General Dennehy, who had served in India and was in charge of them, 'was useless'.

Ponsonby was as powerless himself to curb this new infatuation and when told to increase the Munshi's salary could only obey.

The Munshi soon began to play the role the Queen was pressing on him. At a theatrical performance at Balmoral in 1889 he refused to sit with the dressers behind the guests and went to sulk in his room. Thereafter he always stood apart from the other servants and he accepted the Queen's invitation to join the Household in the Billiards room.

The Duke of Connaught, Queen Victoria's third son, expressed the general dismay to Ponsonby (as the Queen's children often did when trying to use him to influence the Queen whom they did not dare to confront). Ponsonby suggested that the Duke should speak to the Queen himself as he, Ponsonby, did not understand Indian etiquette as well as the Duke did.

Meanwhile the Queen began to learn Hindi (pressing a Hindi vocabulary on Ponsonby), and destroyed all photographs of the Munshi handing her dishes. He was given the official name of the Munshi, Hafitz Abdul Karim. He now moved when the Queen moved and at Osborne had his own bungalow where '"his aunts" and a mysterious friend stayed with him'.

After some years, however, attacks on the Munshi began to appear in the press. In a letter to Ponsonby about one of these the Queen protested at how the feelings of 'the poor good Munshi' had been hurt. To laugh at him in England was particularly out of place, she wrote, when 'she had known 2 archbishops who were sons respectively of a butcher and a grocer', and 'a chancellor whose father was a poor sort of Scotch Minister'.

Government ministers had reason to be concerned. The Queen was showing confidential letters and despatches to the Munshi and he was suspected of passing on what he learned to a disreputable acquaintance in India. But when three senior members of her household protested to her, she refused to speak to them.

Meanwhile the Queen had telegaphed to Frederick Ponsonby, son of Sir Henry, an officer in India, asking him to call on the Munshi's father, who was a surgeon general in the Indian Army. Frederick Ponsonby discovered that in fact this gentleman was an apothecary at the Agra gaol. When he returned to England to become a junior Equerry and told this to the Queen she refused to believe him and he was not asked to dinner for a year.

Finally Lord George Hamilton, Secretary of State for India, told the

Queen that he could no longer send her confidential papers unless she agreed not to show them to the Munshi. To compensate the Munshi she appointed him the Queen's Indian Secretary. This he remained as long as she reigned, but when she died he was swiftly retired.

The Courts of the Houses of Saxe-Coburg and Gotha, and Windsor

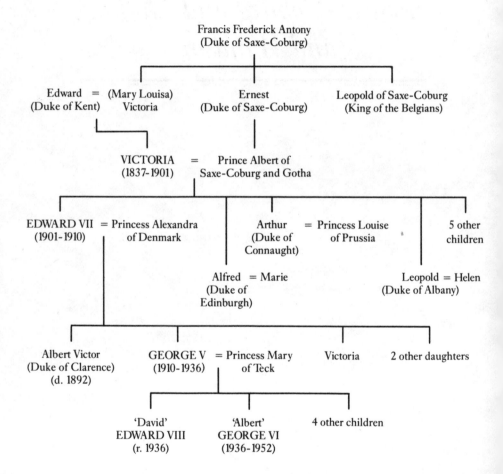

Francis Frederick Antony
(Duke of Saxe-Coburg)

Edward = (Mary Louisa)   Ernest   Leopold of Saxe-Coburg
(Duke of Kent)   Victoria   (Duke of Saxe-Coburg)   (King of the Belgians)

VICTORIA   =   Prince Albert of
(1837-1901)   Saxe-Coburg and Gotha

EDWARD VII = Princess Alexandra   Arthur   = Princess Louise   5 other
(1901-1910)   of Denmark   (Duke of   of Prussia   children
                                     Connaught)

                            Alfred = Marie   Leopold = Helen
                            (Duke of   (Duke of Albany)
                            Edinburgh)

Albert Victor   GEORGE V = Princess Mary   Victoria   2 other daughters
(Duke of Clarence) (1910-1936)   of Teck
(d. 1892)

              'David'   'Albert'   4 other children
              EDWARD VIII   GEORGE VI
              (r. 1936)   (1936-1952)

Edward VII and George V

If Edward VII had not been king he would have 'made his mark as a man of business', Frederick Ponsonby, his Assistant Private Secretary, believed. Edward was already fifty-nine when he succeeded his mother, Queen Victoria, but at once he set about reforming his household in a businesslike way. 'Get this morgue cleared up,' he said about Buckingham Palace. To Lord Esher, the Deputy Constable and Lieutenant-Governor of Windsor Castle, he seemed like 'a man, who, after long years of pent-up action, had suddenly been freed from restraint and revelled in his liberty'.

Superficially Edward, the businesslike King, seems a remarkable contrast with Edward, Prince of Wales, the pleasure-seeking womanizer of the previous forty years, let alone with 'Bertie', the dull-witted, stammering little boy so anxiously over-educated by Victoria and Albert in an attempt to make him 'the most perfect man'.

As he had grown older he had become no brighter; he was also liable to violent fits of temper. 'Afterwards I had to do some arithmetic with the P. of W.,' his tutor, Frederick Gibbs, wrote. 'Immediately he became passionate, the pencil was flung to the end of the room, the stool was knocked away.' When he was seventeen the Queen wrote, 'I tremble at the thought of only three years and a half before us – when he will be of age and we can't hold him except by moral power!' His only hope, she considered, was to rely entirely on his 'dearest papa, that perfection of human beings'. Idleness, his papa considered to be the Prince's chief weakness. 'I never in my life met such a thorough and cunning lazybones,' he wrote.

Gradually people who were not Edward's parents began to find that he was a pleasant young man. 'Nobody could have nicer and better manners,' Edward Lear wrote after showing him his pictures in Rome. '. . . When I said – "please tell me to stop, Sir, if you are tired of so many" – he said "O dear no!" in the naturalest way.' Women, too found the Prince charming, as he did them, and this led to the most serious of the disappointments he caused his parents. When Albert died of typhoid in 1861 the Queen believed that the underlying reason was worry and sleeplessness as a result of Edward's affair with a young lady named Nellie Clifden. The Queen did not forgive her son for what she described as his 'fall'. 'I never can or shall', she wrote, 'look at him without a shudder'.

When Edward married Princess Alexandra she steadily disapproved of the gay social life which the Prince and Princess now began to lead. In 1870 this way of life caused the Prince to be involved in a public scandal when Sir Charles Mordaunt claimed, in divorcing his wife, that the Prince among others had seduced her. The Prince denied it in court, but the public convicted him of loose living in general, even if this time he was innocent.

It was right; besides casual flirtations with young girls, known as 'HRH's virgin band', he had serious affairs with Lillie Langtry whom he helped to launch as an actress, and with Lady Brooke, wife of the fourth Earl of Warwick.

Lady Brooke's loose tongue (she was known as 'the Babbling Brook') probably involved Edward in his second serious scandal, the so-called Baccarat case. At Tranby Croft in Yorkshire ten guests agreed to keep silent about Sir William Gordon Cumming's cheating provided he signed a declaration that he would never play cards again. One of the ten was the Prince. He was therefore a defendant in the libel case which Cumming brought when the declaration became known, and though Cumming lost his case, the Prince was again convicted by public opinion, this time of mixing with habitual gamblers.

Edward's last two important affairs – one with the beautiful Alice Keppel, the other with Agnes Keyser, who managed a London nursing home for army officers, both began in 1898 and ran simultaneously, each of the women giving him something of the love or mothering he needed.

Queen Victoria must in part be blamed for the frivolousness of her son's life. She persistently refused to allow him to play any part in the affairs of the country, or even to see state papers. Where he did have control – at Marlborough House and at Sandringham, the Norfolk estate which had been bought for him – he was already showing the talent for efficient management which he applied to the royal household when he became king.

Within a few weeks great accumulations of junk were destroyed, and modern inventions like the telephone introduced. Cars soon supplemented carriages, including his personal Mercedes and Daimler. Ancient institutions like the royal pack of Buck Hounds were abolished, and tedious afternoon Drawingrooms, at which no food or drink had been served, were replaced by evening 'Presentation Courts', in character more like royal cocktail parties. Private dinners ceased to have the lugubrious formality of the old Queen's and became as conversational as any upper-class dinner party.

Despite this new informality, the King remained obsessively concerned with correct dress and ceremonial. Less endearingly, although he enjoyed laughing at members of his household, like the Italian marine painter, Eduardo Martino, for his bad English, or playing practical jokes on them, like pouring brandy over Christopher Sykes for his obsequiousness, he would take offence if they were familiar with him. On one occasion when a guest called to him across the billiards table, 'Pull yourself together, Wales,' he sent for the man's carriage.

And he remained liable to fits of rage, adult equivalents of his school-room tantrums, or would sulk if he played golf badly or lost at bridge. His restlessness was a more serious problem for his household, which regularly had to follow him on his foreign tours, or to Marienbad where he would go for his health.

This steadily deteriorated and the bronchial condition – of which he eventually died in 1910 – was exacerbated by the huge Corona y Corona cigars he continually smoked.

Every previous Hanoverian king or queen of Britain had quarrelled with his or her male heir. Edward VII was an exception. He and his second son, George (his first, the Duke of Clarence, had died at the age of twenty-eight), were always good friends.

George spent much of his early life in the navy. For the rest of it he looked and behaved like a naval officer. His hearty nautical laugh and blotchy complexion led to a rumour that he drank too much. For all but the last four years of his reign the member of his household with whom he was on the closest terms was his Equerry, Sir Charles Cust, the blunt naval officer he had first met when they were cadets together.

With a naval officer's conservatism, the King retained courtiers who had been members of his grandmother's household. Sir Frederick Ponsonby, once Victoria's junior Equerry, he promoted to Keeper of the Privy Purse, then Treasurer. Arthur Bigge (now Lord Stamfordham) who in his youth had fought in the Zulu Wars then been Victoria's last Private Secretary, he made his own. At Windsor he retained Lord Esher. 'We have reverted to the ways of Queen Victoria,' Esher wrote. 'How the King loves to renew his grandmother's habits in all things. . . . Everything is so peaceful and domestic.'

At Sandringham he was even more domestic, leaving his mother,

Queen Alexandra, in occupation of Sandringham House and continuing to occupy York Cottage, a place so small that Ponsonby had to use either the schoolroom or his bedroom as an office. The King's interests were on the same level: shooting hundreds of driven pheasants and collecting stamps.

It is remarkable, therefore, that he survived the several political crises of his reign so successfully, becoming in the end the ideal constitutional monarch. First came the Parliament Act, reducing the powers of the House of Lords, which the Lords rejected. The King agreed if necessary to make five hundred new peers to pass it.

Next came the Suffragette movement, when much of the agitation was directed against the King himself. Women chained themselves to the railings of Buckingham Palace, and one, Mary Blomfield, told the King loudly at a royal presentation, 'Your Majesty, for God's sake stop torturing women'. She was led away by the Comptroller of the Household. At the 1913 Derby Emily Davison threw herself under the King's horse and was killed.

For the royal household the first Labour government (1924) was even more revolutionary. When Ramsay MacDonald could not find enough members of his party willing to become courtiers. The King agreed that the three great Household officers, Lord Chamberlain, Lord Steward and Master of the Horse, and six other positions should in future become purely royal appointments. But the government retained the appointment of the Treasurer of the Household, the Controller and the Vice-Chamberlain, and the first Labour holders of these positions had once been a tin-plate worker, a miner and a sanitary inspector respectively. They were only persuaded to appear at court in knee-breeches and swords when the King's Private Secretary found for them three sets of Levée Dress, Second Class, from Moss Bros at the bargain price of £30 a set.

In 1935 when the King's Silver Jubilee was celebrated he was astonished to discover how his countrymen liked him. He had become the middle-class father figure they wanted and respected. To his children he was a less successful father. His eldest son, David, considered that he treated them like naughty midshipmen, and when he himself became king, as Edward VIII, he reigned for only eleven months before abdicating. He was succeeded by Albert, George VI, who never overcame his childhood stammer.

Eduardo de Martino, Commendatore

In the 1870s Eduardo de Martino was appointed Marine Painter-in-Ordinary to Queen Victoria. He was a Neapolitan who had served in the Italian Navy till 1867 then settled in England. Frederick Ponsonby considered his sea pictures 'first rate'. Their detail was marvellously accurate.

He was retained in the same position by Edward VII, travelling with the King on his west coast sea trip to Scotland and on several other cruises. Sometimes his dignity was hurt, as when he discovered that he was to be ranked last in the King's suite during the King's first official foreign tour in 1903. To start with Ponsonby, then two other members of the party, offered to be placed after Martino. 'This amused the King very much'. He decided to place Martino next to last.

More often Martino enjoyed making 'quaint remarks in his very bad English' in order to be a butt for the King's wit. In Ponsonby's opinion it was as a court jester that he had been retained by the King, but, 'like all jesters he was really a very shrewd man'.

Alice Edmonstone, Mrs George Keppel (d. 1947)

Alice Keppel's affair with 'Kingy', as her daughters called Edward VII, began on Februay 27th 1898. She was twenty-nine and he was fifty-seven. At dinner with the Keppels that night she and the King seem to have come to an understanding which led to her becoming his principal mistress for the last twelve years of his life.

Their relationship included weekends together at the great country house parties of the period, visits to the south of France with the Keppels as members of the party, and teas at the Keppels' house in Portman Square, where Alice's younger daughter remembered playing a betting game with pieces of bread and butter on the King's trousers. 'He would lend me a leg, on which I used to start two bits of bread and butter (butter side down), side by side. Then, bets of a penny each were made (my bet provided by Mamma) and the winning piece of bread and butter depended, of course, on which was the more buttery.'

Alice, daughter of an admiral, married to the younger son of a peer, was a woman of outstanding beauty and charm. In the many memoirs of the time it is difficult to find a single bitchy remark about her. Lloyd George was one of a number of politicians who were her friends and found her useful in persuading the King to accept Liberal government policies. All admired her 'wonderful discretion'. Osbert Sitwell called her 'a memorable figure in the fashionable world' and described how she would momentarily remove her long cigarette-holder from her mouth and turn on the person she was talking to 'her large, humorous, kindly, peculiarly discerning eyes'. Only the Marquess of Salisbury and the Dukes of Portland and Norfolk considered it wrong to entertain her.

Her husband, George, was also remarkably good-looking, with a large moustache and hearty laugh. He stood six feet four inches in his socks (or nearly eight foot in his Gordon Highlander's bonnet, as his daughter points out). He was apparently happy about his wife's affair with the king. When he was unable to support the life-style which mixing with royalty required, he accepted a job from Sir Thomas Lipton which the King obtained for him.

The Archbishop of Canterbury claimed to be equally satisfied, justifying himself with the none-too-conclusive argument that if she was the King's mistress the King would never have insulted him by always seating her next to him at table.

Even the Queen accepted Alice Keppel's position and function. When Alice grew portly, the Queen once called one of her Ladies-in-Waiting to see the fat King and his fat mistress driving side by side in an open carriage at Sandringham. The Queen and her lady 'burst into peals of laughter'. But in general she realized that Alice always put the King into a good humour – and this was one reason why hostesses would invite her. Typically, when the King was kept waiting at Windsor by Asquith, the Prime Minister (who had gone for a long walk with a Maid of Honour), the Queen calmed him by sending him to drive ahead to Virginia Water with Alice Keppel.

On May 6th 1910 when the King was desperately ill and not expected to live, the Queen sent for Alice Keppel so that she could see him before he died.

Alice was much upset by the King's death and lay in bed where she looked at her younger daughter 'blankly, without recognition, and rather resentfully'.

'Why does it matter so much, Kingy dying?' the young girl asked her father. 'Poor little girl!' the father said. 'It must have been very frightening for you. And for all of us, for that matter. Nothing will ever be quite the same again. Because Kingy was such a wonderful man.'

The Keppels retired to Tuscany, well provided for by the wise investments made on their behalf by the King's financial adviser, Sir Ernest Cassel.

Louisa Jane Grey, Countess of Antrim (1855–1949)

In 1890 Louisa, Countess of Antrim, was invited to become a Woman of the Bedchamber to Queen Victoria, in effect succeeding the Queen's most trusted Lady-in-Waiting, Jane Eley, who had died the previous June. Louisa was thirty-five years old. She came from a family closely connected with the court. Her father, General Charles Grey, had for many years been the Queen's Private Secretary, with an apartment at St James's Palace where Louisa had been brought up. But she was married to an eccentric Irish peer, Bill McDonell, known as the Buzzard, whose ancestral seat was Glenarm on the coast of Antrim. Lord Antrim, who would drive his own cattle to market, once warned his prospective son-in-law that he could do what he liked on his visit to Glenarm except have a woman within seven miles of the castle. He was eventually buried standing upright facing out to sea on one of his own hilltops. Louisa was terrified of him, and although he agreed to her court appointment, he resented her absences during her periods of waiting, and once in rage smashed to pieces her sewing table and threw it into the fire.

Louisa, in contrast, was a lady of 'discreet unruffled calm'. She was tall and thin, and had been known when a débutante as 'Maypole' or 'Knitting Pin'. She spoke with a 'fastidiously well-bred inflection'. She had other qualities to suit her for court life – could ride well, play the organ and paint pretty water-colours.

To Queen Victoria she made a perfect Lady-in-Waiting, attentive, loyal, much liked by her fellow ladies of the court, even-tempered despite piles caused by endless periods of standing. For these the court physician, Dr Reid, gave her laudanum.

But her great days came in the following reign when she was Lady-in-Waiting to Queen Alexandra. Now she went with other members of the royal household on several of the King's foreign tours when, like a great family party, they cruised the Mediterranean, drinking champagne, banqueting and visiting foreign royalty. Many of them were indeed related; Frederick Ponsonby, the King's Assistant Private Secretary, was Louisa's cousin.

Though Louisa's first loyalties were to the Queen, this did not make her disloyal to the King; she considered that 'if she [the Queen] had loved him as much as he loved her he would have been more faithful to her'. But occasional disapproving comments on his mistresses creep into her otherwise discreet journal. At the coronation she noted that just above the Princesses 'was the "loose-box" – and well named it was

– to me the one discordant note in the Abbey – for to see the row of lady friends in full magnificence did rather put my teeth on edge – La Favorita [Mrs Keppel] of course in the best place, Mrs Ronny Greville, Lady Sarah Wilson, Feo Sturt, Mrs Arthur Paget and that ilk . . .'

Louisa left court when Edward VII died, but remained in touch with many friends there, in particular with Queen Alexandra's daughter, Princess Victoria. She survived the Second World War, dying in 1949 at the age of ninety-three.

Captain Sir Charles Cust, R.N. (1864–1931)

George V first met Charles Cust in 1877 when they were fellow naval cadets on the *Britannia*. Nine years later they served together as Lieutenants on *HMS Thunderer* in the Mediterranean Fleet. Already Prince George took a benign view of Cust's outspokenness. 'That brute Cust', he wrote, 'is sitting on the deck of my cabin behind me, because I have got no other chair, abusing both me and my cabin'. In 1892 when the Prince was first given a household of his own, Cust was appointed his Equerry, a position he held till he died thirty-nine years later.

Together in the last years of Victoria's reign, Prince George and Cust would bicycle along the lanes around Sandringham. When the Prince began to make official tours abroad, Cust came too, in 1901 to the Dominions, and in 1911 (now as Equerry to the King) to India.

Regularly Cust made trouble for himself by saying what he thought. In 1910 he criticized the King for leaving his mother, Queen Alexandra, and his sister, Princess Victoria, in occupation of Sandringham while he, Queen Mary and their six children had only York Cottage. Princess Victoria said she would never speak to Cust again, and the King asked Cust what the devil it had to do with him.

In 1911 Cust said that the king should not have telegraphed a message of sympathy to Ramsay MacDonald when his wife was ill. Though Ramsay MacDonald was leader of the Labour Party which already had a number of Members of Parliament, it was still not an official party.

At Balmoral, when the king protested at finding Cust reading what the King thought were his books on the billiards room floor, 'Cust replied, '*Your* books! Why you haven't in the whole of this house got a book that is worth reading. Your so called library is nothing but beautifully bound piffle.' When Frederick Ponsonby told the King that

Cust was right, the King ordered the annual purchase of 'interesting Scottish books' and the weeding out of worthless ones.

In 1931 when Cust died the King and the household missed him. As the King had grown increasingly intolerant of contradiction, Cust alone had continued to be willing to tell him that he was talking nonsense. Ponsonby wrote,

> His great charm was that he was so offensively rude to people he didn't like ... The imposter, the swaggerer, were his particular 'bêtes noires' and he never made any attempt to conceal his dislike. Curiously, the rabbit type he was always kind to, and he generally found in such men unexpected qualities quite alien to their rodent nature. Little children delighted him and flocked to him naturally, while many grown-ups approached him with the utmost caution. To the king he was invaluable; he never hesitated to speak his mind bluntly and even brutally, but His Majesty knew him so well that he never minded even being flatly contradicted by him.

Frederick Ponsonby, 1st Lord Sysonby (1867–1935)

From 1894, when Frederick Ponsonby (known as Fritz to his friends), the second son of Sir Henry Ponsonby, first joined the Royal Household, to 1935, he was constantly in the service of the reigning monarch except when he was released for brief periods during the Boer War and the First World War. When he died, as the editor of his memoirs wrote, it was more like the passing of an institution.

In many ways he resembled his father, Queen Victoria's Private Secretary for twenty-five years, believing in the monarchy as an institution as well as being devoted to his three monarchs in person. But it was as if his father's well-integrated character had started to burst out in certain contradictory directions. On the one hand he had an exaggerated concern with all forms of ceremonial, from correct clothing and decorations to correct forms of address. On the other hand, as an administrator he was highly unsystematic, knew little about book-keeping and rarely kept copies of his own letters. He was also less than resigned to his modest salary, sometimes planning to make himself rich by writing film scripts, sometimes by finding King John's treasure in the Wash.

As a junior Equerry to Queen Victoria when she was at Osborne, Ponsonby found himself in the not unusual condition for courtiers of having nothing to do. He would spend the morning sitting at a desk reading the newspapers and writing private letters. At last at noon the Queen would go out, thus allowing other members of the household to leave the house for a walk. Then, he wrote, 'it was like a lunatic asylum, as everybody went alone in different directions.'

At Windsor Ponsonby helped the Senior Equerry, a forgetful eighty-year–old general, to avoid catastrophe when he forgot to order the Life Guards' band for a ceremonial dinner. To get the band on to the terrace Ponsonby borrowed ladders from the Castle fire brigade. The band was still missing when the Queen arrived so there was no national anthem. 'But as I sat down I saw through the window dark figures climbing on to the small Terrace, and before the Queen had had a mouthful of soup the band struck up an overture.' The Queen had noticed the missing anthem and reprimanded the general but he did not feel that he needed to resign.

At Balmoral Ponsonby found drunkenness common during the last years of the Queen's reign.

> Whenever anyone went out stalking, a whole bottle of whisky was given out, and whatever the guest did not drink became the perquisite of the stalker . . . Whenever the Queen went out driving, a bottle of whisky was put under the coachman's seat and was supposed to provide stimulant to anyone who had had an accident . . . Innumerable bottles of whisky must have gone astray in this way . . . Another occasion when whisky was freely given out was the anniversary of the Prince Consort's birthday. All the stalkers, gillies, and people on the estate were expected to attend in top-hats . . . and black coats. A prayer was said in front of the Prince Consort's statue . . . then whisky was sent out as light refreshment at the back of the wood. The result was that the whole community was three parts intoxicated and when we went for a walk in the afternoon it was no uncommon sight to find a man in a top-hat and frock-coat fast asleep in the woods.

When the Queen's eyesight began to fail she asked Ponsonby to make the lettering of his messages and transcribed cables blacker, so he developed a much larger handwriting, bought some special black ink like boot polish and used a device heated by a spirit stove to dry the ink without his needing to blot it. When the Queen was still not satisfied he got still blacker ink. Unfortunately this went through the paper so he took to writing on only one side. But as a result the Queen complained of the daunting quantity of papers he was bringing her. So he reverted to using both sides of the paper but took much trouble to get special thick paper from the stationery office. The Queen now complained that the cables were too bulky to fit the case in which she kept them before sending them to the archives. Ponsonby therefore reverted to ordinary ink and ordinary paper – and received a message from the Queen asking him to write blacker.

Though Ponsonby was re-appointed Assistant Private Secretary to King Edward, he had difficulties with Sir Francis Knollys, Edward's Private Secretary for the previous thirty years, who at first gave Ponsonby nothing to do. Knollys and those who had worked for Edward at Marlborough House believed that the Queen's staff at Buckingham Palace were useless and their methods hopelessly out of date. Later Knollys would often fail to brief Ponsonby, and in the end had a second Assistant Private Secretary appointed, so for a time reducing Ponsonby's service to six months a year and his salary by £200.

But Ponsonby often went with the King when he travelled, and was with him in the first year of his reign when he visited his sister, the Empress Frederick, in Germany. Here Ponsonby was commissioned by the dying Empress to smuggle her letters out of the country. She believed that they would be destroyed when she died since they gave her side of her quarrel with her son, the Kaiser. Ponsonby agreed, imagining a few small packages, and was dismayed when, in the small hours of the morning, four stable hands in breeches and riding-boots arrived with two large and conspicuous trunks. Nevertheless he managed to take them home, and twenty-seven years later published a selection from the sixty volumes of which they consisted. For this he was much criticized; the Kaiser tried but failed to have them suppressed by claiming the copyright.

Ponsonby was also with the King in 1903 on his first official foreign tour when with the final phrase of one brief speech – 'Paris, where I always feel as if I was at home' – he, in Ponsonby's opinion, transformed the alignment of the nations of Europe. Crowds which had previously shouted at him '*Vive Jeanne d'Arc*', now cheered him wherever he went.

Earlier, in Rome, Ponsonby had been given for cyphering a furious cable from the King to Arthur Balfour, the Prime Minister, who had advised the King against calling officially on the Pope. Late at night, unable to reach the King, Ponsonby rewrote the cable in diplomatic language, believing that if he had not done so the government would have resigned. The Prime Minister replied that if the visit was a private one, this was a matter on which it would be impertinent for him to offer any observations and a political crisis was avoided.

When the King, on the same trip, cabled ahead that he would like to arrive incognito at Naples, Ponsonby considered this 'rather absurd', since 'no other human being in the world would come with eight battleships, four cruisers, four destroyers, and a dispatch vessel'.

'I never quite understood', Ponsonby wrote about the King,

> why he made people so frightened . . . but there can be no doubt that even his most intimate friends were all terrified of him. Abroad . . . I had only to mention his name and at once all resistance vanished. . . . Whenever he expressed any wish there was never any opposition, for he was by far the biggest man and the most striking personality in Europe.
>
> I have seen Cabinet Ministers, Ambassadors, Generals and Admirals absolutely curl up in his presence . . . In his business room . . . I was quite at home . . . and found no difficulty in arguing with him, but when at luncheon or staying at a country house he got cross over a matter I knew little about, he fairly scared me.

Ponsonby had reason to be anxious; in 1907, when the King ordered a silver cigarette case to be given to a Paris race-horse owner (he had run out of gold ones) Ponsonby cancelled the order and wrote that a gold one would be sent from London. The King was enraged, reducing Ponsonby to 'speechless terror', ordered the silver one to be sent and showed Ponsonby the gentleman's letter of gratitude. When Ponsonby asked how else he could have replied the King was furious again and for two years Ponsonby was in disgrace.

George V found Ponsonby as useful as his father had done and in 1914 promoted him to Keeper of the Privy Purse. When Ponsonby was offered the position of Governor of Bombay, the Prime Minister, Asquith, intervened on the King's behalf to prevent him from taking it.

Though George V travelled less than his father, Ponsonby went with him on several visits to France during the 1914–18 war and was close to him on the occasion when he was inspecting the Royal Flying Corps and the second-in-command ordered three cheers. The King's horse 'quivered with terror and crouched down on its haunches. Then suddenly springing up it reared straight up in the air and, its hind legs slipping, it fell back right on top of the King'. Ponsonby allowed the

King to rise to his feet as soon as he expressed the wish to do so, but admitted that medically this was a serious error.

Ponsonby was created Lord Sysonby in June 1935, but died suddenly in October, three months before the King, whom he had by then served for twenty-five years.